# I'm an English Major—Now What?

How English majors can find happiness, success, and a real job

TIM LEMIRE



WRITER'S DIGEST BOOKS
writersdigestbooks.com
Cincinnati, Ohio

 Published by Writer's Digest Books, an imprint of F+W Publications, Inc., 4700 East Galbraith Road, Cincinnati, Ohio 45236. (800) 289-0963. First edition.

10 09 08 07 06 6 5 4 3 2 1

Distributed in Canada by Fraser Direct
100 Armstrong Avenue
Georgetown, ON, Canada L7G 5S4
Tel: (905) 877-4411

Distributed in the U.K. and Europe by David & Charles
Brunel House, Newton Abbot, Devon, TQ12 4PU, England
Tel: (+44) 1626 323200, Fax: (+44) 1626 323319
E-mail: mail@davidandcharles.co.uk

Distributed in Australia by Capricorn Link
P.O. Box 704, Windsor, NSW 2756 Australia
Tel: (02) 4577-3555

Library of Congress Cataloging-in-Publication Data
Lemire, Tim.
I'm an English major—now what? : how English majors can find happiness, success, and a real job / by Tim Lemire. -- 1st ed.
p. cm.
Includes index.
ISBN-13: 978-1-58297-362-3 (pbk.: alk. paper)
ISBN-10: 1-58297-362-8
1. Vocational guidance. I. Title: I'm an English major. II. Title.
HF5381.L3525 2006
650.1--dc22

2005035555

Editor: Jane Friedman
Designer: Claudean Wheeler
Cover Illustration: Caitlin Kuhwald
Production Coordinator: Robin Richie

# Dedication

To majors in English everywhere:
past, present, and future

# Table of Contents

# Introduction

If you graduated from college with a degree in English, the first thing you should know is that there's no need to panic. Have a seat, take a deep breath, and read on, Macduff.

People typically choose to major in English because they love literature, reading, and writing. Then, when they enter the workforce, they discover they also love eating, preferably something other than cold baked beans out of a can.

Not to worry.

This book offers information and guidance to English majors who wish to translate their skills into a job in their field—even if they don't exactly know what that field will be. This book also dispels common fears about the major in English, primarily:

- that English majors' career options are severely limited
- that English majors will never make good money
- that English majors' skills have no currency outside of academics

This book addresses common questions among English majors, including:

- Do I need to go to journalism school?
- Should I get my MFA in creative writing, and when?
- How do I begin a freelance career in editing or writing?

This book will also refute misconceptions held by English majors, such as:

- the fatalistic belief that all you will be able to do in the world is teach English
- the idealistic belief that you can make a reasonable postgraduate living from writing the kinds of poems and novels you read as requirements for your major

The latter belief, if not more common, surely runs deeper. Some undergraduate English majors I talk to refer to their future of writing plays as if there were an office building somewhere in midtown Manhattan crammed with scribbling playwrights working against deadline; and at least one young person has shared with me his crafty strategy of taking an entry-level job in book publishing to advance his chances of getting his own (yet unwritten) novel published. Suffice to say that you are ill-served by your college or university if you walk out of its gates (as I did) thinking that one day, as you are filling out a form, you will enter Literary Novelist or Poet under Occupation.

As for teaching, we'll address that noble occupation—and others—in the pages to come, which feature interviews with English majors who have gone on to establish themselves in a variety of occupations.

A disclaimer: My opinions do not necessarily reflect those of the professionals I have interviewed, nor should their willingness to participate in this book be interpreted as a tacit endorsement of my views. The information in this book is based on my own experience: If what I write does not sound kosher to readers' ears, I encourage them to talk to more people, research, investigate, and put my information to the test.

Or, as is said more succinctly in journalism: If your mother says she loves you, check it out.

# CHAPTER I I'm an English Major

English, huh? Well.

Good for you. So …

What are you going to do with that?

After all, physics majors become physicists; psychology majors become psychologists; and even history majors become historians. What do English majors become?

Englishists? Englishologists?

Waiters?

To be sure, majoring in studio art or medieval philosophy or medieval studio art prompts a stronger parental spit-take than the declaration of a major in English: for, surely, Mom and Dad have some acquaintance with the English language and can imagine, vaguely, that English may prove useful in a white-collar office environment where you can earn a good salary and get a decent dental plan. The English major involves a lot of reading and writing, and people *do* do that, don't they—I mean, in real jobs?

Indeed they do.

This fact alone should encourage you and give you hope for gainful employment. The jobs are there, as is happiness and success—provided you know who you are, what you can do, what you want, and where to look.

## So, What Can English Majors Do?

Before we examine specific jobs, let's break down the major in English into its fundamental skills. Obviously, each of the colleges and universities across America has a different set of requirements for the major in English, but it's fair to say that, to earn a degree in English, you must be able (at a bare minimum) to read two three-hundred-page novels and write a five-page paper about them. If you can do this, you can:

- assimilate and synthesize large amounts of information
- identify and summarize important points
- translate large concepts into succinct language
- do all of the above against a deadline

Writing papers requires you to develop skills in:

- research
- information management
- argumentative or persuasive writing
- proper grammar and usage
- acting as your own editor when revising and correcting your work

Taking on a variety of writing assignments trains you to:

- customize your style and voice for particular audiences
- develop a versatility in planning, thinking about, and executing assignments
- develop skills in multitasking and project management

Luckily, these skills are wanted in more than just the teaching profession. So where are they? Where are the jobs to which such skills could be applied?

## Where the Jobs Are

In my own teaching days, I told my students that where there are words—in newspapers and magazines; in magazine ads; on cereal boxes; in the instructions to your MP3 player; in books, brochures, and on billboards and in junk mail—there are people who write the words. There are people who check for factual accuracy, correct spelling, and proper grammar. There are people who then rewrite the words, and there are people who incorporate graphics and visuals with the words. There are people who see to it that the words are printed and published and delivered into your hands. There are people who write words in order to market and sell the products that have words on them.

Where there are words, there are jobs for the English major.

But don't think the only jobs for English majors involve words.

Because the preferred mode of communication nowadays is not semaphore or smoke signals but language, it may be said that where there is lingual *communication*—speeches, presentations, commercials, ads, podcasts, and broadcasts—there are jobs for the English major.

Consider that many people, despite being graduates of the finest institutions of learning this country has to offer, cannot always use words to communicate effectively—or even correctly. Sometimes they themselves admit it: They say they don't have a way with words or a command of the English language (as if language were a dog to be brought to heel, to do one's bidding).

When I was a teacher, foreign-born students would come to me at the start of the semester to apologize because, they said, being new to America, they were still struggling with the English language. I always reassured them: *Don't worry. You'll fit right in.*

Where there are people who need help using words to communicate, there are jobs for the English major. Those jobs may be found in corporate America just as easily as in schools.

But don't think the only jobs for English majors involve communication.

When health care or social agencies need to translate valuable information about policies or procedures for their non-English-speaking audiences, they depend on someone who not only knows Spanish or Chinese, but also knows English. Book publishers translate English-language novels, nonfiction, and textbooks into other languages, and this requires a knowledge of English, as does teaching English as a second language.

Consider, too, how bursts of technological innovation have introduced to people of all ages not only new gadgets, new hardware, and new software, but also an attendant avalanche of new words, terms, and phrases to learn, adopt, and use.

When the government publishes an eight-hundred-page white paper or a federal court hands down a ruling that is recondite and complex, the media consult with someone who can put into plain language what is anything but plain.

Where there is English, there are jobs for the English major.

And there's more.

## *Jobs Beyond the Obvious*

This is where you come in. Your own interests, strengths, abilities, hobbies, and obsessions play an even greater role in determining where you will find—or make—a job. Here are some quick examples from actual English majors.

A woman told me she wanted to write for magazines, but she didn't know which ones. I asked her what her areas of expertise were. (I think the notion of having expertise threw her a bit, since we commonly associate expertise with a formal degree or professional certification.) She said she knew a lot about wine. She also told me she was bilingual, as fluent in Spanish as in English. I suggested to her that Hispanic people drink wine, too, and probably wanted to read about it: She could research wine magazines and newsletters, write columns or features, and market herself in two languages—to both English and Spanish publications. She was very excited to hear this; the idea seemed never to have occurred to her.

A young man told me he wanted to be a writer, but he didn't know what to write about. I asked him what he did in his spare time: snowboarding, it turned out. "Can you tell me the top ten places in America to snowboard?" I asked. "Oh sure," he told me. He had snowboarded all across the country. "Well," I told him, "go online or use *Writer's Market* to research publications geared to snow-

**Most Important Skills**

Throughout this book, I will identify the most important skills you need to succeed in the profession under discussion. Because this chapter doesn't address any one profession in particular, let's look at some skills you'll need for a successful job search.

***Cold-Calling.*** English majors (or at least stereotypical ones) tend to be bookish, reticent types—not the kind of people who are comfortable telephoning strangers out of the blue to ask for information. The good news is, no one is comfortable doing this—not right off the bat, anyway. In time and with practice, you will get used to pursuing job leads, setting up informational or formal interviews, and just following up with contacts by using Mr. Bell's great invention. And remember: One thing a person can give you that a job listing cannot is a new lead.

**Presentation.** Four years of wearing sweatpants and backward-facing baseball caps to class doesn't exactly prime you for what is de rigueur in the job marketplace: a clean, professional presentation in your clothing, your hair, your speech, your résumé and portfolio, and your follow-up and thank-you communications. If you want to know how businesspeople dress, it's as easy as getting yourself downtown to where all the office buildings are, waiting for the lunch whistle, and taking notes as people walk by.

**Detective Work.** As good a resource as the Internet is, don't limit yourself to online job listings. Look in trade magazines and newspapers and read up on the state of the industry you're interested in. (You might find, for instance, that layoffs are leading to a spike in contract work.) Investigate your state's career center in addition to your college career center, and most of all, talk to people. Talk, ask questions, and pursue leads. It's called a job *hunt*, and a hunter doesn't go after his prey sitting in a chair looking at a computer screen.

boarders, write a short feature on where the best snowboarding is, and query their interest in it—if one little magazine bites, there's the first line on your publication résumé." The young man looked at me hopefully and asked, as if seeking permission, "Can I do that?"

One young woman I spoke to was not only an English major, but premed as well. She spoke as if she had to choose between the two concentrations. "Why not combine them?" I asked. "Hospitals have communication departments. Look into being an editor at a medical journal or a member of a medical center's marketing or communication team." The young woman looked surprised at the notion—and happy!

To your fundamental skills, you add your own strengths and interests and the areas about which you wish to learn more. It's a constant process of evaluating yourself, gaining experience, and learning new skills.

## What an English Major Is Not

It's an English major, not a super major.

When people praise the major in English, one word that always comes up is *versatility*: the major in English is a great major because it's so versatile, so flexible. I agree. I would add, however, that you could call versatile or flexible any program of study that doesn't prepare or train you for any particular vocation. The major in English is one such program (and the book's final chapter will address the ramifications of the fact that a major in English does not include any type of professional training).

Suffice to say for now that the versatility of a major in English—while genuine—is easily exaggerated and romanticized, as when you encounter the belief that four years spent analyzing literature gives English majors some kind of mystical insight into the human condition, which is somehow applicable in the marketplace. Good luck applying for a job in social work with the argument *Believe me, I know people. I read* Bleak House *three times.*

While a major in English does not prepare you for any specific occupation, it does provide training in critical thinking. But although English majors may exhibit skills in critical thinking, they don't own the copyright; some critical thinking comes into play in the sciences, as well. English majors know how to write, but there is a variety of written forms in which students of English get no classroom training whatsoever: financial grants, technical writing, and corporate communications, to name a few.

This book contains interviews of English majors who are now working professionals, and among those English majors, several referred to the major in English as a *good foundation.* One individual, who today interviews young people for jobs, put it more frankly: "Great, you majored in English—but what *else* you got?" That is, what other experience, skills, and abilities do you bring to the table?

You can answer this question better than any book can, and seeing how other people have answered it will inspire and motivate you.

## *Happiness in a Real Job*

The subtitle of this book, as you have no doubt already noticed, suggests that I know how English majors can achieve happiness and success in life, in addition to finding a real job.

Here's the thing: I would call a *real job* any job that pays you a livable wage for doing something that you would do even if you weren't paid to do it. It's the job that is a natural extension of who you are and what you want to become. It's the job that draws on and develops the skills and knowledge that help define you as an individual.

Some people talk about this kind of job as if it were a far-flung fantasy, but I believe and trust that there is a job like that for everyone, and that if it is not out there, you can create it.

Now, as for happiness and success …

(Pardon me a moment while I strike my gong.)

Happiness is both a condition and a philosophy—an attitude, a perspective, or a way of thinking. Success, while quantifiable by any number of material measurements, is more meaningful in terms of the degree to which you find happiness. And of course, happiness and success are not necessarily the byproducts of having that *real job.*

But having that real job sure as hell helps you attain happiness and success.

You want happiness, success, and a real job? Let's start with the real job, and see how closely the other two come on its heels, okay?

Let me close this chapter by telling you that it was only when I entered the workforce that I realized what was the biggest mistake I ever made in my education. My biggest mistake was believing that everything I needed to know, I would learn in school, and that what I learned in school was everything I needed to know. I stuck to the assigned reading list, and I studied to the test. I waited for assignments, and, like a good boy, I did them—on time, in full, and as requested. Unfortunately, I didn't develop the initiative to make and find my own challenges and thus take charge of my own education. I was passive.

Surely, I thought, school would not take me in and then send me out into the world without telling me or teaching me what I needed to know. As befits a school being *alma mater* ("fostering mother") or *in loco parentis* ("in the place of a parent"), I trusted school like I trusted my own mom and dad; I had no reason to do otherwise.

As it happened, school did teach me many things I needed to know—and a few things I initially didn't want to accept. I'm grateful for that. But nearly twenty years of sitting quietly, taking notes, raising my hand when I had an answer more often than when I had a question, and learning as I was told may have gotten me As, but the As did not stand me in good stead once the last class of the last day of school was over.

## TRY THIS

At one career night event, an English major told me he didn't know what he wanted to do for a living, but he *did* know what he liked: He liked animals—all sorts of animals! And he liked helping people. He liked to write, too. And he liked that experience you get when you're in a restaurant and the service is really good? And they just make the whole evening memorable? He liked that.

As he's talking, my brain is spinning, thinking he could get a job writing menus at exotic restaurants where they serve crocodile, buffalo, and shark.

Kidding aside, this young man was on the right track, and I told him so: He was thinking in terms of skills, abilities, likes, dislikes, strengths, and weaknesses. I suggested to him that zoos have education and communication departments; perhaps there he could satisfy his love of writing and his love of animals. Perhaps he could explore the travel industry, to see if writing and customer satisfaction and animals could somehow combine in that area. Ultimately, I suggested to him the exercise below.

### Strong-Suit Brainstorming

- ***What You Need:*** index cards, markers, a hat (or something) to put the cards in, a big table, and supportive friends and family. (And it won't kill you to make hors d'oeuvres.)
- ***What You Don't Need:*** The parent who will say "You want a job? Take over the family creosote business. There's your job, smart guy."
- ***What You Do:*** Give each person a bunch of index cards and a marker. Ask everyone to write down four or five things he thinks you're good at (one item per card): It could be writing, or fixing things, or working well with children—anything. No ability, skill, or talent is too small. And do the same for yourself.

Ask each person to write three of your strongest suits (again, one on each card), e.g., kindness, generosity, intelligence, a giving nature, sympathy, organization. Also do this for yourself.

Put all the cards in a hat, and stand or sit around the big table. Take out the cards one at a time, and place each card on the table. Ask who wrote each card, and ask that person to explain why he wrote what he did.

You may be surprised at what people think your strong suits are and what they think you're good at. Listen to their explanations, and try to see how other people see you.

Start to arrange the cards into patterns of your own choosing, and brainstorm with your guests about what jobs place a high priority on your strong suits (generosity and organization, for example) and would allow you to do what you do well (such as fixing things).

Your family and friends have experience and perspective worth seeking out and listening to. When you think in terms of skills and abilities, you're free to mix and match and brainstorm.

Have fun. Put the pieces together like a jigsaw puzzle and see what picture they make.

# CHAPTER 2 Perchance to Teach

Ah, the obvious question: *Oh, an English major—planning on teaching, are you?*

When friends or family ask this of English majors, they ask it not so much with genuine curiosity as with an automatic expectation that the answer will be yes—teaching being the assumed normal, natural next step for anyone who graduates from college with a BA in English.

Perhaps this shouldn't come as a surprise. English majors spend their college years reading novels, poems, and plays and writing papers about same, and no job outside of teaching requires you to punch the clock, plant yourself behind a desk, and get right down to work analyzing symbolism in *The Great Gatsby* or "The Rime of the Ancient Mariner."[1]

Of course, there is nothing wrong with English majors becoming English teachers: we need as many capable teachers as we can get. If, however, you are thinking about teaching as a career, you must answer two crucial questions right off the bat:

- Has the undergraduate English major curriculum adequately prepared you for a career in teaching?
- Are you considering teaching because you've heard that teaching is what English majors do, and, quite frankly, you can't think of anything else to do?

[1] Or perhaps you're thinking of becoming a book critic. Sorry, but the career of book critic doesn't fit the bill. English majors write long papers about literature written mostly by dead authors; book critics write short features about books, mostly by living authors. English majors write about books to analyze and interpret; book critics write about books to recommend or discourage purchase. English majors are full-time writers; book critics typically have supplemental incomes or other newsroom duties. English majors write for an audience of one (their teacher); book critics write for an audience of thousands.

This chapter, in its discussion of teaching responsibilities and challenges, mainly focuses on teaching kindergarten through high school. English majors interested in teaching on the college level should refer to the chapter on higher education, since full-time tenured teaching positions on the college or university level require a post-graduate degree.

## *Undergraduates, Underprepared*

The answer to the first question above is no, and not just because requirements for the English major do not include teacher training.

The answer is no because the skills necessary to craft a lesson plan; generate assignments and discussion topics; administer tests; grade papers; and deal with the daily disciplinary, interpersonal, and political challenges of teaching are not abilities easily extrapolated from four years of reading novels and writing papers about them. (Some people would argue that the aforementioned skills are not easily extrapolated from a major in education, either, but that's a whole other debate.)

It's also one thing to have *studied* English; it's an entirely different matter to *teach* English.

Knowledge of a subject—even expertise in a subject—does not, alone, qualify you to be a teacher: excellent, good, or mediocre. And just because you enjoy reading and writing does not mean you're going to enjoy teaching it or be any *good* teaching it. Surely you've had a teacher who knew the subject through and through, but who was hopeless when it came to teaching that subject: disorganized, disengaged, uninspiring, uninspired, too lax in discipline or too draconian, digressive in lectures, unhelpful in answering questions or giving one-on-one guidance, or just dull as dishwater.

If you are considering teaching because you can't think of anything else to do (regardless of whether teaching is a career you plan to stick with your whole life or a job you intend to try for only a year or two), stop. You should not enter the teaching profession by default or with a sense of resignation. Doing so will make you a lousy teacher, and lousy teachers produce worse students—and, in case you haven't heard, we have quite enough of those already.

## What Makes Teaching Unique

More than any other profession addressed in this book, teaching is a confluence of opposites. Teaching draws on instinct, and it draws on acquired skills. Teaching involves routine, and it involves improvisation. Teaching is prose surprised by moments of poetry. Teaching is applied pedagogy, tested by trial and error. There is no better way to learn something than to teach it, and teaching itself is a continual learning process—a methodology that changes every time new students walk in the door and sit down at their desks.

In every job, a barrier exists between you and the end user of your good or service. Newspaper reporters and magazine editors don't see people reacting to their work, and although they hear from some of their readers (often in the form of complaints), they seldom hear from all their readers; book editors work for a year or more on a single title, but it's not easy to

**Most Important Skills**

The four most important skills for any teacher to develop are:

- ***Organization.*** Your effectiveness as a teacher is greatly influenced—some might argue, totally dependent on—your ability to plan your lessons, manage your time, pace yourself and your work, and maintain order (if not in your classroom, then at least in your day planner).
- ***Focus.*** It's all too easy, in evaluating your students and their needs, to become overwhelmed by what they appear not to know. It is then that the job feels unmanageable. Each student is different: Not all are at the same ability level, and not all have the same desire to learn. Meanwhile, the clock is ticking for the class, the semester, and the year. The effective teacher can focus, simplify, and move from one student's needs to the class's needs and back again.
- ***Detachment.*** Teachers share something in common with emergency room doctors: They do their work on a stranger, stay with that person for a while, then release that person from their care. How well that person is going to do from now on, who knows? As a teacher, your job is to care about your students, and yet, within a year or a few months, those young people will

have moved on. You may never hear from them again, you have no way of knowing if what you taught them sank in or meant the least bit of difference in their lives. A measure of detachment, cultivated over time and with experience, is a necessary thing.

- ***Patience.*** This is the big one. Even if you think you are, by nature, a patient person, I guarantee that your patience has never been tested like it is tested teacher-style. On a daily basis, your patience is tested with your students, with their parents, with the other students in the school, with your colleagues, with your administrators, with your state government and the federal government, with the people who make the books and with the people who develop the tests. Of course, your patience with yourself is tested, too.

Depending on where and what you teach, your students come to you for a relatively brief amount of time: You have only so many months in which to administer the lesson. Frankly, sometimes you just hope that something sticks and they walk away having learned something. Where they walk to is anybody's guess; whether you made a difference is also often anybody's guess. You do what you can, while you can, with what resources you have.

You surely have, in your mind, memories and a mental picture of the best teacher you ever had; you may want to become just like that teacher. What you *didn't* see is how long it took for your favorite teacher to get that good. It took long hours, hard work, a lot of frustration, trial and error, and a long series of little steps.

And patience, patience, patience.

tell if students are learning from the textbook or if adults are enjoying the novel; and writers and editors who work in business communications aren't there to see people open the letters or brochures they developed.

Teaching provides greater immediacy and interplay between you and the person you're trying to reach. You are right there with your students, facing them, looking over their shoulders and taking them by the hand to help them learn (in some cases, literally). If you find satisfaction in that immediacy, in seeing the effects of your work, and if you feel comfortable standing up in front of a group, then rack up a few points in favor of teaching.

Most of all, if you yourself like to learn—if you love that feeling, that intellectual and emotional sensation, when something complex suddenly becomes simple or when something unfamiliar becomes familiar—and you like the idea of sharing that experience with someone else, then you score another point.

With teaching, you become involved with your students intellectually, psychologically, and emotionally. You see them every day and think about them on the weekends. Depending on their age, you literally may be drawn into their confrontations with each other and into their troubles at home. You're part of the picture. Even when I taught college, I had students come into my office to discuss their essay assignments only to have them burst into tears and tell me about their personal lives. (Note to self: Always make sure your office has a tissue box. Either you or your students will be using it.) You worry about the students who fall behind, and you worry about the students who excel.

This attachment and proximity to your students can have its benefits, and these, I find, are often what people talk about when they talk about the rewards of teaching. You become involved with your students and their development, so when you see them succeed and learn and surprise even themselves, that payoff makes up for all the other stuff—the stress, the anxiety, the taxing of your patience.

Teaching is arguably far more collaborative than any of the other professions discussed in this book. You are exchanging information, skills, pedagogy, and practices with your colleagues and with great minds of the past and present. Your daily work with your students is a collaborative effort.

In most of the various jobs I have held, I could walk out at five o'clock and check out mentally. I could leave the newsroom in the newsroom and the office at the office. Teaching was hard to leave behind when the time came to punch out. In the shower, in bed at night, driving to the supermarket, watching TV, mowing the lawn, eating dinner: I found myself thinking about my kids, about lesson plans, about papers that needed to be graded. Sometimes it was thrilling to know that I cared so much about something that it had become such a large part of my life; other times, I was desperate to turn it off and stop thinking about it.

And yet, part of me didn't want to stop thinking about it.

Why? Because after journalism, teaching was the job in which I most felt like I made a difference in people's lives. You cannot know the gratification and emotional impact of that until you experience it firsthand, as a teacher. The smallest victory with one student can make your week.

Other characteristics common among capable teachers are strong organizational skills combined with an ability to improvise; a facility for multitasking; patience and forbearance; and a tolerance for, if not an appetite for, politics.

What about a love of young people? All the really great teachers in the movies and on TV really seem to love kids. Do you need to love kids in order to teach?

## *Teach First, Love Later*

First of all, not all teachers teach kids. Adults need to learn, too: a new skill; a new language; or the subjects they didn't have the time, opportunity, or money to learn in their youth. Adults in every type of profession need to be trained and are interested in furthering their education; they all need to be taught.

Second, even if you do teach children or young people, you don't have to love them to be a good teacher, though it certainly would help the development of your patience, flexibility, and understanding. It may not even be necessary to *like* children, either in general or as individuals.

You might say that you need to love teaching more than you need to love your students.

One teacher I spoke to for this book reflected that if all she had was a love of young people, she might have become a social worker or a pediatrician. But although she loves the company of children and interacting with children, she loves, above all, teaching children and helping them learn. That's why she teaches fourth grade.

Like many of her colleagues, this teacher is motivated by a desire to help—and not just to help in an abstract sense, but to really sit down with a student or students and work through a problem, an assignment, a challenge.

You need, then, not so much a love of children as a sense of responsibility toward your students—perhaps even a sense of duty, if you care to think of it in those terms—manifested in an eagerness to work with them; a willingness to make sacrifices for them; a tolerance for their mistakes; and a fundamental belief in the importance of learning and the value of what you're doing every day.

If you believe there is some correspondence between your personality and what makes for a good teacher, you're probably wondering what teaching is like.

## Caveat Instructor

If you have never taught before, your perception of teaching is largely defined (or, let's say, skewed) by your experiences as a student: You think about teachers you have known or have had—and have either loved or hated—and from that, you imagine what teaching is like. This may be only natural, but it's not the way to determine whether you want to teach.

For example, I've known people who say they don't want to teach high school because they didn't *like* high school—as if every high school in America is like the one they went to fifteen or twenty years ago and, as a teacher, they would face the same problems they faced as a teenage student. Similarly, people who attended public schools assume that teaching at a private school or a charter school or a community college would be pretty much the same thing.

Being a student does not give you a sense of what it is like to be a teacher any more than being a hospital patient gives you insight into what it is like to be a doctor or a nurse.

Okay, then what else do you have to go on? Well, you've seen TV shows and movies about teachers: TV dramas such as *Boston Public* or movies such as *Pay It Forward, Mr. Holland's Opus, The Emperor's Club, Stand and Deliver, Dead Poets Society, Mona Lisa Smile* or (going back a little ways) *To Sir, With Love.* Funny how these movies always take place either in elite, leaf-strewn prep schools and colleges or savage inner-city high schools. Both have good scenery, I suppose, but movies tend to serve up the teaching profession with a heavy helping of schmaltz. In these charming set pieces, the hard-to-reach student is invariably reached; the cold and unfeeling administration is confronted with the errors of their ways; the kids who deserve As get them; the class is, finally, appreciative of all the teacher's efforts; and all discover that somewhere between the assignments and the papers and the grades, they must remember the most important thing, love.

You may have already figured out that these movies are no more representative of real-life teaching than *Rocky* is of real-life boxing. Movies and television are often about wish fulfillment—confirming on-screen our hopes, our dreams, and other lies we like to tell ourselves—and the aforementioned teaching-themed movies comfort us with the assurance that the teacher really did care about us as people, and we did, in the end, learn something valuable and useful in school. If we are parents, the movies soothe our anxieties by having us think that teachers who care are alive and well.

But if you want to get a realistic look at what teaching is like, movies aren't going to help. You could talk to working teachers, be they family, friends, strangers or your own teachers, but remember two things when talking to people about their job: First, as a general rule, it is easier for most people to express complaints about their job than to articulate its rewards and satisfactions. Second, when you talk to a teacher, her experience is specific to the school, district, city, and state in which she works, as well as to her own background, experience, credentials, and proximity to retirement.

You may hear that teachers are unappreciated and that teaching is a thankless job. (Psst: Almost everyone, in every profession, feels unappreciated. Everyone from the lowliest beat police officer to the president of the United States feels like she isn't shown enough gratitude or respect.)

You may hear that teachers are criminally underpaid. (Psst: When was the last time you heard someone complain, *You know, to be fair, they really do give me too much money in this job*?)

You may hear that the teaching profession does not attract the best and the brightest. (Psst: Have you read *Dilbert* lately? Incompetence can be found in every profession, company, department, and office.)

So how do you know if teaching is right for you and if you are right for teaching?

Ultimately, there's only one way to find out: teach. And depending on how seriously you wish to pursue the profession, you may want to consider giving it more than one semester. In her book *Ms. Moffett's First Year: Becoming a Teacher in America,* author Abby Goodnough identifies a school of thought that suggests that it takes a person between three and five years to truly get to the top of the teaching game—problem is, most people drop out before they clock three to five years.

Why?

Teaching is one tough job. There may be tougher jobs than being a teacher—the job of an emergency room doctor leaps to mind—but these jobs (because they are so difficult) are likely to require lengthy and intensive training. ER doctors, for instance, have to go through medical school and internships, which prepare them for what they face every day. Not a few people come into teaching with little or no training, preparation, or mentoring, and the natural result is a speedy burnout.

And pay? Sure, the only teachers driving to school in Jaguars are the stuck-up ones in the movies, who get what they deserve when the football team douses their car with paint, but given the challenges of teaching, you could double the pay for some people, and they'd still drop out.

**The Best Advice I Ever Got**

I could fill another whole book with advice from teachers for teachers, but I have selected the tips that follow because they were the most helpful to me in my classroom career.

- ***Gauge your discipline.*** It's easier to start the semester as Hitler and get nicer than vice versa.
- ***Call on students.*** If you address a question to the entire class, no one will answer, so don't ask questions that way: Call on students regardless of whether they have their hands raised. Tell your students at the outset that you will ask direct questions directly. If you say "Somebody better raise their hand or I'm just going to start calling on people," you sound petulant and threatening.
- ***Set clear grade expectations.*** Give the students—preferably in writing—a clear and concise guideline as to what constitutes an A paper, a B paper, and so on. You could even try letting the students themselves determine how their written work will be judged. Spend a class discussing what makes

good writing. Break the students into discussion groups and have each group reach a consensus on two or three basic qualities of good writing. Put responses on the board, discuss them, and agree on the three most important qualities. Tell the class that these three qualities—e.g., succinct expression, perfect spelling, persuasive argument—will be the basis for judging their written work.

- ***Keep your distance.*** Once, after a class, a few of my best students invited me to attend a festival of some kind the school was holding that weekend: They seemed really excited at the prospect of my coming and hanging with them. Politely, I declined. Other teachers may disagree, but the best policy (and safest one for all parties) is for you to see your kids in the classroom and in office hours—period. This is true whether you teach grades K–12 or college. Anything else risks a compromise to the teacher–student relationship, and down that path lies madness. And lawyers.
- ***Have some class.*** On tests and in papers, some of your students are going to give you answers and statements that are so absurd or laughable, you'll be tempted to share them with your teaching colleagues under the heading *Students Say the Darnedest Things.* Teachers get e-mails like this: dopey responses or sentences that are a comedy of errors. Your students may laugh at you behind your back and talk to their friends about what a dork you are, but that doesn't mean you should do the same to them. Don't become known as the teacher who holds up her own students as objects of scorn and smug, superior laughter.
- ***Leave the door open.*** Never hold office hours with the door closed. There is nothing a student needs to tell you that she cannot tell you with the door open a crack. Better safe than sorry.

Most people, when they take a new job, expect to hit their stride within the first month—two months on the outside. When that doesn't happen in a teaching job, some people bag it and say teaching's not for them.

But teaching itself may not be the whole problem. It could be that they're not teaching the right material at the right level to the right kind of student in the right kind of school supervised by the right administrators in the right city in the right state.

## *Teacher, Test Thyself*

Simply saying *I want to teach* isn't specific enough.

Do you want to teach in the United States or abroad?

Do you want to teach in the city or in the suburbs?

Do you want to teach full time, part time, as a substitute, or as a tutor?

Are you interested in teaching elementary, secondary, or high school?

Do you want to teach in a public school, a private school, or a prep school?

Do you want to teach in an all-girl school or an all-boy school?

Do you want to teach in a parochial school, a magnet school, or a charter school?

Do you want to teach in a vocational school?

Do you want to teach children in an accelerated program, children in special education, or children with a mix of physical and mental abilities?

Do you want to teach children of wealthy families or children of middle-class or underprivileged families?

Are you willing to be assigned to teach subjects you know nothing about? (It happens: I know a Spanish teacher who was assigned to teach a class in Latin, and she literally kept one chapter ahead of her students.)

Are you willing to live in a dorm with your students, as part of your teaching responsibilities? Are you willing to coach a sport, as part of those responsibilities?

How willing are you to relocate to a different town, city, or state to continue your career?

Of course, there's no correct answer to any of the above questions, but there is an incorrect answer to all of them: *It doesn't make any difference.*

When I considered teaching as a career, I had a pretty good mental image of the kind of teacher I wanted to be, but what your guidance counselor and the want ads don't tell you is that *what* you teach, *how* you teach, and *whom* you teach will change from assignment to assignment, school to school, and class to class.

Example: You may have grown up being taught spelling or phonetics or grammar in a certain way—a way that you liked and that you would like to use when you become a teacher. By the time you get in a classroom, you may not have the liberty to choose or use that method. Why? Because the method that you were taught under is twenty years old. It's out-of-date, old-fashioned, not the current pedagogy. You will likely have other teachers and administrators telling you how you will teach: Teach this subject, teach these skills, teach in this way, and (perhaps) teach to this test. You may have to collaborate with other teachers, or you may teach at a school that has a certain mission or style of teaching.

What's more, regardless of what kind of teacher you become, you may find that the job title *teacher* is slightly misleading because it suggests that all you will be doing is teaching: i.e., drawing up a lesson plan, writing on the chalkboard, asking questions of the class, handing out assignments, and grading papers and exams.

Would that the job was that elementary, but not even teaching elementary school is that elementary.

## Who Is the Teacher?

You are also a disciplinarian. You are a referee. You are a counselor, psychiatrist, nurse, detective.

You are a field trip organizer and leader, fund-raising coordinator, and substitute teacher in a subject you know nothing about.

You are an advocate: for yourself, for your kids, for your subject, for your school.

You are the intermediary between your students and their parents. To some of your students, whether you asked for the job or not, you are also a surrogate father or mother.

You may be a mentor to some of your students. It's nice to think that you will be a role model or even a hero. Some teachers, in their teaching style, try to be friends with the students. (The ones who try to be more than friends are recognizable by their orange jumpsuits and handcuffs.)

You will be a union member, committee member, unpaid volunteer, and, at some point in your career, you may be either a striker or a scab.

At a private school, you very likely will be called upon to be a coach (as in, of a sport) and/or a resident assistant. You may be named director of the school play or musical, regardless of your experience and whether you even like *South Pacific*.

Sounds like a lot of work, doesn't it? And you thought you'd cut loose at 2:45 P.M. every day and get summers off. So, to do all this, what do you need?

## *That's Certified, Not Certifiable*

In order to become a teacher, you need to be certified—except in those instances in which you don't need to be certified. To be certified as a teacher, you must fulfill federal- and state-mandated requirements to teach a particular subject or to teach at a particular kind of school. Different states have different certification requirements for different levels of teaching; a detailed explanation of these is easily obtained from your state's department of education or from an Internet search.

Teaching certification and licensure will likely involve passing an exam or a number of exams, taking a practicum in teaching (sometimes called student-teaching), and undergoing a performance evaluation (observation in a classroom setting). Your state may also require you, post-certification, to participate in professional development programs, and you may, after a period of time, be required to recertify.

Not all teaching jobs are full time. If you get a part-time position at one school, you may find that, in order to cobble together a living as a teacher, you need to take supplemental work at another school five miles away. Unfortunately, your certification to teach English at the first school may not preclude you from having to obtain certification all over again at the second school, especially if the second school happens to be just across the state border.

Not all teaching opportunities require state certification—or any certification at all. It may also be within a school's discretion, if it needs to hire someone quickly or in an emergency, to take someone without certification.

It may vex your mind to comprehend why you do not need teaching certification in English to teach at an expensive private school, although you do need teaching certification in English to teach at a low-quality public high school, but there it is. Similarly, you may find that a college or university cannot allow you to teach certain courses because you do not have a master's degree or PhD, but the same college can allow you to teach the same course in the summer studies program.

You may find yourself rejected for a job teaching English composition at a high school because you lack credentials and experience, but if, the following year, you are accepted to a master's program in English, you automatically become qualified to teach English composition to a group of college freshmen, who are paying a much higher price to benefit from your wisdom (even if you aren't being paid much at all).

As contradictory and absurd as the teaching certification process may be, you are subject to its regulations and requirements (though loopholes and allowances may exist, depending on the school's need for teachers).

## *There's Pay, and There's Payoff*

A friend of mine, a teacher of English, once told me about a day when everything went so well in class—the kids were involved and asking questions, everyone was enjoying the material—that he could not get in his car and go home. He considered himself in no condition to drive; he was that elated and excited. He had to go for a long walk to burn off some energy, he felt so terrific.

The headaches and long nights grading papers can evaporate in an instant when you see the light of understanding brighten a student's face. There is simply no substitute for knowing that a difference has been made in a young person's life. (I suppose you could be an egotist and claim all the credit for yourself, but most teachers I know say instead that learning made a difference, the resources or program made a difference, the poem made a difference, the stretch of that student's reach beyond her grasp made a difference.)

To teach successfully requires creativity, patience, indulgence, persistence, determination, and skills in storytelling, organization, and empathy not taught in a class on the nineteenth-century British novel. Perhaps for this reason, people like to say that teachers are born, not made. This, of course, is romantic claptrap because its logical conclusion is that teachers need no ongoing education or tutelage and that any failure on the part of the teacher is the result of poor genetics. Teachers are taught, nurtured, cultivated, and grown, just as their students are.

All sorts of people can be excellent at their jobs and still think of them as what they do on the days between weekends. But the truly excellent teachers, the ones who make a long career of it, think of teaching as fundamental to who they are as people. This is in part why they think of teaching as their vocation, their calling in life: Teaching taps into and is an extension of qualities that are basic to their personalities and desires in life, whether they desire to help people, to enrich someone else's life through education, or just to work with kids because, for all the grief and anxiety they cause, teachers want to be with their students.

## *If Not Teaching, Administration*

My father earned his master's in education from Boston University, took a job teaching, and discovered he didn't like it. He couldn't get accustomed to standing up in front of kids every day and meeting all the challenges teachers must face—it just wasn't an arrow in his quiver.

Instead of becoming a shoe salesman, he tried guidance counseling, and he found he liked that better than teaching. He was still interacting with students, but he did better one-on-one with young people. He founded the guidance department at a high school in a small North Shore town in Massachusetts, and in 1965, he applied for and was hired to an administrative job in Rhode Island: director of special services in the Warwick School Department. He stayed in that job for twenty-three years. He oversaw special education and the gifted program, and supervised the guidance counselors, nurses, and other non-teachers who came into daily contact with the schoolchildren.

Although a career in school administration can be an option for those who don't wish to teach, keep in mind that professional requisites for administrative positions such as the one my father held often include time spent as a teacher. There is much—much—to say about school administration, so much that I could take up another whole book discussing the politics, the labor negotiations, and the budget battles. Suffice it to say, if you're an English major and you don't want to teach, it doesn't mean you can't go into education.

## TRY THIS

There are ways to get a taste of what it's like to teach. Stand up in front of a group and teach something. Hold an informal class for your friends or classmates in your dorm room or apartment. Turn your weekly study group into an opportunity for you to teach, or teach your friends how to make a dinner in ten minutes, how to tap a keg correctly, or how to apply makeup. What you're teaching is less important than the fact that you are experiencing teaching.

If you are no longer an undergraduate and you work in an office, ask your supervisor if you can hold a lunch-and-learn or brown-bag session—a voluntary noontime meeting at which your colleagues eat their lunch and listen to you make a presentation on a given topic, business-related or not. Pick a topic of interest to you that you think will be interesting to others; build a presentation or lesson plan, using visual aids; and allow time for questions. Your co-workers will be a familiar and (quite likely) forgiving audience.

The caveat to these techniques for getting a taste of teaching is that you must recognize, even if you cannot yet appreciate, the difference between standing up in front of a group of friends, neighbors, and colleagues and doing the same in front of a roomful of strangers who, given the choice, would rather be outside playing or hanging out at the mall. One group is predisposed to support you and wants you to do well; the other is made up of people who don't give a whit whether you succeed or fail, and even if you succeed, they'll find something to complain about anyway.

Consider tutoring the child of a friend if the child is having difficulty in an area you know something about. Teaching one child is vastly different from teaching an entire classroom, but it's a form of teaching nevertheless. Ask around at work to see if anyone is a paid or volunteer tutor. If you find someone who is, take her to lunch to pick her brain and hear her story.

Volunteer at your local school. If you happen to be free during the day, help out with reading and writing in first grade. Get involved. Talk to teachers: See what you'll be doing and what you'll be up against.

## GLOSSARY

### WHAT'S THE DIFFERENCE BETWEEN ...

PTA and PTO?

*PTA* stands for Parent Teacher Association. There is a local PTA for your school, a state PTA, and a national PTA. Your local PTA comprises parents of schoolchildren who work with teachers, administrators, politicians and policy makers, and other members of the community to advance the education, safety, and well-being of the schools and its schoolchildren.

*PTO* stands for Parent Teacher Organization and refers to a local group that acts independently of the local and national PTA. Although a PTA and PTO do fundamentally the same work, the former charges dues for membership and the latter does not. (It's not uncommon, in fact, for parents to refuse to join their PTO because they mistakenly think they have to pay dues.)

If you're curious to know what major issues a school district is facing, your most accessible source may be the PTO or PTA president. Take her out to lunch.

Teaching Certificate and Provisional Teaching Certificate?

Requirements for both vary from state to state and from subject to subject. A *provisional teaching certificate* is a temporary license to teach, pending completion of required teaching hours, observation in the classroom, and completion of curricular requirements. Your state department of education has all the details; go online or call them for information.

**Public School, Private School, and Prep School?**

A preparatory (or prep) school is a private secondary school, usually comprising grades nine through twelve but sometimes starting as early as grade five. A private school is owned by a person or persons rather than a government agency, and its officials are not publicly elected. (A public school is operated by publicly elected officials.)

Not all public schools are disaster areas, not all prep schools pay meager salaries, and not all private schools are religious schools.

**A College, a University, and a Community College?**

My own alma mater, Boston College, could very well call itself Boston University, if the name weren't already taken. Strictly speaking, *college* refers to the school's undergraduate program, and *university* is a term for an institution of learning that comprises an undergraduate program and other colleges (e.g., law, medical, and other graduate-level programs).

A *community college* is usually a two-year public institution offering programs suited to community needs. Admission may not have the entrance requirements that a college or university would.

## *Q & A*
## WHAT YOU TEACH, WHO YOU ARE

Tim Beneski has a lot of children—seventy-five or eighty, approximately.

Four of those kids live at home with Tim and his wife, and the others may be found at the Avon Old Farms School in Avon, Connecticut, which, as it happens, is where Tim and his family live.

Tim and his children eat lunch together and play sports together. Tim serves them their dinner. He knows the personal details of their lives down to the names of their pets. On a daily basis, Tim talks to these youngsters about writing and literature and language and moral philosophy, and when night falls and it's time for bed, Tim is there to turn out the light.

Though it sounds like it should be one-room, belfried building painted barn red, the Old Avon Farms School is a prep school for 380 young men. Eighty percent of these students are boarders, and the remaining twenty percent are day students.

Beneski, who is forty, starts a typical school day a little before 8:00 A.M. After classes, club meetings, committee meetings, sports, lunch, dinner, and study hall, he finishes up a little after 11:00 P.M. He teaches English, Latin, and moral philosophy, and he's been at the Avon School for more than a decade.

**Tim, when did you decide you wanted to major in English?**

I declared my English major in eighth grade. I just knew that's where my talents were and that's where my interest was, in reading and writing. I knew that I was not a great math scholar. I just knew that literature excited me as a child and I knew that's what I wanted to get into. When I was in high school, I took as many English electives as I could.

Did you know, just as early, that you wanted to teach?

I remember distinctly a conversation I had when I was going into my senior year [of college], and [someone] asked me what my major was, and I said English, and he said, "Are you going to be a teacher?" and I said, "*No way!*" [laughs]

Why not?

I knew that I wanted to make much more money than I thought I could make as a teacher, and I knew, by that time, my schooling was more or less done, and the idea of going back to it was not appealing to me.

So what did you do instead of teach?

I thought about law school. I ended up working as a claim manager for CIGNA life insurance.

How did that work out?

[laughs] I realized I didn't like it. So I sat down and made of list of what were the things that I liked best—making presentations to groups of people, helping people to learn things to their maximum ability. . . .

In other words, teaching!

I knew that in order to teach public school in Connecticut, I'd have to be certified. I went full time to graduate school to get a teaching certificate.

And you taught while you were in graduate school?

I took on any kind of teaching job I could. I coached while working as a substitute teacher in the Hartford area. I subbed like a crazy person. I could have subbed every day if I wanted.... I was listed as a sub in four districts. What I did was, I worked every angle and I talked to every secretary and everybody I thought would get me to the top of the [substitute teacher] list. The key is making yourself available and getting people to like you enough and respect your work as a sub enough to request you.

Then you got a job as adjunct faculty at Tunxis Community College in Farmington, Connecticut, and by this time, you'd fulfilled the curricular requirements to receive a provisional teaching certificate. I see from your résumé you also held a job teaching at the Morse Business School—a class in proofreading for court reporting?

It was a class for which I had only the minimum requirements. I knew grammar, but I learned a ton about punctuation and rules that I hadn't given much thought to.

How did you hear about the Old Avon Farms School?

A buddy of mine called me and said, "I'm teaching at this school, Avon Old Farms School, and I think you would like it more than me."

Sounds as if you like it just fine.

I like the idea of a prep school, which was something out there beyond my experience when I was a student. When I saw it, I thought, *This is intriguing*: the idea that the kids are always there, you're always there, and you're always a teacher.

*Always* a teacher? Don't you need a break?

I read as a senior at Boston College, "Don't let what you do define who you are." But I want to be what I am, and what I *do* should be what I am! The idea of being a teacher all the time was appealing to me, and being at a boarding school, you are always on.

It's this idea that the kids are always there, you're always there, and you're always a teacher. Teaching became my life.

And you prefer teaching private school to teaching public school?

I'm there to tuck [my kids] in at night, for crying out loud, so I know my kids way better than I could in a public school system.

You sound like a surrogate parent to these kids. And a pretty good one, too.

[laughs] Love, baby. It's all about the love.

## *Q & A*
## THEY'LL NEVER FORGET YOU

At a certain point in her career, Kelly Cowan found that the most helpful teacher meetings were the ones she managed to get out of.

In the late 1990s, Cowan was in her early thirties. She had moved from Texas back to her native state of Maine and was on a short-term contract teaching Spanish at a small rural school. Difficult students were making her wonder if teaching was the right career for her.

Because of her short-term status at the school, Cowan was able to get out of regular teaching meetings—or, as she saw it, to escape what she considered bureaucratic conferences unhelpful to her development as a teacher. The free time allowed her to sit in on the class of a colleague, a German language teacher, who seemed to be enjoying great success with her students.

Cowan showed this teacher her lesson plans and asked, *What am I doing wrong? Or right?*

What was her big secret?

> What I learned from this teacher was primarily better and more exciting pacing, how to confidently hold to high expectations, practical ways to turn the problem and responsibility for a solution back on the student, the importance of convincing students that I am on their side and working for them and not against them, the ability to move from the imagination to the concept seamlessly, and activities that give warmth and magic to dry material without downplaying the centrality of factual material.

You were actually a double major in college, I see: English and human development. It doesn't sound like you were determined to become a teacher.

I kind of feel I've been directed spiritually along this path.... I had an idealistic love for learning, . . . [but] I don't know where it came from. I came from a pretty poor family. We didn't have any books at home. But I graduated fifth in my [high school] class, and I just always loved ideas. I really like trying to figure out what is the truth about things.

You took education classes as an undergraduate. What did you learn there?

[laughs] I remember I took a class called Methods of Teaching English. I don't remember anything [about it]. I couldn't name one single method that an English teacher uses.

Classes in statistics, adolescent psychology, pedagogy, and the history of education—not helpful?

I think a lot of these ideas have good intentions, but they're not helpful to the practical stuff.

If you want to be a good teacher, don't be an education major. The best thing you can do is be really good in your subject.

What do you find, day to day, makes for a good teacher?

You really do have to be the kind of person who will roll up your sleeves and get to work. You can't be snobby, because you're flying by the seats of the pants most of the time. You don't have a secretary. It's this weird mixture of being an upper-level manager with lots of responsibility, but you don't have a lot of support or freedom or control over the ways things go. But then you shoulder all the responsibility if your kids don't do well.

At the moment, you're finishing your second year teaching tenth grade at Crockett High School in Austin, Texas, but I see you've taught everything from Spanish to special education to English.

Once you know yourself and you know what you want to teach, it clicks. [Figuring that out] might take a while.

And figuring out your own style, too, yes?

In my undergraduate education classes, they told us that lecturing was inferior to hands-on activities. But no one lectures to [students] anymore; nor are students prepared to listen well to lessons—or to one another. Students need to learn how to listen, and they need to be given practice in sustained listening. So I read to my kids, and they respond.

You figure out what works.

You can come to [teaching] with different strengths. A colleague of mine, a woman fresh out of college, will come into school more focused on her relationship with her students than on the minute details of the day's lesson plan. But she loves people, she goes out of her way for her students, she doesn't judge them, and she tells them she loves them.

[laughs] She tells me, "They might hate you, but they'll never forget you."

## *Q & A*
### TEACHER OF THE RISING SUN

When I asked Nikolai Yasko, thirty-seven, how he chose Japan for a teaching abroad experience, he replied, "Japan chose me."

Yasko worked in Japan for a total of twelve years: two years as an assistant language teacher (ALT) at public junior high schools, and ten at private high school. Along the way, the former English major also held part-time positions at a university and at a couple of "cram-exam" schools.

Currently, Yasko lives with his Japanese-born wife and their two children in his native state of Wisconsin, where he teaches on the high school and university levels.

The option of teaching abroad literally opens up a world of choices. How did you choose Japan, and how would you advise someone go about choosing a host country?

I was a young English teacher willing to go anywhere. A small Catholic school in northern Japan had an agreement with a private college in Minnesota to provide them with teachers, but nobody at that college wanted to go that year [1991], and so they posted an opening with the University of Minnesota, where I had gone to school. I applied, interviewed over the phone, and was offered the job.

Is that a typical entrée into the system?

In Japan, most Westerners go on a program called JET, sponsored by the Japanese government, which takes young people from English-speaking nations and places them as assistant language teachers in public schools. Some of these ALTs also come from sister-city or sister-state programs, including myself, who used the Wisconsin-Chiba sister-state program as a starting point on my second tour of Japan.

Some people have written books and studies of the JET program, and the consensus seems to be that, while the ALTs have value, they are so marginalized that any potential impact from Westerners is negated. Moreover, there is no nationwide standard of just how to use these people (who are usually limited to a three-year contract), so no two ALT experiences are ever quite the same. Hit-and-miss.

Other Japan teachers find jobs with corporations (a field that largely dried up after the bubble), language schools (almost no one has a positive experience with these), private high schools (high pay but impossible working conditions), and private universities (mostly terminal contracts, but good pay and vacations), as well as cram schools (for students who are still attending or who have graduated from high school but who want to enter a university that requires a strenuous examination).

### What's so impossible about the impossible working conditions at private high schools in Japan?

The private high school in Japan is a closed environment. It gets musty and dank, and strange things start popping up. The public schools are a bit better because teachers and principals are forcibly rotated every few years, but most students and staff members are on autopilot there, too. The private high schools pay well, but they want your soul in return.

Education and classes are simply not important to anyone in any high school—it's all about socialization. See the chapter about education in a book called *Dogs and Demons: Tales From the Dark Side of Modern Japan* by Alex Kerr.

Serious-minded kids study outside of school, at cram schools, or on their own. Walk by most classes in most high schools (class size is usually forty to forty-five) and you will see about half the kids sleeping or talking while the teacher recites a memorized lecture directly at the blackboard.

### Does that make teaching easy or hard?

Teaching is the easy part. For teachers, the socialization is very labor-intensive. Everyone is expected to do their part for coaching, clubs, and festivals—the stuff that the parents get to see. I imagine American schools have some similarities in this regard, but I would argue that it's a matter of degree. The Japanese are a people who accept polite fictions, and one of these is that kids go to school to learn.

I worked at one of the top twenty high schools in the nation when I was in Kyoto. We had good, bright students and did absolutely nothing with them. That they got into good universities was entirely a result of their own efforts.

Most teachers at private schools in the States have to coach a sports team, in addition to teach. Did you have to do that?

Coaching is one of the biggest jobs a teacher can have. Teachers are assigned sports to coach, whether they have any experience with it or not. Most sports clubs practice year-round, and most teachers are expected to be sort of hard-nosed. Sports, especially baseball, are treated as martial arts. The teacher has to give up weekends and summer vacations. How much is a comfortable salary worth if you never see your own family?

Some other people I've spoken to who have taught abroad say that among their students, there was an initial fascination with "the American," but that this fascination quickly wore off, and that among parents, other teachers, and community members, there was often a suspicion of the American's motives for teaching abroad. Some teachers, for example, would dismiss the American as a wayward youth looking for "an experience," only to return one day to the wealthy home nation. Did you find this at all, teaching in Japan?

There is an interesting dynamic concerning American teachers abroad. On the one hand, we are symbols of Western culture, and so are viewed with feelings of resentment along with, to some degree, respect and an initial fascination. A Filipino or Korean in Japan, for example, has a very different experience. On the other hand, the English teacher is also a paid servant, and subject to the whims of employers, who often view their employees with thinly veiled contempt. Again, what is this person doing here? "Real Americans" stay home.

Students always viewed me with initial fascination. Later in my career, when I spoke Japanese well, there was always some disappointment at this. Many Japanese view Americans who speak the language with a good deal of suspicion. The popular conception (in the States as well as in Japan) is that Japanese is a very difficult language and only Japanese can speak it well. A Westerner who speaks the language will confuse and anger people because the Westerner, whenever he opens his mouth, is challenging their conceptions and making them think. That's always dangerous.

As a young man reading Steinbeck's *East of Eden,* I found the character of the Chinese servant unbelievable—no one would demand that someone speak pidgin English, I thought. After my Japan experience, however, I find that character the most interesting creation within the novel.

**It is possible, though, isn't it, to make friends with students, teachers, and parents?**

Some students who hate English will be pleased that you can speak Japanese, and will make an effort to be friendly. Teachers in Japan have to take care of a homeroom, and these homeroom teachers are counselors, vice-principals, coaches, and advisors wrapped into one. So you get pretty close to the kids. In fact, too close. In my high school life, I dealt with extortion, bullying, theft, violence, and sexual harassment. A lot of Japanese teachers these days will try to hush these things up, since that's what the school wants.

Colleagues appreciate language ability, and will be less likely to shunt you off to the side if you speak the language. Still, some will make fun of you. You spend a lot of time with Japanese colleagues at the high school level, and it is important to have people around you that treat you with some modicum of respect.

Parents in Japan these days are very vocal. In the postwar days, most of them did not have degrees, and the idea of the teacher as a respected figure in society was real. That's not so much the case these days. Most parents don't have realistic conceptions of their child's ability. Like other institutions that one finds in Japan, a lot of families are very busy trying to fit squares into round holes. I saw one kid run away from home and live on his own for two months because his father wanted him to become a doctor, and he didn't want to. His older brother had committed suicide for the same reason, and still the old man wouldn't give up. Try dealing with a parent like that.

You note that in addition to teaching, you did translation work, writing and editing, and even judged speech contests. Were these opportunities you found on your own initiative, or were they opportunities readily available for someone in your position?

Speech contests are part of being a secondary school teacher. You get anywhere from fifty to two hundred dollars for watching junior high kids recite a speech, or perhaps an original speech that the local Westerner wrote for them.

When abroad, it is always easier to get published. English textbooks always sell, and every once in a while a Westerner makes a lot of money with an original approach. As for non-academic writing, local tourist magazines or friends with Web sites offer opportunity. Someone may ask you to contribute.

How did you obtain a public school teaching license in Japan, when such a thing is prohibited by law?

Japanese law is funny. Japanese rules are funny. Things appear to be set in stone, and, just as you have given up, someone will say, "Oh, about that thing you wanted to do? It's against the rules, but we can make an exception this time." On the other hand, things that appear fine will hit snags. Everything is on a case-by-case basis.

Regarding my license: The director of my school in Hokkaido was impressed that I had an American teaching license, and applied on my behalf. He must have known someone. I didn't care much about the license, but it did save me some paperwork later on (since foreigners get special, temporary licenses). There are a few Koreans working in public schools, but not many.

Once you were in Japan, did you maintain a relationship with the state sponsor program in Wisconsin? Peace Corps teachers, for example, need to file reports on their work and progress.

The Japanese run the JET program. Any sort of support comes from the Western side of it all. You are at the mercy of the local *gaijin* handlers (*gaijin* is a pejorative term for any non-Japanese), who usually resent the fact that they are saddled with this responsibility. That's why the program is so hit-and-miss. Other than that, you're on your own.

I understand your teaching salary in Japan wasn't anything to sneeze at. What occasioned your return to the United States, and has your teaching experience in Japan helped you in any way, back in the States?

The most I made was $85,000, at the private high school in Kyoto. I would be approaching six figures there, if I had stayed. The JET program pays about $30,000. The salary hasn't changed since its inception in the 1980s. Language school teachers can expect to make between $20,000 and $30,000, with much longer hours. University three-year positions usually pay about $40,000 to $60,000 a year.

I left because it's true when people tell you that money isn't everything. I did not believe in Japan anymore, and I didn't like it anymore. There is a constant sense of hostility that the long-termer feels, and it's wearing on a person. I was not without resources in the United States, and it was time for a change.

Moreover, I have two Japanese-American kids, and did not want to send them through the Japanese school system. International schools are so costly that sending two kids through them would have taken about half my salary every year.

What was the most gratifying part of teaching abroad?

I learned another language. I learned a new way of looking at the world. I see things in America that I would never have seen had I not gone abroad. I have a better sense of what is important in life and what is not. I have a wonderful Japanese wife and two bicultural and bilingual kids. I have an interesting set of international friends: Northern Irish, English, New Zealanders, and Japanese. You don't meet these kinds of people too often in [my home state of] Wisconsin.

As far as classroom teaching, I found that teaching Japanese-to-English translation was fun, even if the kids didn't always like it. Still,

I believe that teaching in America is better that teaching in Japan, because teaching here has more meaning.

What advice would you give someone considering teaching abroad?

As far as choosing a place, I would look at Internet sites where teachers talk about their experiences, and stay away from the places that seem to garner more than their fair share of negative responses. Poland is not too bad, I hear.

If possible, I would talk directly with someone who has taught in a particular place. An experienced voice can save you lots of grief.

# CHAPTER 3 *Higher Ed: Nobody Goes Back to School*

As an English major, you're probably more accustomed than other people to the insular environment of libraries, classrooms, and reading rooms, which may lead you to consider the groves of academia as your natural habitat. Where else, after all, do book lovers go—especially if you graduate into a job market that is less than welcoming?

First of all: If, after graduating from college, you decide you want to go back to school, then turn yourself around, re-enroll as a freshman, and do the whole four years all over again. Graduate school is so different from college, you're not going *back* to anything; you're walking into an entirely new situation, with a wholly different set of demands, expectations, and challenges.

Second, as you think about grad school, if you call to mind all your favorite things about college—keg and bong parties, games of Ultimate Frisbee on the quad, that breezy elective you took in Gods and Goddesses of India, spring break, the informal palling around with professors, Greek life—and you assume that some version of those things awaits when you go back to school—forget it.

## Do You Need the Degree?

When I'm asked about advanced degrees, the question is typically phrased *Should I get a master's or PhD?* or *Do I have to go to journalism school?* These are interesting ways to phrase the question, because *should* and *have to* imply obligation or duty, as in *Should I call my mother every weekend?* or *Must I floss after every meal?*

Phrasing the question in terms of *should, ought,* or *have to* also suggests an end result, something to be obtained or procured from earning a postgraduate degree; that is, there's an unstated suffix to the question: *Should I get my*

*MFA [in order to become a successful author]?* or *Do I have to get a PhD [if I want to get a job in book publishing]?*

Thinking about end results and obligation is not bad. In fact, it's as good a way as any to approach the question of graduate school. Think about what you might want to do and where you might want to end up, and through research and reflection, figure out, as best you can, if graduate school is the best, most advantageous, inevitable route to achieve that end.

Phrased another way, can you get away with *not* going to graduate school?

Consider this: If you walk into someone's office and diplomas are displayed so prominently that there is no missing them—e.g., in the office of a doctor or dentist, a lawyer, a psychiatrist or psychologist, or an architect—then yes, you do need a postgraduate degree for that job. Not only should you get one, state and federal law probably insist that you get one.

For everyone else, if you don't see that diploma on the wall, then no, you probably don't need a postgraduate degree. That goes for journalism, book and magazine publishing, and corporate communications. If you're still unsure, go online to job search engines and enter a job title. Examine the job descriptions that come up and look at professional or educational requirements: See if an advanced degree is required, preferred, encouraged, or irrelevant.

An ad for a position as a newspaper or magazine editor might express a preference for graduates of journalism school, but the degree itself is not strictly necessary to building a career in the field. In book publishing, advanced degrees are not usually required. However, an advanced degree in a foreign language would work in your favor if you wanted to edit ESL (English as a second language) or foreign-language textbooks or work in translation services. An advanced degree in linguistics would work in your favor if you were interested in pursuing a career as an editor of dictionaries.

An advanced degree alone cannot help you get a job any more than the fancy clothes you wear to the interview or the expensive paper on which you print your résumé can. *You* help you get a job—by networking; by acting professionally; by learning how to present (or market) yourself; by seeking out opportunities; and by remaining flexible with respect to your criteria for a job.

Degrees can be helpful, but they are not magical. They are not sheepskin tickets to the echelons of success; you won't do well just because you have one. The finest schools in this nation graduate doctors who are sued for malpractice, lawyers who are disbarred, and professors who plagiarize for their books. A students and D students hang the same diplomas on their wall and put the same stickers on the rear window of their car.

## What Makes Higher Education Unique

The graduate experience is very different from the undergraduate experience. Before you decide to enter grad school, make sure that you need an advanced degree and that you can meet the higher expectations of a graduate program, as discussed below.

**Focus.** Undergraduate study, even with its majors and concentrations, is not as focused and as directed as graduate study. College gives you latitude to wander, explore among the various disciplines, and take that cool class in Tolkien. But there are no blow-off classes in graduate school, where you will be more focused on why and how each class will serve your personal and professional goals when you graduate.

**Workload.** I like to say that graduate school is where you finally start taking your studies seriously. The amount of reading alone is a cold bucket of water to any undergraduate notion that you are well read. Add to this your writing requirements, your teaching fellowship, and the second job you will probably have to take. They give you your undergraduate degree because you complete the requirements; they give you the graduate degree because you earn it.

**Social Life.** Because graduate students usually live off-campus or in housing that may be a couple of miles from campus, and because graduate students often have spouses and children, the campus life to which you became accustomed in college (naked beer slides, panty raids, destruction of property) doesn't exist on the postgraduate level.

I'm sure there are fourth-year PhD students out there who would contest that assertion and say that they really let their hair down from time to time. Yes, graduate students take breaks from their studies and go a little wild, but given how much work there is and given obligations to teaching and to their families, taking a break and going wild usually means a rented movie and a nap. Graduate students tend to be more solitary, and the university's idea of a function to amuse and allay their anxiety is a sherry hour in the faculty lounge.

**Time.** College you can finish in four years or less—anything longer than that, and people suspect either penury or indolence, perhaps a drinking problem. Graduate school, on the other hand, lasts as long as it takes for you to finish your dissertation and have it approved: A three-year-program could take five years, or six, or eight.

Urban myths and legends abound about how much time some people have frittered away working over their dissertations. One of the more amusing (and true) stories has a doctoral candidate showing up an at academic conference with a lapel button of his own making that reads, "Don't Ask: It's Not Done."

**Teaching.** Your tuition expenses at graduate school may be paid, in part, by your work as a teacher. As a teacher's assistant (TA), you are attached to a professor with an auditorium-sized class, and your job is to show up at the class (another difference from college!), take notes, do the reading, and grade the flood of papers. You may also be asked to lead a discussion group, as the professor breaks up his giant class into sections. Leading the discussion group will require you to write lesson plans and evaluate performance—in other words, be a teacher. As a teaching fellow, you lead and teach your own classes—probably 100-level courses or English composition.

Your college English professor may never have told you, but he is more than happy to foist the job of reading and grading your papers onto a graduate TA. Those teachers who can pass 'em off, do. Some TAs will read papers and recommend grades to the professor, who then puts his X on the last page, with the grade. Approaches vary, but you'll find that these teaching and grading responsibilities take up a fair amount of your time and energy.

Why, you ask, is the education of undergraduate freshmen and sophomores entrusted to young people who have no formal training in teaching, no advanced degree in their field, no time to dedicate themselves fully to the task of teaching, and perhaps no desire to be in the classroom teaching in the first place?

I'm glad you asked that. It's an excellent question. Now, on to the next topic. . . .

**The Union.** When I went to college, the student union was a building that housed the cafeteria and bookstore. In my first weeks at the University of Michigan, someone recommended to me that as a teaching fellow,

I might want to attend an informational meeting of the graduate student union, or GSU.

I went and listened to a young man explain how graduate TAs like me were no better than servants indentured to our professor overlords and that, from time to time, grad student TAs needed to assert their integrity through dereliction of their teaching duties (i.e., a strike). The best part of the meeting was when he pitched to us the spiral-bound GSU academic calendar, which featured such important dates as the founding of the GSU and the execution of Sacco and Vanzetti.

(If my memory is faulty—if, for example, the GSU calendar did not mark the execution of Sacco and Vanzetti and, say, instead marked the Triangle Shirtwaist factory fire—then I apologize, but the underlying point is the same: The grad student TAs I knew tended to see themselves as victimized and overworked, undercompensated for their efforts and in thrall to the university machine.)

The cynical view would be that the members of the GSU were mostly privileged white kids who liked nothing more than griping about work and their students, all the while flattering themselves in the thought that they were legitimate kindred to members of the local chapter of the clothing and textile workers union.

That said, I once met with an administrator in the English department who asked me if I had joined the GSU, and when I replied that I saw no need for it, that whatever problem I had with administration was one I could handle myself, she felt very comfortable laughing in my face.

**The Dissertation.** A dissertation is the ultimate term paper, and is required if you are pursuing a PhD. (A thesis, in contrast, is a long academic paper you write for your master's degree.) The dissertation experience, if you will, is eight-fold: (1) soliciting faculty to serve as your advisors; (2) deciding on a topic; (3) having the topic approved; (4) researching the topic; (5) writing the paper; (6) submitting it and awaiting approval; (7) rewriting it as many times as necessary, per committee edits; (8) and defending it to a committee that, with approval of the dissertation, greenlights the degree.

That's as many steps as an octopus has legs, and there is just as much ink involved.

The dissertation is without doubt the single largest and most challenging academic assignment you will ever undertake. Somewhere, surely, there is a dissertation about dissertations and how consuming they are of your time, energy, and sanity. The dissertation is, in fact, the best way to distinguish between college and graduate school. In college, you're there to do a lot of things. In grad school, you're there to work. Complete your dissertation, and you'll have a new appreciation for why, in *Austin Powers: International Man of Mystery*, Dr. Evil says, "I didn't spend six years in Evil Medical School to be called *mister*, thank you very much."

You do not necessarily need to write a dissertation to achieve your career objectives: If you completed all your coursework alone, you would be what is called ABD—all but dissertation—and again, depending on your circumstances and your personal and professional goals, that may be enough.

People may joke about going to graduate school to stall for time in finding a job, but the graduate school commitment—in terms of money, time, and energy—is simply too great to allow for an intention that frivolous. If you genuinely want to stall for time in finding a job, you'd be better off taking four years and joining the armed services, where there's more opportunity to travel and a hell of a lot less reading. (What's more, with the training you get in the armed services—particularly in a field like com-

**Most Important Skills**

- ***Knowing what not to do.*** It didn't take me long, as a graduate student, to feel overwhelmed by the amount of reading I had to do. In desperation, I called a friend of mine who is a lawyer—no, not to sue the school, but to get advice on how to handle the workload. He told me he had a similar experience in law school, being overwhelmed by all the assigned reading, and he said, "It's not what you read: it's what you can get away with not reading. They don't expect you to read every single word. They're purposefully overloading you so you can develop the skill of selective reading and figuring out what you need to know." Now that is good free legal advice, ladies and gentlemen.
- ***Sitzfleisch.*** In his 1991 book *One of Us: Richard Nixon and the American Dream*, author Tom Wicker quotes a friend of

the thirty-seventh president as saying that Nixon had what it took to be a great lawyer: an iron butt. In other words, good lawyers—like good grad students—are able to sit for inhumanly long periods of time, reading and writing. The Germans call it *sitzfleisch*, "flesh where one sits." You get the picture. (I must mention, though: Because you're going to be sitting on your behind reading or standing in front of a classroom for at least four years, and you'll be more stressed out than you ever were in college, so do your sanity—and your body—a favor and exercise regularly. Really.)

- ***Stamina.*** If you told people you took ten years to complete your undergraduate degree, they would look at you like you were either drunk or insane (possibly both). If, however, you told people you took ten years to get your PhD, the worst they could think is that you pursued your degree part time. Completing the curricular requirements, fulfilling obligations as a teaching fellow, and, most of all, surviving the dissertation process takes stamina—you may find yourself reminded of that moment in *Rocky* when one of the announcers incredulously cries, "What is holding Balboa up?"

puters or engineering—you're more likely to get a job when you're done than if you went to graduate school.)

## All in the Timing

What's the best time to attend graduate school?

There is no best time, just as there's not a best time to get married or to have children or to buy a home. Doing any of those things at different times in your life carries different responsibilities, different outcomes, different pluses and minuses.

One argument holds that you should go directly from college into graduate school while you are still young, still accustomed to an academic schedule, eager to continue your education, and charged with momentum; the counter-argument posits that you stand to gain by obtaining experience in the workplace and taking some time to consider whether graduate school is something you are interested in and can afford. This counter-argument also suggests that after sixteen or seventeen years of school, you deserve a break, and that at least a few years of your twenties should be spent seeing the world, trying out jobs and places to live, and just plain enjoying yourself before settling into such a long-term commitment.

Naturally, the longer you are away from an academic schedule and the *sui generis* demands of an academic program, the harder it may be for you to acclimate back to them. Then again, with age, you may come to master organization skills (and find more discipline) that you didn't have while you were in your twenties.

I have found that people who enter their forties and fifties, having become well-established in their own personal routine and that of their family, find it challenging to go back to school. Taking classes at night, on top of working during the day and being a good spouse and parent, is a lot of work—so much so, that it takes longer to complete the degree. A one-year program turns into a three-year program, and a three-year program turns into a five-year program. Some people work for companies that will give them time off to advance their education because the company sees it as professional development. Such companies may even foot the bill or subsidize the tuition, which of course is a sweet deal.

In addition to asking yourself if you are prepared to enroll in graduate school—financially, intellectually, emotionally—you should ask if your spouse, boy- or girlfriend, or life partner is prepared for your enrollment and all its demands on your time and energy. You may have matriculated to college because your parents wanted you to, but people already partnered matriculate to graduate school because their partner agreed to it.

## Popular Graduate School Options

As an English major weighing grad school programs, your instinct may be simply to keep on keepin' on: You did well majoring in English, so let's go for the master's and the PhD in English, too.

Don't make it that simple.

Think beyond merely *English*. Some universities, for example, offer graduate degrees in English with an emphasis on composition. You could get what is called your TESOL: a master's degree in the science of teaching English to speakers of other languages. (Thank heaven for initialisms.) Arizona State University offers a graduate certificate program in scholarly publishing. You could also pursue a degree in library science, American studies, or other literature or education programs.

The most strategic way to choose among graduate programs is to determine, as best as you are able, which programs provide the knowledge or certification that will help advance your career path. Always investigate whether your employer, as a matter of policy, will help defray the cost of your continuing education as professional development.

That said, here are some of the more popular graduate programs for English majors.

## MASTER'S OR PHD IN ENGLISH

If all you want to do is teach on the college level, then get a master's degree in your subject.

You may be asking, *Don't you need a PhD in English to teach English on the college level?*

You do not.

While I was earning my MFA in creative writing, I received a fellowship that allowed me to teach classes in English composition and 100-level English literature, and after I graduated, I stayed on for a year, teaching those same courses. Boston College hired me to teach a class called Writing for Publication to a mix of first-year and sophomore students—an appointment based on my nonacademic credentials in journalism and the publishing industry.

Now, if the question is *Do I need a PhD in English to teach upper-level literature full time on the college level or to secure a tenure-track position?* then the answer is yes.

Again, specificity concerning your professional and personal goals will help you decide what to do. *I want to teach college* isn't specific enough.

As an undergraduate English major, I had it in my mind that I wanted to be a college professor. Basically, I didn't see a future for myself working in a cube (little did I know), and I warmed to the idea of wearing tweed jackets, having summers off to write my novels, and being respected by my male students and adored by my female students. Now, if you asked me what

I saw myself teaching, I would have said something like "James Joyce, the American short story, Modernist novels, and maybe a little T. S. Eliot"—the very things I enjoyed studying, at the time.

What I did not appreciate then is that the job market for professors is not a salad bar. You don't just pick and choose what you want to teach and where and when to get a job. Thousands of prospective professors would like to teach James Joyce or *The Sound and the Fury*, but colleges don't just hire more professors to teach those subjects because the more, the merrier.

What you teach, where you teach, how you teach, and to whom you teach are not governed by your choice alone. These things are governed by a college's need for someone to teach a particular subject, the curriculum committee's approval of this course or that one, student interest in this course or that one, pedagogical trends, popularity of certain authors interpreted and taught in a certain way, tenure, budgets, class size, and on and on.

Of course, you shouldn't enter a PhD program trying to second-guess which subjects or authors will be popular or desirable by the time you get out; not only is that impossible, it's no way to structure something you'll be handing over your life to for several years. Study what you're passionate about. But always remember the anecdote in Henry David Thoreau's *Walden* of the Native American basket weaver who started knocking on doors in Concord, Massachusetts, expecting people to buy his beautiful baskets: He was rebuffed by someone informing him, "My good man, we don't *need* any baskets." (That Native American is now teaching English comp and John Dryden at a small college in Missouri.)

## JOURNALISM SCHOOL

Consider this excerpt from the article "The J-School Debate," which appeared in the *Christian Science Monitor* on August 1, 2002.

> Journalism training is a bit like playing piano. A pianist who only hits the notes seldom "makes music" of the same caliber as a person who also knows composition, musicology, theory, and music history. In journalism, it's a given that a reporter can write about, report, and edit the news. But to approach the craft with an informed profession-

> al perspective—to "make journalism"—aspiring journalists need to study media ethics, law, history, global communications, and theory.

Got all that?

Now consider that the article appeared in the opinion section and that the author, William A. Babcock, is chair of the department of journalism at California State University, Long Beach. Mr. Babcock's point deserves consideration, his analogy holds some water, and, to be sure, his résumé in journalism makes mine look as if it were scribbled on the back of a napkin. But personally, I don't know how much law or history you need to know to cover tomorrow night's city council meeting, how much media ethics you need in order to realize that it's wrong to make up facts and quotes and to libel people, or how much theory you must assimilate before you can get your behind down to the scene of a five-alarm fire at the town nursing home and safely start asking people "What happened here?"

Some people attend journalism school because they believe it hones their skills, broadens their horizons, deepens their knowledge, and enhances their qualifications; other people consider their journalism school to be the newsroom and their local beat, much like a whaling ship was Yale and Harvard for Ishmael in *Moby-Dick*. (Tuition is certainly a lot less on whaling ships.) Plenty of people on staff at the country's leading newspapers went to journalism school, but millions of people who preceded them never saw the inside of a classroom. If there is some independent study that shows a sudden spike in the quality of journalism produced in this country after the development of journalism schools, I'd love to see it.

Do you need to go to journalism school? Of course not. You don't need to go to college or high school, either. Going or not going will simply steer you in the direction of one opportunity versus another. I know what is meant by the question, though: Will going to J-school improve your chances of getting a good job in journalism?

Let me adduce my own experience, briefly.

A couple of years out of college, I walked through the door of a small community newspaper conglomerate, armed only with some clips from my college newspaper: an arts review and a humor column. Little did I know community newspapers were not crying out for humor columns.

The editor in chief gave my clips a quick look-over and asked me, "Did you go to journalism school? Or take any journalism classes?" I told him the truth (which was no), fearing that would conclude the interview.

It did. He said, "Good," and he hired me on a steady freelancing basis.

All he wanted to know was: (1) was I a quick study; and (2) could I tell a story? My academic credentials were not as important—not to this guy, anyway, who helped me secure full-time positions later on down the road.

He happened to subscribe to the belief that journalism school favors theory-based academic classroom work over in-the-field reporting. The way his philosophy ran was: All you need in order to be a good reporter is a phone; a pad and pen; storytelling ability; and the skills of persistence, boldness, and curiosity.

Contrast my experience, though, with that of William Donovan, an English major interviewed at the end of chapter four. Journalism school afforded him opportunity and experience that many writers would give one arm for.

Look at the graduate programs. Ask about internships and what percentage of the student body gets them and where. Ask to see names of alumni, especially those who are willing to be contacted by prospective students. Research the program as you would research a front-page story. Find alumni from your college on staff at a newspaper, and ask them how many of their colleagues hang up their J-school diploma in their cubicle.

You could go to J-school and find that most of your education is bogged down in theory; or, you could

**The Best Advice I Ever Got**

- ***You are not your thesis.*** And your thesis (or dissertation) is not you. Despite the fact that this giant project is going to make terrific demands on your time, energy and sanity, it is not who you are. So when you need to resubmit it to the review committee for the fourth time, understand that this is not a judgment on who you are as a person.
- ***Just get it done.*** Think of your thesis as a child you need to baby-sit for two hours a day. Think of your thesis as a holy mission. Think of it as a game, a puzzle, an exercise, whatever: But think of your thesis in whatever way will *get it done.*

make a go of it on your own and find that your hands-on, self-taught education is spotty, erratic, and unreliable.

Depending on the location of the graduate program and what, if any, internships you manage to swing for yourself, going to journalism school may also offer you the opportunity to make a lot more contacts and collect a lot more clips than you would be able to do on your own. And that itself may make all the difference in the world.

## MASTER OF FINE ARTS (MFA)

MFA stands for the master of fine arts degree and is commonly associated with degrees in creative writing: fiction or poetry. MFA programs usually combine writing workshops with required credits in graduate-level English courses, and teaching fellowships are often available to help defray the tuition cost. Most MFA programs are two years in length, although if you consult *The AWP Official Guide to Writing Programs* (AWP stands for Association of Writers and Writing Programs), you will find that some programs are one year in length and some are three.

The MFA program's advantage over, say, a writing workshop held out of someone's home or through your local adult education center is that in a workshop, you may only get one chance to circulate your work and receive group reactions to it, while in the MFA program, your turn comes around several times in the course of one or two years. MFA programs may also give you teaching experience and, upon graduating, some kind of teaching accreditation (although it's difficult to get a job teaching college-level creative writing unless you've published a novel).

The application and selection process for the MFA program is competitive and rigorous. You can be confident that your colleagues in the program have been adjudged to be writers of talent, promise, and dedication, and not just people who could pony up workshop tuition.

If you're thinking about applying to an MFA program, keep the following factors in mind.

**Strength of the faculty.** Think twice about choosing a particular MFA program because you like the novels of one or two of the faculty members. Someone can be a great writer but a lousy teacher of writing.

Conversely, don't be prejudiced against the faculty if you've never heard of them or their books.

**Value and style of workshop critiques.** You take a gamble when you gauge your writing by comments from your colleagues in the program: They may not represent the kind of people you want to write for in the first place.

Then there is the issue of the tenor of a workshop—that is, the extent to which its critiques inspire people to nod their heads or to run from the room in tears. The tenor of a workshop is largely determined by the faculty member presiding over it. Before you commit to an MFA program, talk to the director of the program and ask flat out how the workshop is run: What kind of comments or behaviors does he consider inappropriate or unprofessional? If he has rules or guidelines for critiques, what are they and how are they enforced?

One of my MFA advisors told the story of a time he interviewed a prominent writer for a teaching position in the program. He told her that he made a point of maintaining civility and mutual respect in the weekly workshops. This other writer happily disagreed with that philosophy and said she liked it better when the students mixed it up like cats in a bag.

That interview was over.

**A focus on short stories.** Because most MFA programs are structured around weekly workshop meetings, they favor short stories—it's not easy making a judgment on an isolated chapter of a novel or on a 175-page novella. Short stories will scarcely pay the rent, so you are shelling out a great deal in tuition for a program that nurtures your skills in writing in a form that can't possibly earn you back your tuition expense.

**No guarantees.** The MFA degree does not certify expertise or credibility as an artist; neither is it a guarantor of publication. While it is true that admission to high-profile MFA programs (such as the programs at the University of Iowa and at Stanford) may increase your visibility to agents and editors, you sign a contract based on your writing, not your diploma. I also would not recommend banking your tuition on being taken under the wing of a sage professor-author who introduces you to the right people and forwards your work to the right agents or editors and who makes it his mission in life to see that you receive all the honors and grant monies and opportunities that your genius is due.

**Time to write.** When people sing the praises of their MFA program (especially while they are still trying to pay off their loans and justify the expense), they often comment that the program gave them time to write. I believe it's more accurate to say that the program gave them an excuse to claim time to write, as in, *Sorry, I can't do the dishes or waste the evening relaxing because I have to write—I'm in an MFA program, after all.* How much you want to dedicate yourself to your teaching fellowship, your other required classes, and the job you may need to defray the cost of your tuition will influence how much time the program "gives" you to write fiction or poetry. You can give yourself time to write with or without an MFA program. And even given the time within an MFA program, you may find you don't work well in an erratically structured environment, in which you have two hours free in the morning, a class to teach, then a half-hour, then four hours of a job, then office hours, then....

Finally, do not go to an MFA program hoping that your professors will be able to tell you, once and for all, whether you have what it takes to be a writer or whether you're wasting your time with creative writing. The only person who can answer those questions is you.

## Which School?

When you're choosing a graduate program, the wealth of reference materials online and in your local library and bookstore can help you narrow the field in terms of price, location, available scholarships, student body size, teacher–student ratio—the same factors you plugged into the equation when you chose your undergraduate program, right?

Right?

When you evaluate graduate schools, you should take a closer look at the faculty—your potential dissertation advisors. One graduate school may have a universally revered department or faculty member, a good reputation, or an academic climate that you find more attractive than another. Your choice should be based also on how you want to concentrate your course work: medieval lit, American studies, Russian literature of the absurd, or what have you.

Geography can certainly enter into the equation—whether, for instance, you can tolerate summers in the Southwest or winters in the Midwest—but consider, too, that you'll be working so hard when you're in graduate school, you won't be seeing much of the outside world anyway. Think of the geographical location of your graduate program in terms of its proximity to things related to your field of study or the industry you want to join.

---

**TRY THIS**

Do your homework. Find out: (1) if going to graduate school fits in with your personal or professional goals; (2) what financial resources are available to you; and (3) which graduate program will afford you the education, experience, and convenience you want.

Find the people who are doing what you would like to do, professionally, and get enough of their time to ask if graduate school would be a necessary or helpful step in getting a job like theirs. You're bound to encounter differences of opinion, but as in the Supreme Court, all you may need is a simple majority vote.

Research scholarships, fellowships, grants, loans, and loan-structuring strategies that will ease the toll exacted on your wallet. You might try getting on *The Apprentice* and making Donald Trump take enough of a shine to you that he offers to pay for your education; that may involve less paperwork and only slightly more ass-kissing.

Take advantage of the abundance of choices in graduate programs. Don't pick one the way you picked college—'cause you liked the campus and its proximity to a cool city. Talk to professors, students, alumni, administrators, the janitor—anyone who can help you make an informed choice.

And while you're at it, learn to have fun by taking GRE practice exams. Those logic problems are a hoot.

## GLOSSARY

### WHAT'S THE DIFFERENCE BETWEEN ...

Teaching Fellow and Teaching Assistant?

Both are graduate students, but while the *teaching assistant* helps a professor grade papers and leads discussion groups, the *teaching fellow* typically teaches a class and holds office hours.

GRE, GMAT, LSAT, and MCAT?

These are the admission exams for graduate school, business school, law school, and medical school.

Assistant Professor, Associate Professor, and Full Professor?

An *assistant professor,* commonly, is untenured, although possibly on the road to receiving tenure (called the tenure track). An *associate professor* has received a promotion with tenure. *Full professor* is largely a ceremonial title, meaning the professor has tenure and got a raise, to boot. The coveted academic prize is tenure or a tenure-track position. The etymology of the word *tenure* comes from the Latin for "to hold," and when you are a tenured professor, you are assured employment until death, departure, or retirement. A tenure-track position may or may not lead to tenure, depending on performance and scholarly achievement (hence the adage *publish or perish*). Tenured faculty sit on committees that give promotions and issue tenure to assistant professors. *Adjunct* is a Latinate term meaning "no medical benefits." Colleges and universities save money by hiring part-time (adjunct) faculty, who don't receive the benefits full-time professors do. You often see teachers cobbling together a living (or, trying to, anyway) with several adjunct engagements at different schools.

## *Q & A* THE CLOSEST JOB TO COLLEGE STUDENT

If English majors needed a poster boy, Colin Wells would be solidly in the running. He started out in college in the school of management, until, two years into it, he decided to take a popular interdisciplinary humanities course.

That changed everything. Now Wells found himself rethinking his plans and his life, and confronting his mom and dad with the difficult news that he didn't want to be a businessman after all. He wanted to be an English major. After changing majors, Wells doubled up his course load and graduated in four years.

That was about twenty years ago. Today, Wells is a tenured associate professor of English at St. Olaf College in Northfield, Minnesota. Wells is the author of *The Devil & Doctor Dwight: Satire & Theology in the Early American Republic.*

Colin, how did you parents react to the news that you were switching from the school of management to a major in English?

My father was hesitant because he didn't know what English majors do!

At what point in your undergraduate studies did you consider graduate school?

As soon as I became an English major, the idea was, I would go to graduate school and become an English professor.

Sounds simple enough.

I was in love with the idea of college. And I think this is true for a lot of academics. I never wanted to leave, and becoming a college professor was the next best thing. Also, probably, I wanted to deal with students at a higher level [than high school]. I didn't want to be in a classroom where you had bullies and stuff like that.

My career ended up being like an English major. In other words, there's not much difference between writing your paper in your [English] class and writing a paper for a conference. This is the one job that's closest to being a student.

You were born in England, educated in New England—how did you end up teaching in Minnesota?

This was the job I got after I applied to seventy jobs in my field! [laughs] Out of all the jobs in America, and I got one offer. I've been here since 1995.

You must like it, since you've stayed.

Right now, I'm at the point where I have tenure and I have [a family]. Now I'm at the point where I can enjoy the purity of the literary stuff that I dreamed of back in college ... what I dreamed the career would be about. For most of my career, I found that graduate school and the early days of being a college teacher were very much like having any other job, the difference being it's about literature.

Besides teaching, what are your responsibilities as an associate professor?

I participate in between one and two committees, and there are about ten or fifteen committees: the tenure and promotion committee, the committee reviewing general education, the committee approving new courses, and one that deals with admission and financial aid.

Do you enjoy that part of the job?

The thing about a college, it's kind of like a communal operation where we're all partners and we all have to participate in the administrative duties.

The main thing for us [professors] is the research. I would say, in the academic year, teaching takes up 70 percent of my time, research is 20 percent, and administrative is 10 percent. And in summer, research is 80 percent and preparing for teaching is about 20 percent.

Do the English majors you teach know what they want to do with their major?

They still just do not know what to do [for a career]. I kind of think they know, early on, if they want to teach, because it's the first thing they think of in relation to English—or secondly, a writer. The one thing that students who end up going into publishing do, which helps them a lot, are these seminars for recent graduates, like the one in Colorado.

What advice, based on your own experience, do you give them?

I have always had this feeling that in every job, in every profession, success was really really hard to achieve. As I get older, I realize that that's far from the truth. When you're young, you think of everyone closing their door on you. I kind of felt that way about girls I asked out, too. I didn't realize that girls wanted to meet guys.

## *Q & A*
### MAN MADE FOR LAW

When I contacted Shea Doyle, he told me he was on his way to the wedding of a lawyer friend of his, whose undergraduate major was music. So much for having to be pre-law to get into law school.

Shea Doyle, thirty-seven, has worked as counsel at Modern Woodmen of America in Rock Island, Illinois, since 1994. His legal experience also includes working at a general practice and as a prosecutor.

Shea is also a published poet, and his plays are performed in his hometown of DeWitt, Iowa.

Is there any one major that is more serviceable than another for law school?

English majors may have some built-in advantages in terms of the ability to write well or to read critically. Certainly, other majors ask the undergraduate to do the same thing. But law is fundamentally an exercise in reading (sometimes a very large volume of reading) what others have said on a particular topic, be it statutory, case law, or regulations.

In what ways did your English major studies serve you in law school?

English gave me the confidence with language that perhaps other majors would not have. In most English curricula, there are opportunities to express yourself critically and artistically. Legal writing also takes many forms, and having the opportunity to explore various genres provided a level of confidence that each new form of legal writing was attainable.

Studying literature also broadens the perspective and allows a person to see other viewpoints. This experience helps, in that a lawyer is called upon to advocate a client's position and not necessarily the lawyer's own position.

You've said that you became a better writer because of law school. How so?

Legal writing is different from creative writing. But the study of law is often how a particular word turns in a statute or a case. Law school made me a closer reader and improved, I think, my work as a poet. Judges often value brevity above all else. You may have a hundred thousand words you could say on a topic but need to express them in five pages or less. It's the difference of making yourself clear in a novel versus a short poem. The trick, if you want to still write fiction, is to be able to live in the world of legal writing and the world of fiction writing. They are two very different animals.

Why do you refer to law school as *intellectual boot camp*?

In some ways, law school is a process of breaking students down from the old way of thinking to something akin to thinking like a lawyer. I have never been through military boot camp, but the Socratic method and constant challenging by the law faculty quickly make you perform in the new arena of law studies. In law school, you don't necessarily learn the law as in what the fine is for speeding. You learn to think and write in a certain way.

What is the most valuable thing you got from your English major? From law school?

The most valuable thing I got from my undergraduate degree was a phenomenal reading list. My undergraduate program was basically a great-books program. At law school I learned a trade. I love working in the profession with all the challenges and opportunities it provides.

Is law school only for people who want to be lawyers? Or does the degree have applications in other fields, as well?

A JD is a great degree to have for working in business, government, the nonprofit sector, as well as many other fields. I don't work as a trial lawyer. My own career went from a small town general practice to an in-house corporate practice. In law school, you do have the opportunity to intern at various jobs, and in my third year I worked as a prosecutor in a district attorney's office under the supervision of their prosecutors.

My own job revolves around consulting with the people in my company and overseeing litigation around the country. We have a small corporate legal staff and so my job still resembles a general practice within our company, since whatever comes across my desk I handle.

**You've done some hiring on a board of business administration. What advice can you give young people, now that you're on the other side of the desk, so to speak?**

I'm on the board of the Rock Island Arts and Entertainment District, which is a business development agency. My advice is that your undergraduate degree should be a foundation. Take advantage of internship opportunities if you can. If you need employment while at school, choose something that can give you added skills. Even if you think you are in a fairly standard job, try to differentiate yourself. There is a concept called *job crafting* that suggests that individuals make their jobs what they want. Add value to your résumé by going above and beyond the expectations of your job. Develop a new procedure; or document the best practices you find, even in your own job, so that it can be passed on to others.

**You're now completing your doctorate in business administration. Is that something you planned for all along, or is your career (and careers in general) more serendipitous than that?**

I decided to pursue some business studies because as an in-house attorney, the business issues are often as prevalent as the legal issues. I never planned to go to business school; but once I began my in-house practice, I realized there could be benefits in understanding where the business people were coming from. The English degree was helpful in the business studies also. With the doctorate, the thinking is very much at the theoretical level. Again, the same dynamics were at work as with the legal writing. I am finishing up my dissertation, which is about 150 pages long. I do think that the English major helped with the dissertation, since the same fundamental skills are at work in the long paper as in the short class paper. You still need clear sentences and paragraph structures that lead the reader through the work, even if it is 150 pages.

# CHAPTER 4 *Breaking (Into) the News*

People today get the news from their phones, from blogs, and from the Comedy Central cable channel. For English majors interested in joining the fabled Fourth Estate, however, the most permeable point of entry is the newspaper: This is where this chapter on journalism will focus, instead of breaking into news as a TV anchor, a broadcaster, or an international correspondent.

When news spread through my family that I was doing my part to help English majors find their professional way in the world, word came back via my wife that friends of her parents were interested in having me talk to their son. The young man was soon to graduate from college, and he had expressed an interest in becoming a reporter.

*Well,* I thought, *at least the kid knows what he'd like to do.* I loved being a reporter more than I loved any other job I've had, so my immediate response was an enthusiastic, "Sure, I'll talk to him!"

Then my wife added that the parents wanted me to talk their son *out* of becoming a reporter. I suspect that, like all good parents, this mother and father were concerned that their child would not make a livable wage, which is understandable, if not entirely accurate.

The fact is, dissuading someone from joining any profession is easy: Trot out half of the facts, insert a few choice stereotypes, and pepper it with some colorful personal bias.

For example, I could have told this young man that as a reporter, he'd be earning chicken feed to perform a thankless job. I could have thrown around some terms like *conglomeration* and *profit-driven management* and argued that such conditions have made it near impossible these days for the press to do its job. I could have told him horror stories about unions, contract stalemates, and the death of freedom of speech. I could have warned him that he would be better off telling people he was a defense attorney or a bank officer who issued farm foreclosures than telling them he was part of the media.

I declined the invitation to talk to this young man. If journalism was truly what he wanted to do—if he got his feet wet in the industry and found he liked it—nothing I could say to him would change his mind. That kind of determination, I find, is among the qualities that make a good reporter.

## What Makes a Good Reporter?

Do you know someone in your family unafraid to ask questions?

Let's say it's your dad. Imagine you're on vacation by the ocean, and you stop in one of those saltwater taffy places where they make the taffy on the premises, right in front of you. People are coming in with their kids, watching them make the taffy, buying their boxes of taffy, and leaving. Meanwhile, your dad has already made friends with one of the women at the taffy machine, and he's asking her, "Why do they call it salt water taffy, anyway—is there salt water in it? How long has this building been here? Are you the original occupants? Is this a family business? How old is this machine? How much taffy do you make in a day?"

You may be watching all this, dying of embarrassment and thinking, *Dad—let's just get the candy and go.* Meanwhile, Dad and the woman are laughing it up and having a wonderful chat, and Dad has learned a lot (which, God help you, he's going to share on the car ride home).

You may think of Dad as nosy or a royal pain, but he has one of the fundamentals of being a good reporter: He has no problem walking up to perfect strangers, introducing himself, and starting in with questions. And every answer to one of his questions spawns another question, and another. Dad puts the woman at ease, maybe by telling her a little bit about himself. He jokes, he kids, he's friendly—and in the process, not only does he wheedle information out of her but he gets a free sample, too. He's determined. He may not be as sweet as taffy, but he's just as sticky.

Dad shrugs off your embarrassment and says he just likes meeting people and hearing their stories. He's a people person. He likes to learn things. He likes history, anecdotes, first-person narratives. He's always eager to know the inside story, the dirt, the skinny. He likes hearing other people's stories so that he can have stories to tell.

What Dad may lack is the ability to ask relevant and challenging questions, to filter out unnecessary information, write down quotes as fast as people deliver them (or, better, remember them verbatim in his head), and make all his notes cohere into a readable, informative, entertaining narrative.

All that aside, learn from Dad. Observe the master at work. Watch how he disarms people—people who are accustomed to not talking to other

**Most Important Skills**

- ***Storytelling.*** As an English major, you probably associate the word *stories* with short stories (i.e., fiction) and think that all newspapers and magazines print *articles*. The ability to get and maintain a reader's attention, tell a compelling and informative story, connect to a reader's intellect as well as the reader's emotions—all with careful attention to detail, word choice, and style—is not exclusive to fiction writers. Journalists and reporters do this daily.
- ***Determination.*** Reluctance and outright resistance to talking to the press are nearly universal. (In my own experience, the people most eager to talk to the press were those who wanted publicity.) A reporter needs dogged determination to track down information, get quotes, and obtain the necessary ingredients for a good story despite being blocked all along the way. If you were on the track team in high school and ran the hurdles, you're in good shape for the Fourth Estate.
- ***Balance.*** In the newsroom conversations I had, the general consensus among reporters was that the legendary objectivity of the press was a bunch of baloney. No one is objective: not the person on the street, not a judge in the highest court in the land. What reporters can be, however, is balanced—that is, to the best of their abilities, in the best interest of their stories and their readers, and under the constraints of time and available space, they can provide opposing points of view and present facts, perspectives, and data to allow readers to make up their own minds. That is one tall order, especially on deadline, but it's what the best people in the business aim for every day.

people. Notice how he chose his subject carefully: the woman operating the machine, as opposed to the woman at the cash register. Listen to the questions he asks, and listen to how he listens. Dad will tell you that when you're listening to someone talk, listen to what they *don't* say as well as to what they do say. Listen to *how* they answer questions: the words they choose, their tone of voice, how quickly or slowly they speak. Listening can be an art and it can be hard work.

Reporters are active listeners: They listen respectfully but ask penetrating questions. If they were listening to someone tell the story of the boy who cried wolf, they'd pipe up after the story was over and say, "So, would you say there was a wolf problem in that village? I mean, how many wolf attacks are we talking about? And who put that kid in charge of the sheep in the first place? Can you give me a name, and how to contact him?"

Reporters are not trying to be wiseasses in doing this (though to some, it comes naturally); they're simply trying to fill in missing details or put the story in a larger perspective or make it relevant. If you are this type of listener, then you may have what it takes to be a reporter.

Think about how you are (or were) in a classroom. If you rarely raised your hand, if you rarely participated in group discussions, and especially if you bit your tongue because you were afraid of asking a stupid question, you should think twice about being a reporter.

Reporters know that there is no limit to how many questions they could ask. Like Professor Kingsfield says in the movie *The Paper Chase,* each question prompts yet another question, ad infinitum. Part of a reporter's skill, then, is determining which key questions to ask, because depending on the situation, the reporter may have the opportunity to ask only one or two. The last thing you want to do is ask a question that you could easily answer yourself.

You might say that good reporters are good note-takers; better reporters are good listeners. Good reporters ask good questions; better reporters often know (or suspect) the answer to a question before they ask it.

## *The Reporter's Personality (Such as It Is)*

A word or two about the reporter's temperament is deserving of our time, in the event that you find yourself either simpatico or opposed to it. Not all reporters have the same disposition, of course, but you're more likely to find a certain personality type in the newsroom.

By virtue of what they do for a living, reporters find themselves at an arm's length from their subjects—politicians, public figures, private individuals, celebrities big and small—all of whom are on their guard around the press because they don't want to divulge information, they don't want to be misrepresented, or they don't want to risk being taken advantage of. Reporters, therefore, find themselves on the outside trying to get in.

When you're treated like that on a daily basis, you tend to see yourself as disenfranchised. If you're romantic, you may see yourself as a rebel, a thorn in the side of power, a troublemaker. This can make a person sardonic and cynical. Add to the mix someone who is underpaid and underappreciated, and you have something like the common reporter's disposition. News people tend to enjoy black humor, gallows humor, cynical wit. It should come as a surprise to no one that Mark Twain was a journalist.

If you, by your nature, are an optimist—someone who is instinctively trustworthy and willing to give people the benefit of the doubt—and you are also upbeat and sunny, a team player who's big on boosting group morale, you may find yourself isolated in the company of reporters.

Example: When I was a newspaper editor, our editor in chief would corral the troops for a meeting once a week to call attention to major stories that week, talk about the week ahead, and so on. One week, our editor in chief praised a new reporter, a young woman and recent college graduate, by saying, "Amy had her first body this week!" There followed a cheerful round of applause.

What our editor in chief meant was that Amy had written her first news story involving a dead body: one of those stories in which people started smelling something weird coming from the house next door (and flies were actually gathering at an upper corner of the house's exterior). When police broke down the door, they found a woman and her elderly mother in an apparent double suicide.

"Aw, why couldn't it have been a murder-suicide?" one other reporter asked aloud in the meeting. "That would have been terrific." Several colleagues laughed and agreed.

If you already think reporters are cynical and jaded, it's easier to think of them as being bad people for making jokes about murder-suicides, but I would bet you that doctors, nurses, EMTs, police officers, firefighters, and funeral directors also enjoy black humor every now and then, either to inure themselves against the pain they witness daily or just to get a break from it.

People complain all the time that there's no good news in the news, that it's all murder, death, crime, natural disasters. Obviously, many news outlets exploit calamity and tragedy and live and breathe by the adage *If it bleeds, it leads,* but fundamentally, crime and natural disaster and corruption affect the daily lives of more people than the little girl down the street who rescued a cat from a tree. There is good news in the newspaper, but bad news tends to have better visuals and gets people talking more: talking, discussing, arguing, debating.

People enjoy good news, but good news does not sell, and papers that don't sell don't attract advertisers, and papers that don't attract advertisers go out of business. Happy endings sell, but not good news. Call it the sad truth about good news. (One could argue that if you want good news, you should read about the bad news and then go do something about it.)

Now, you may be saying to yourself, *Oh, it's not a big deal if I work with people who like to grouse or who assume human beings are fundamentally evil. Lots of people are unhappy in their jobs, and I'm used to it.* The difference is, reporters aren't necessarily unhappy in their jobs. They're cynical for a living. If your personality is at odds with that, then working in a large room all day with dozens of professional cynics surrounding you may be more unpleasant and dispiriting than you think.

Reporters are doubting Thomases. They are all born in Missouri, the Show Me state. They may hope for the best, but they anticipate the worst. People in power hate the press if they cannot use the press for their own ends, and being the object of people's hatred does something to you after a while.

That said, news people are some of the most collegial people I know: when they're not on deadline, they love to sit and trade stories, chew the fat, talk about other people they know in the business and who you could call to find about that and a colleague who's down in Alabama now covering the state house, and what's going on and what might happen. There is no other crowd I'd rather go out for drinks with than news people.

So, that's news people. Let's talk about the profession of journalism and examine some of its pros and cons.

## Reporter's Rap

Everyone knows that American movie heroes are typically: (1) police officers or detectives; (2) soldiers or vigilantes; (3) maverick lawyers fighting the system; or (4) Tom Cruise (who, as it happens, has portrayed all of the

**What's in a Name?**

The name of a newspaper is usually the name of the city or town it serves, followed by a word meant to describe the paper's nature or character: e.g., *Reporter, Register, Press, Chronicle, Press-Chronicle, Herald, Inquirer, Post.* Some newspaper names suggest that within their papers you will read about the *Globe*, the *Times*, or the *World*. Some newspapers consider themselves a *Beacon*, a *Sun*, or a *Star*, while others look upon themselves as a *Leader* (or, in Manchester, New Hampshire, a *Union Leader*).

Some newspapers aspire to be the official paper of record in their community; some papers just call themselves the *Record* and leave it at that. Ditto for being a *Standard*.

A *tribune*, in ancient Rome, was an official whose job it was to defend the interests of ordinary citizens against magistrates. The word also means a platform from which you address a congregation. *Sentinel* is an ancient word meaning "sentry," or "soldier at a post."

A newspaper may call itself a *Telegram* or a *Dispatch*, suggesting an urgent message, or it could simply call itself a *Messenger* (a handy name, given the adage *Don't shoot the messenger*).

The publishers of the New Orleans *Times-Picayune* would not want you to think their content is picayune in the sense of "having little to no value"; rather, a *picayune* was a form of Spanish currency in the South.

My favorite name for a newspaper suggests industry, activity, and productivity—*Bee*.

above). Seldom is the hero in a movie a reporter (and seldom is a reporter portrayed as a hero).

Quite some time has passed since American movies presented reporters in any kind of favorable light: *All the President's Men* (1976), *The Killing Fields* (1984), and *Salvador* (1986) spring to mind. True, Peter Parker is a freelance photographer for the *Daily Bugle,* and Clark Kent is a mild-mannered reporter for the *Daily Planet.* But if you see a reporter or journalist at all in the movies, she is more likely to be a liar (as in *Shattered Glass*), a lush (as in *Bonfire of the Vanities*) or so peripheral to the action of the film that she could as easily be a door-to-door salesperson or be played by a Jack Russell terrier.

Every politician from the president of the town council to the president of the United States inveighs against the media for being biased, ill-informed, disrespectful, quick on the draw, and short on the facts. (Richard Nixon went so far as to say "The press is the enemy.") Exacerbating the problem are recent scandals swirling around professional fabricators Stephen Glass and Jayson Blair, whose fictional fancy footwork further imperiled the reputations of prominent newspapers and magazines.

Do a little asking around, and you are likely to encounter negative buzz around working for newspapers: The pay is lousy; the hours are erratic; plum assignments are already taken or are doled out based on seniority and nepotism; and the work is thankless. What can be most discouraging is that you hear this trash talk from reporters and journalists themselves.

Reporters and journalists are also not tops with the average person. Put bluntly, lots of people (and not just politicians) hate reporters. Why? For starters, you spelled their kid's name wrong in the article about the junior league soccer game and now he's in his room, crying. The city councilwoman you interviewed disavows something she said to you that puts her in an unflattering light, and even though you have notes to prove that she said it, the fact that it saw print means that you are out to get her and you'll be sorry.

The local restaurateur thought your review wasn't glowing enough. Don't you realize how much she spends in advertising with your newspaper? Why, she knows the publisher personally, and you'll live to regret it, once she's spoken to her. Remember that article about local business development you wrote? One local shoe store is angry that you wrote about her competitor instead of her, even though she never returned your phone calls.

Meanwhile, everyone in the community thinks that you don't write about what's *really* important to the community—a subject that varies from household to household: property taxes, school supplies, noise pollution, snow plowing, neutering pets.

Then, of course, there are the allegations that reporters are liars, that they don't live in the communities they cover, and on and on and on.

Actually, for all the animosity between politicians and the press, the one thing that both groups could commiserate over is that their jobs give them a privileged insight into how incredibly unhappy and dissatisfied everyone is in their community, and how the people's unhappiness is all their fault.

So why consider newspaper journalism as a career choice?

**The Best Advice I Ever Got**

This advice served me both as a newspaper editor and as a reporter.

- ***People want to read about people.*** Whatever you decide to write about, identify the human angle. People like reading about people, especially if those people are themselves. It helps them connect to an issue or an event and, as they say, put a face on it.
- ***If your mother says she loves you, check it out.*** This adage is frequently cited as a principle of the Chicago school of journalism, whatever that is. Take nothing for granted; assume nothing; always investigate. Get a reliable source, and if you have a secondary source, ask the primary source if the secondary source is accurate. Don't rely on the Internet as the wellspring of truth. Develop an index of names or a list of places to confirm particular data, and update and add to it constantly.
- ***If you can say it better yourself, do; otherwise, quote.*** Novelist Elmore Leonard once observed that fiction readers don't skim over dialogue. Similarly, news readers seldom skim over quotes, so get and include as many as space and good storytelling will allow; but, if you can say something better than the person you interviewed, paraphrase.
- ***Don't ask a question you don't already know the answer to.*** Skilled reporters, like skilled attorneys, approach their subjects knowing what they'd

like them to say and then asking questions that will get them to say it. So go to the interview prepared. Know what you're talking about, even if your subjects don't know what they themselves are talking about. You do want to allow for some spontaneity, so once in a while, ask a question your subject doesn't know the answer to.

- ***Save difficult or challenging questions until the end.*** The last thing you want to do is kick off the interview by stumping or alienating your subject, which may prompt her to walk away. A great example of this is in the book *How to Lose Friends & Alienate People* by Toby Young, in which our hero lands a plum interview with actor Nathan Lane and decides, for the sake of being different, to ask him straight off if he's gay. Young didn't get a response, unless you count the announcement that the interview was over.
- ***Never let a subject review your piece before publication.*** Someone, always, will ask; always say no. You are a member of the press—you are not on a publicity team. This is official editorial policy of any publication worth a damn.
- ***Don't tell the reader how to react.*** This principle is a variant of *Show, don't tell.* Present the facts, the quotes, the information, the story. Don't call the story or its details *interesting, shocking, appalling,* or *fascinating.* Let the reader make up her own mind.
- ***Save your notes.*** At least up to a year after you cover a subject.

## Reporter's Reward

In the introduction to his 1999 book *Fat Man in the Middle Seat: Forty Years of Covering Politics,* journalist Jack W. Germond has an answer: *because,* he says, *it's fun.* I always wonder if Germond's statement was inspired by the scene from the movie *Citizen Kane* in which millionaire playboy Charles Foster Kane muses, "I think it would be fun to run a newspaper."

Germond is right: Journalism is fun, regardless of the medium—print, radio, TV, or online. Then again, any profession is fun for people who are either so good at it or so deficient in other skills that they couldn't imagine doing anything else.

Journalism can be deeply gratifying work for people who wish to be involved in their community and in the issues that affect the community, because therein lies the possibility of making a difference. While reporters are fond of styling themselves as an unsentimental, even cynical crowd, they remain in the business to bring an ignored problem to the attention of the public; to put a human face on suffering or victory; or to make sense of a complex issue.

When you are given a forum to craft and to tell a story—one that's entertaining or sad or moving—that is when journalism's rewards are deep and lasting.

The majority of reporters and newspaper editors I've known were remarkably intelligent and well-informed people. They were great to talk to, to learn from, to use as resources or as sounding boards. They were great people to be around, and the newsroom environment, being informal, could be a great place to be every day.

Journalists also like being in the know, wherever that may lead; they like being able to inform their readership and present points of view to them. They like the turnover of assignments and the variety of voices and faces they encounter. Most of all, they love stories.

*Love,* on reflection, may be too mild a word.

Reporters thrive on stories: They never tire of hearing someone say, "You know, a funny thing happened last week." Stories are a reporter's heroin. Reporters can't get enough of stories big and small and in-between.

It's true: There really *are* eight million stories in the naked city, even if that city is Cranston, Rhode Island. Working for a newspaper puts you in the thick of them, and it can be a heady place to be.

## What Makes Newspaper Journalism Unique

The beauty about teaching is that you can do it at any time in your life. But there is an optimal time to pursue journalism: when you're fresh out of college; when your lack of attachments allows you to pursue opportunities wherever they may lead; and when your energy, drive, and lack of dependents allows you to work hard for low pay.

With few outside demands on your time, you have greater flexibility to cover events (provided you're not, at 21, already married or married with kids); the low pay doesn't sting as much; and you're probably as eager and as idealistic as you'll ever be. This is not to say, of course, that the journalism game is exclusively for the young or that people don't find second careers either as full-time or (more often) freelance writers for the local newspaper. If you stick with it long enough to work your way up to editor in chief (or higher), then you can move out of your apartment into a home.

Journalism is an industry in which everyone tends to start at the bottom. Chances are excellent that everyone in the newsroom, from the full-time reporter to the publisher, has logged hours writing obituaries or covering town hall. It can be a slow climb, especially if you're interested in working for a daily newspaper, where you may be required to work split shifts and late hours.

Journalism is an ephemeral business. Your hard work this week will be lining bird cages the next (if it isn't pulped and recycled back into blank paper). If you're the kind of person who needs new assignments, and lots of them on a regular basis, you'll find journalism appealing, but you may have to remind yourself of the benefits of your work—service to the community, the integrity of pursuing the truth, etc.—because you may not see them day to day. Your readers are out there, somewhere, and who knows how much they read or what they think about your work—unless they don't like it. (Believe me, people make it their business to let you know if they don't like what you're doing.)

## *Enormous Changes at the Last Minute*

If you spend any time at a newspaper, you'll discover that you'll have to make some changes in how, why, and what you write.

As you go through college, the papers you write become longer and longer. Journalists, on the other hand, can tell a story that delivers all the pertinent facts in five to six hundred words. This requires a succinctness and immediacy of expression challenging for someone accustomed to building an argument over five to ten pages. English majors measure their papers in pages; reporters measure their writing in inches.

English majors select sources based on how germane they are to the central thesis and on the source's intellectual pedigree; journalists know a quote from a janitor is as good as one from a PhD, provided it serves the story being told.

Academic papers and essays advance a strong thesis, but news articles often give equal time and balanced coverage to opposing points of view.

English majors come up with two or three paper topics per class per semester; journalists must come up with several ideas a day.

English majors unearth information in books and in periodicals; journalists unearth information mostly through cold-calling, a skill little developed in the classroom. You must learn as a reporter to assert yourself, your presence, your demands, and your inquiries.

When English majors put titles on their pages, they usually come up with toe-tappers like "Being and Becoming in *Tess of the d'Urbervilles*: A Case Study of Postmodern Marxian Analysis"; reporters like to include verbs in their titles (headlines), which tend to be shorter and punchier: "Town Nixes Prop 3" or "Head Dem Sez: 'It Ain't Over!'"

Finally, while you may be used to receiving edits from professors, you may not, as a reporter, be accustomed to your editor telling you that last-minute cuts need to be made because the piece is running too long.

## Types of Newspapers

Let's take a look at some of the different kinds of publications that may be in your area.

### THE DAILY NEWSPAPER

After six years in journalism—three, as an editor—I applied for a job at my city's daily newspaper. In the interview, I was told the hours: 11:00 P.M. to 7:00 A.M.

"I'm sorry," I said, "Could you repeat that into my good ear?"

No, my hearing was fine, which was also a suitable adjective to describe my experience in journalism up to that point—fine, not bad, average—at least as far a daily newspaper was concerned.

All dailies are different, depending on their size and the size of the city they cover, but by and large, the dailies are the big leagues, and many daily papers will not consider you unless you have five years of clips for them to look at. This is why I encourage undergraduate English majors first to pursue freelance reporting or jobs at smaller community newspapers in their area.

This is not to say, of course, that you stand no chance of getting a job at the daily newspaper. Internships will help. Contacts you make through

**Attention Fiction Writers**

Among literary-minded writers, journalism is often disparaged as a lesser form of writing which will dissipate and ruin the fiction writer's energies. Despite the fact that both fields require a mastery of storytelling, journalism and fiction writing are seen (at best) as distant relatives, or (at worst) as feuding strangers. More reporters may dream of being novelists than vice versa; perhaps reporters want to become novelists so they can look down their nose at reporters, which is what novelists tend to do—the smug and superior ones, anyway.

Journalists pride themselves on relevance and telling stories that matter to people. Novelists fault journalists for writing in a form that allegedly requires less creativity and imagination.

Journalists who write books about current events or history tend to outsell literary novelists. Novelists criticize the media machine for giving them publicity or air time only if their novel has an interesting hook.

Journalists write every day and pound out stories in six or eight hundred words. Novelists may take a more muse-inspired approach to the act of writing. (Although Hemingway assiduously maintained a daily word count, regardless of what form he was writing in.)

The antagonisms only get more ridiculous, the more the two parties have at each other. I'm happy to stay out of the fray. I wish only to alert jejune readers to the fray's existence—I certainly knew nothing of it when I was an undergraduate. I will say, though, that if colleges and universities are truly interested in helping students learn creative writing, I do not understand why they concentrate on hiring fiction writers and poets to do the job. Journalists know a thing or two about how to tell a story and how to edit a piece of writing, and confining journalists to the communications department to teach classes in news reporting makes no sense.

journalism school will help. Starting out in a department other than editorial—such as sales or marketing—will help.

If you live in a big city like Chicago, Washington, Boston, or New York, the daily newspaper is Broadway. You can make it if you try, but straight out of college, you're not up for the lead.

## THE COMMUNITY NEWSPAPER

In addition to the daily newspapers published in major cities, you may find other newspapers (most likely weeklies) servicing the needs and interests of smaller towns and cities. If you are starting out in journalism, knock on this door first.

The aspiring journalist fresh out of college may be surprised to learn that the most important parts of the newspaper are the police log, the children's sports pages, school lunch menus, bus schedules, senior menus, obituaries, and classifieds. You may find yourself having to write about issues that have never before meant much to you, like property taxes, public school budgets, street repair and snow plowing, gentrification and land development, and the race for city council and mayor. These issues, as well as the sections mentioned above, are of tremendous interest to the average community newspaper reader.

If working at a community publication makes you feel small-time, remember this adage from former Speaker of the House Tip O'Neill: *All politics are local.* You are dealing with issues and events that have the most immediate effect on the lives of your readership, and people are reading you closely.

To be sure, some community newspapers are perfectly dreadful—unimaginative articles, toothless political coverage, few photos, and weekly poems by the town's oldest resident—but you may have a community weekly that is outstanding, made so by an editor with vision and a caring staff.

## THE (SO-CALLED) ALTERNATIVE MEDIA

If you live in a big city that is ethnically or culturally diverse, you're likely to find at least one small newspaper that brands itself *alternative.* This paper is likely to publish a weekly or a bimonthly; cater to a readership of college students and young singles; provide listings for the local music, nightclub, performance, and visual arts scene; have a relaxed policy concerning vulgarity in its articles and features; and basically compliment itself for being contrarian, bold, shocking, in-your-face, and opposed to conservative Republican politics.

If you are considering working for this kind of publication, here are a few words of caution.

**Don't be fooled by camaraderie.** It may be the case that the average age of this publication's editorial and sales staff falls somewhere between twenty-two and twenty-seven. It's an office of young people like yourself: People are wearing jeans, the CD player is playing The White Stripes or the neo-punk band of the moment, people are laughing and telling dirty jokes (not that there's any human resources department to complain to), and the environment is full of youth, attitude, and a liberating excitement.

Be warned: Just because someone is your peer or someone you'd knock back a few with after hours does not mean that person is philosophically opposed to taking advantage of you.

Being on the ground floor of a publication like this may be fun and informal and cool, but do not allow that to influence you when they tell you there's no need for something so formal or stuffy as a contract. Even if you have a freelance agreement with them—especially if you have a freelance agreement with them—do not take the editor's word for how much she will pay you just because she treats you like her college roommate. (In fact, you may be her college roommate.) Ask for things in writing.

If you are submitting an invoice, do not make one copy and drop it off on the editor's desk. Make two copies—one for the editor and one for yourself—and stand there and wait for the editor to sign both.

I have seen people get screwed out of money, some to the tune of thousands of dollars, because they believed and took the word of a brash young editor with a vision.

**Don't be fooled by the alternative pose.** I once applied for a job with an alternative newspaper, one of secure standing, and most of my interview was conducted by a deputy editor, a guy who looked to be in his fifties. I sat in this gentleman's office, which was spacious but sparsely decorated: a few posters on the wall, a plant here and there, some doodads on the desk. At one point in the interview, he turned my attention to a crudely framed photograph on the wall: "See that?" he asked me in a fairly challenging tone.

"Yes," I replied. It was a black-and-white photograph of Joe Strummer, the lead singer of the punk band The Clash, standing at the microphone and giving his audience the finger. The editor proceeded to enlighten me that this picture represented his general attitude, which was certainly in keeping with the rebellious, devil-may-care alternative style of his newspaper.

This picture was for show. It did not mean this fellow embodied the punk alternative fuck-you attitude; this is merely what he wanted people who came into his office to believe. Indeed, he was too old to be a rebel. He had a wife and children, a career and a mortgage to protect, and flipping everyone the bird does not get that accomplished. (Next to the picture of Joe Strummer, in fact, was a much bigger framed picture—a movie poster of *Casablanca*—that told me that beneath his rough exterior he was, in the words of Captain Renault, "at heart a sentimentalist.") However, making a profit from the paper was a good way to protect everything he had built for himself at home, and posing as a rebel helps when you're the editor of an alternative paper.

The editor of an alternative paper might be young or older; she might appear to be a peer or a protector. But appearances can be deceiving. She wants as much from you as she can get at the lowest cost.

Remember that the alternative nature of these publications is mostly a pose, a marketing strategy. In some instances there might be sincerity behind the pose, but it's a pose nevertheless, meant to court advertisers and readers who belong to a key demographic. If you walk into one of these operations thinking these people are too cool, too nice, too *alternative* to do you harm, you will be taken advantage of. Remembering this fact is not paranoia. It is a healthy and self-respecting way to protect yourself.

## Types of Jobs

Writing for your student newspaper or some other campus periodical is a smart thing to do. You'll learn something about the business, you'll build some clips, and you may get a good idea of what kind of reporter or writer you want to be. But there's a catch. The catch is that the kinds of writing jobs you do as an undergraduate reporter may not be as readily available in the postgraduate marketplace.

By way of explanation, let's review some of the jobs undergraduate newspeople tell me they're interested in.

## SEX ADVICE COLUMNIST

Permit me to dash a hope gently: Your chances of getting a job after college as a sex advice columnist fall somewhere between *not bloody likely* and *yeah, right.* I refer you to the satiric vehicle the *Onion,* which justly parodied this aspiration in the September 15, 2004, article "College Sophomore Thinks She Would Make a Good Sex Columnist," in the September 15, 2004, issue.

Dan Savage, who writes the syndicated sex column *Savage Love,* once responded to any and all readers who dreamed of having the easy life of a sex advice columnist by pointing out that in college, graduation ensures a reliable and steady turnover at the student newspaper, making the columnist jobs relatively easy to come by. Not so in the real world, where, more often than not, the only thing that opens up a columnist position at a newspaper is death. Savage correctly argued that established columnists (who, if they are full-time employees of a paper, often do the column on the side) hold on to their jobs for dear life and do not gracefully relinquish their duties to members of the next generation, who think they know more about the mores of fellatio.

If you want to write a sex advice blog, though, knock yourself out.

## SPORTS REPORTER

The one thing an undergraduate periodical and ESPN have in common is their coverage of the college sports scene: football, basketball, hockey. The graduating college sports reporter may find, however, that her counterpart at the daily newspaper, who has been there since the previous century, has no immediate plans to retire.

If said reporter gets a job at a smaller daily community newspaper, she may find herself assigned to write about the athletic scene in high schools, secondary schools, and even elementary schools—still football, basketball, and hockey, but also soccer, field hockey, and track. Community weeklies usually freelance out the sports coverage.

In the suburbs, youth athletics is a big deal: They want the games covered, the photos printed, and the kids' names spelled correctly. Discussing strategy and the finer points of the game is fine for ESPN and your dorm-room sofa, but the community (and its newspaper) has a different focus and set of priorities.

If you love sports and writing about them, there's no problem.

## ARTS/ENTERTAINMENT CRITIC

Being a critic of some kind—food, music, book, theater—might impress the undergraduate reporter as being fun and even easy. You're sure to have read movie reviews in major newspapers and thought, *Pffft! I could do that.* You probably can, but sadly, you probably won't.

The critics at the newspaper where I worked had plenty of other tasks to occupy their day—namely, writing all sorts of other articles. Furthermore, full-time critics worked under either a cloud of indifference (*Who the hell cares what she thinks about the latest Ben Affleck movie?*) or else intense scrutiny (*Do we really need to keep a music critic on staff?*). The food critics, who I supervised, were freelance, and as was our policy regarding freelancers, we made every effort to pay them, respectfully, as little as possible.

If you manage to become a critic, remember a lesson from FOX's short-lived animated series *The Critic,* whose star was television personality Jay Sherman, a stumpy and bald movie critic whose oft-repeated verdict was "It stinks!"

In one episode, Sherman is upbraided by his Ted-Turneresque boss Duke Phillips, who reminds him that negative reviews don't make for great ratings. Sherman is paid, Duke tells him, to rate movies "on a scale of good to excellent."

"But what if I don't like something?" Sherman shrugs.

Duke replies, "That's what *good* is for."

Art and entertainment reviews, as you find them in newspapers and magazines, are seldom excoriating—for good reason. Harsh dining reviews encourage restaurateurs to withdraw advertising support from the publication. Crushing movie reviews can cost the writer access to upcoming celebrity interviews. The writer of a music review trashing a local band can come home to an answering machine pulsating with threats of violence, either from diehard fans or the band members themselves. Bad reviews in general can lead to the writer not being invited to parties, press functions, receptions, and the like.

Is the solution, then, to rate on a scale of good to excellent? No. Well-written and well-thought-out reviews are not mere airings of opinion, positive or negative. The well-written review is analytical, succinct, and helpful to the reader, who may be ignorant of how to evaluate the subject in question.

The problem is, beginning critics often believe that disliking everything is evidence of good taste, and when they put their hand to writing reviews of a new CD or movie, a desire to be noticed and talked about can translate into paragraph after paragraph of invective. Writers of this kind are especially vulnerable to falling in love with the resonance of their own zingers.

The converse problem is the review that gushes with praise without showing aesthetic discernment or perception. The middle ground is not ambivalence; it is an opinion based on knowledge, experience, examples, and reasoned argument.

Granted, if you're penning reviews for a slick frat-boy skin mag, you might get away with variations on *It stinks!* or *Dude, this rocks!* But if you do so, not only are you not being a critic, you are not being someone difficult to replace.

## How Do I Increase My Value to a Newspaper?

**Diversify your subjects and writing style.** In the normal course of your work as a reporter, you may write a sports article, a business profile, political coverage, and a local color feature. If you're in college and writing for school or community publications, branch out into new territory as often as you can. And even once you have a job in reporting, take a stab at new sections (but avoid rudely infringing on others' turf).

**Learn the business.** Typically, in any newsroom, there's a levee between the editorial side and the sales side. The sales people don't understand why the editors and reporters can't appreciate that the newspaper runs on advertising revenue; and the editors and reporters don't understand why the sales staff can't grasp that without copy, there'd be no paper and no ads. The sales people want a high ad density for each page, but that would make for less content in the paper; the editors want a big paper (lots of copy) one week, but that would mean an average ad density of less than 50 percent, which is not good for the sales people. The sales people want the restaurant reviewers to give favorable reviews to the big advertisers, and the restaurant reviewers want to scoop the competition by reviewing out-of-the-way places that can barely afford a quarter-page ad.

Your interest in learning different aspects of the business will be noticed, and, if you're fortunate, encouraged, which could lead to your being considered for higher positions in the company.

**Learn page layout and editing.** If you're interested in developing your skills and value as a reporter (and you should be), consider learning more about pagination, copyediting, and proofreading. Paginators lay out the newspaper using programs such as QuarkXPress and InDesign, and chances are good to excellent that management is interested in developing paginators who also know something about editing. But be warned: Paginators often work late nights, and you could be corralled into helping out in a pinch after you've already logged a full day as a reporter.

If you're still in college, the best way to learn more about pagination is to help out at school publications. Or you could volunteer to help with a club or department newsletter. You're likely to find additional opportunities in your community; many organizations and churches need volunteers to help lay out and edit all manner of bulletins, brochures, and flyers.

---

## TRY THIS

You could do these little exercises alone, but I'd recommend doing them with a partner.

### Listen

The next time you are at a party, bored out of your skull as you stand in a circle of people or slump on a sofa (or perhaps as you sit in shamed silence at the dinner table after family members have asked you what you plan do to after you graduate), try this: Listen. Listen to what people say, and sift through their sentences for good quotes.

Then try to retain in your brain the best quote or quotes. Give it a minute, then excuse yourself to get a refill or hit the bathroom. Then take out your trusty pad and pen, and write down the quote as faithfully as you remember it. If you try this with a partner, after the party, check with that person to compare what quotes you identified as the best and how well you both remembered what the person said.

At some point in your journalism career, someone will be talking too fast for you to type or write down what she says, and you will have to use the pad in your brain to take down the quote. This exercise will help you learn to do so. One more thing to remember: Never—*ever*—leave home without your pad and pen. Even if you are out walking through the park or on your way to the dentist, the last thing you want to have to do is hunt maniacally for something to write with and something to write on.

**Slice and Dice**

Grab a magazine or a newspaper and one of those colored highlighters. If you have a partner, find some articles for the both of you: one long, one short, one medium, an interview, a sports article, whatever. Mix it up. Then make two copies of the articles, and sit and read them.

Ready? With your highlighter, cut that article in half. Highlight what you think is unnecessary information, extraneous detail, or purple prose—get rid of any adjective that overstates its case. Get that ten-inch article down to five inches. Then compare and contrast what you decided to cut with the editorial decisions your partner made. Discuss why you cut what you did, and why you left in what you did. This exercise familiarizes you with what editors and reporters do when copy needs to be cut because those pesky ads are taking up too much space.

**Live in Five**

Okay, this one is going to seem terrifically geeky (or like something you would see on the TV improv comedy show *Whose Line Is It Anyway?*), but bear with me. The next time you are at an event with a fair amount of action—a basketball game, a fire drill at your office building, a cookout, or a big sale at a clothing store—position yourself well so that you can see most everything that's going on, and then imagine that a person with a camera runs up, points at you and says, "We are live in five, four, three, two, one."

Pretend you are a reporter live on the scene, and narrate in your mind what you would say. Look at the scene, assess what is happening, and formulate in your mind, as quick as lightning, how you would put it into words or into the arc of a story. Identify action. Relay the importance and relevance of the event. Describe details that set mood and speak to what people may be thinking and feeling. Make up the questions you're being asked over the feed.

This exercise will speed up your ability to look, listen, and translate events into words—into a story. Do this enough times, and one day you will be able to run into the newsroom, sit at your desk, and pound out a six-hundred-word article in fifteen minutes. And to think it used to take you an hour to write the first two pages of an English paper.

## GLOSSARY

### WHAT'S THE DIFFERENCE BETWEEN ...

Publisher

The *publisher* of a newspaper oversees everything. The various heads of editorial, sales, marketing, production, etc., answer to this person, who may own the company that publishes the newspaper or may represent the owner. Do not send your résumé to this person—she is busier than you know.

Editor in chief

The *editor in chief* is the head of the editorial department and the person to whom the editors of various departments or publications report. This person develops editorial vision, shapes editorial policy, and takes angry phone calls from public figures, advertisers, and people threatening to sue.

Managing editor

The *managing editor* is charged with executive organizational responsibilities within the editorial department. This involves the interviewing and hiring of new editors, the resolution of grievances or problems among the editorial staff, the coordination of major editorial projects, and the like.

Contributing editor

A *contributing editor* is someone who likely does not physically show up at the editorial office; instead, she is sent submissions or articles chosen for publication to read, review, or edit. Put bluntly, this person is probably a friend of the editor in chief or a former staff editor who wants to pick up a few extra dollars and have her name on the masthead. A *contributing writer* may be a regularly featured freelancer, usually someone of name or reputation.

**Editor**

The *editor* is to the editor in chief what a cabinet member is to the president of the United States: answerable and accountable but in charge of her own domain.

**Reporter**

A *reporter* (or *writer*) is a full-time, part-time, or freelance writer for the publication. Usually, if a newspaper byline reads *Special to the [name of paper]*, it means the writer is either a freelancer or a staff member on another publication that is a member of the same syndicate.

**Stringer**

A *stringer, string correspondent,* or *correspondent* is a part-time writer who files copy from another location, be it California, Rome, or the front lines of the latest war. Some reporters have people who fetch them quotes, information, or other material for their articles, and these stringers may or may not receive a byline or credit.

**Freelancer**

A *freelancer* may be published anywhere between once and a hundred times in a publication. Freelancers are not considered staff in a strict sense—they receive no medical benefits, and they are not often invited to the office Christmas party.

**Prefixes**

Prefixes such as *associate, senior, junior, deputy,* and *assistant* (e.g., assistant editor, associate editor) indicate seniority and authority more than any difference in the kind of work performed.

The further you head up the food chain, the greater the concern for ad revenue, circulation figures, and other non-writing-related financial matters.

## *Q & A*
## LICENSE TO BE CURIOUS

George Donnelly is editor in chief of the weekly *Boston Business Journal.* At forty-six, he has spent twenty-two years in journalism—in newspapers and magazines—and the profession, he says, has given him "a license to be curious." Donnelly speaks with a dulcet voice and assured delivery—he is every inch the man who knows of what he speaks.

George, what did being an English major mean to you as a young man?

[In 1976], being an English major was a statement that you were a citizen of the literary world. You went into it as a leap of faith. You weren't thinking of what you were going to do four years later.

There's a literary world?

I wanted to be a writer. I basically felt like I would live F. Scott Fitzgerald's story: Inspiration would befall me and I would carve that into some astonishing work of art, and the best thing I could do to prepare for that was to read the greatest writers who ever lived. That's what I thought, if I thought about it at all.

The major in English provides a great foundation, which you can leverage in many different ways. Reading literature is inherently valuable as a way of discovering how others made sense of the universe.

Your father, Richard A. Donnelly, was a weekly columnist for *Barron's* magazine. What influence did he have on your career decisions?

My father reinforced that college was not a vocational experience. He wanted to be a literary guy, and he wanted his [five] children to be like him. He wanted all his kids to be intellectuals. He disapproved of the notion that a major in English should translate into a clear career path.

Your first job in journalism was selling advertising for a biweekly community newspaper. What did that job teach you about journalism?

I learned a lot about what I was bad at: selling ads.

From there, you became a reporter for the *Somerville Journal*, then its editor. George, how does a reporter become an editor?

> A good reporter thinks like an editor. The reporter thinks for his editor: generating ideas, figuring out which stories will draw reader interest. . . . Most [reporters] are promoted because they're receptive to the idea of managing others.

If you could redo your journalism career, what would you do differently?

> I'd be more aggressive in seeking out internships. Now, as the editor in chief, I interview candidates for internships, and I find young people are savvier and more competitive for those few available slots.

What advice would you give to young people seeking internships?

> It's the kids who are comfortable taking initiative who take the jobs. It doesn't matter what school you went to, and it doesn't matter if you have brains, especially—it's how well you imagine yourself in the position. What we're looking for is what they call in the legal field preponderance of evidence that you will succeed.

In other words, research the place you're applying to and make a case for a good fit. Do your homework, like a reporter.

> I can tell inside of ten minutes if [applicants] will do well in a newsroom. This woman who's going to be with [the *Boston Business Journal*] this summer is going to be great: I know she is.

It sounds like she convinced you.

> When I interview kids, I know. I know.

## Q & A
### OF CLIPS AND CONTACTS

William Donovan says that, when he declared an English major as a freshman in 1974, he knew he wanted "to do something involving writing." Then, by graduation, things got a little clearer: "I knew I wanted to work at a newspaper."

Did he ever.

You've said that you didn't get involved in internships as an undergraduate.

I [graduated] really unprepared in terms of having clips or any practical experience. So when I got out of [college], I did the usual thing: I worked for nothing that summer at a weekly paper in Arlington, Massachusetts.

How long did that last, working for nothing?

They hired me after about three months to work at a sister weekly in Winchester, Massachusetts. I stayed there for two years—becoming one of two editors—before I made a quantum leap in my career: I went back to school. I wanted to go back and study journalism not so much to soak up more theory in a classroom, but to land an internship that would secure me clips, contacts, and experience. The logical place to go seemed to be Washington, DC. That's where all the national newspapers had bureaus, because that's where all the action was.

You were accepted to American University's master's program in journalism—then what?

I walked over to the Washington bureau of my hometown newspaper, the *Boston Globe*. I interviewed with Bob Healy, who had been the *Globe's* man in the nation's capital since 1957. I figured a fifteen-hour-a-week internship would leave me enough time for classes, so when Healy telephoned me a couple of days after the interview to tell me I got the internship, I agreed to start that coming Monday. I said to Healy, "What time should I come in?"

He says, "Well, we start at about eight or nine o'clock in the morning."

I said, "Okay, and what time could I punch out?"

Healy says, "Well, we work all day."

[*laughs*] I said, "How many hours a week do you see me working there?"

Healy says, "Well, forty, of course!"

How on earth could you go to grad school and hold a forty-hour-a-week job?

I didn't tell the people at American University the amount of hours I was working at the *Globe*. I reorganized my class schedule to work forty hours a week and still go to class. I got some fantastic clips there and worked with guys who, in my mind, were fantastic journalists.

Such as?

In the cubicle next to me was Tom Oliphant. Three cubicles down was Curtis Wilkie, and working his way through various jobs before assuming the throne at the *Globe* was [future publisher] Ben Taylor. Healy, Oliphant, and Wilkie were all prominently featured in *The Boys on the Bus*, Timothy Crouse's book about the press coverage of the 1972 Nixon-McGovern presidential race.

You got your master's degree in 1982. You must have gotten some good clips along the way.

I had clips from the White House, clips from Congress.... When I started sending those around, papers that hadn't been interested in me a year earlier were starting to call me back.

What about the *Globe*? They didn't hire you straight out of the internship?

Bob Healy and Jack Driscoll, who was executive editor, were really helpful and gave me some good career advice. But I was still green. My next job was in Vermont, covering the State House in Montpelier.

Was that a comedown, after the Beltway?

It was great to be a young reporter there! Montpelier is the smallest capital, and Vermont is one of the smallest states, but it's still a state and it still had many of the major issues California would deal with.

I took the national issues we wrote about in Washington, DC, and wrote about them in Montpelier—including economic issues no one else there was covering.

You can find great stories on the business page because business news has everything that goes into great drama: greed, loyalty, betrayal, ambition, achievement.

You worked briefly at *New England Business* magazine and then at the *Providence Journal*, where you stayed as senior business writer for fifteen years. You did pretty well. What's the secret?

It all happened because I went down to grad school and I got that practical experience. It's all about the clips. And the contacts. Talk to as many people as you can. Through the years, be proactive in going where the opportunity is. Getting the contacts and getting the clips were the tangible results of going to grad school.... The fact is, I went where the opportunity was. I found the place to go that was going to give me the clips and the contacts.

You're more independent these days, with your own writing and consulting firm for corporations, small businesses, and nonprofit organizations. Are you a hard boss for yourself?

I love being on my own. It's far more challenging and a lot more fun, because what I do now is custom publishing. I look for customers who could use an editorial product of some sort to get their message across, and I try to think of an angle, a real fresh approach—only it's in editorial form. Even if they don't go for it, I really get a kick coming up with that idea.

To learn more, see the second part of William Donovan's interview in the chapter on freelancing.

# CHAPTER 5 *Magazines*

Ask someone to name a dozen newspapers in thirty seconds.

Unless he's an infomaniac, a journalist or a librarian, he will probably start stammering after six or seven: the *New York Times,* the *Boston Globe,* the *Wall Street Journal,* the *Washington Post,* their local community weekly ... the *Chicago Tribune* ... uhhh ... the *New York Post* ... how many is that?

But ask someone to name a dozen magazines in thirty seconds, and you're more likely to get a breathless rundown of titles, as the person visualizes either the magazine rack or the coffee table at the doctor's office. If you're a college student, chances are you would rattle off names such as *Sports Illustrated, Cosmopolitan, Maxim, Playboy, Vogue, O,* perhaps *Wired,* or the *New Yorker.*

What if you could name one thousand magazines?

You would still be naming about one-third of the number of magazines published in the United States. What you see on the newsstand or in the bookstore is a mere glimpse of all the magazines out there.

## *Mapping the Marketplace*

Magazines are not for everyone, but for everyone, there is likely to be a magazine. Unlike newspapers, which appeal to a broad spectrum of interests and a more general reader, magazines are written, edited, and published to appeal to a very targeted readership.

### CONSUMER MAGAZINES

Most college undergraduates are familiar with consumer magazines, even if they're not familiar with the term *consumer magazine.* You find consumer magazines on newsstands and in bookstores, airports, supermarkets, and other heavy-trafiic retail outlets. While consumer magazines such as *Cosmopolitan* and *Time* appear very general in their content or appeal, they are targeted to a particular demographic.

Have you ever opened a magazine to find a reader survey, asking you (among a hundred other questions) to identify your age, gender, salary range, hobbies, education, and whether you rent an apartment or own your home? The magazine doesn't want to know these details because they're just gosh-darn curious as to who you are: they are conducting marketing research to clarify and focus their target readership. Decisions about articles, graphics, and ads are all made with that targeted readership in mind.

The more you understand that, the more you understand the difference between one magazine and another, the more advantaged you are in your search for a magazine job.

## TRADE MAGAZINES

Not long ago, I was in a hotel in New Hampshire, playing in the swimming pool with my kids, and I noticed that one of the parents sitting poolside was reading a magazine dedicated entirely to log cabins and the people who owned and built them. It was called (what else?) *Log Cabin.*

Ladies and gentlemen, there is a magazine called *Log Cabin.*

Do you like yoga? Me too. Now, do you subscribe to *Yoga Journal, Yoga International Magazine, Yoga, Ascent* magazine, *Enlightened Practice* magazine, or *Life Positive* magazine? Perhaps you just read one of the several online-only yoga magazines.

Trade magazines are more focused than consumer magazines. Trade magazines contain highly specialized content for hobbyists, collectors and enthusiasts, professionals in particular fields, owners of businesses and consumers of particular products. There are magazines about dogs, magazines about cats, magazines for gun collectors, magazines for enthusiasts of every stripe and color. Lots of magazines, lots of markets.

Business trade magazines are sometimes referred to with the shorthand B2B, for *business-to-business.* They are published by people in a particular business for people in a particular business, whether that business is computers, recreational vehicles, or hot tubs.

Of course, in your job search, to B2B or not to B2B—that is the question. (Sorry.)

You needn't feel bad about not having heard of *Log Cabin* magazine, because you're not apt to see it on the newsstand: the woman by the pool got it through a subscription, which is how most trade magazines reach their readers.

Another trade tale, to illustrate this point:

Back in the days when I was applying my major in English to serving people lattes and cappuccino, a friend took a job at a new business venture, a kind of info café that served coffee, provided Internet access, and sold somewhere on the order of about, oh, five hundred magazines and newspapers—a caffeinated world of media at your fingertips. My friend was in charge of ordering the periodicals, which rapidly became the job of returning unsold copies of the periodicals.

What was going on? Didn't people read magazines?

The problem was, the café was trying to sell too many trade magazines in a consumer magazine point of sale. The reason why trade magazines are sold largely through subscription is it's easier to send the magazines to the targeted buyers than to plop a café in the middle of a big city and expect all the targeted buyers (fewer in number and farther between) to beat a path to one door.

Since that café is no longer in operation, I recommend you visit your local library instead and peruse *The Literary Market Place* (LMP) or *Writer's Market*. These resources will clue you in to the breadth, depth, and sometimes comical focus of the magazine industry. You can also use the Internet and call up the sites for magazine publishers such as Reed Business Information, Condé Nast Publications, Ziff Davis Media, the Meredith Corporation, and Hearst to view their vast holdings.

## Which Is Better: Trade or Consumer?

Many English majors I meet and talk to are interested in working for magazines—and why not? Magazines are sexy: they're colorful, they're glossy, and they can seem either more intellectually stimulating and more plain fun than a newspaper. Magazines may have more allure as a place to work because with their targeted content focus, they seem to be speaking directly to *you* and what you're interested in, whether it be computer technology, health and beauty, guns and ammo, stocks and bonds, or the latest celebrity love couple.

But which to work for: trade or consumer?

Trade magazines, being smaller operations, are seldom as glossy and slick as their higher-profile consumer cousins. The content's micro-focus may have the appeal of simplicity, but perhaps you want more variety than a magazine dedicated only to hamsters and gerbils.

Working for a consumer magazine may be attractive to you simply because doing so carries more cachet: everyone knows *Cosmo,* and everyone knows its allure and appeal. The only thing is, the more high-profile and popular a magazine is, the harder it may be to break into. It's also worth noting that just because a magazine is full of hot women or good-looking men, it doesn't mean its offices are, too.

It's impossible to say which kind of magazine, trade or consumer, is "better" to work for, but undoubtedly, the trade magazine industry represents more titles and more kinds of magazine than the consumer industry. More titles, more diversity, more opportunity. And you're more likely to find a trade magazine focused on a field which you're passionate about, which not only will make you a more attractive candidate, it'll make working there more pleasant.

On the other hand, it could be that a trade magazine is so small that it cannot support a paid internship or the hiring of additional staff, at least in editorial. A larger consumer magazine may be better positioned to offer more opportunities, and don't rule out looking for jobs in sales, marketing, or advertising as an inroad to the editorial department.

## Working for Magazines: What's It Like?

English majors tend to end up in the editorial department; that's where they see themselves ending up.

Editorial staff members of a magazine are editors, charged with different departments or sections of the magazine. While it's not unheard of for magazines to have writers on staff, a more common practice is to contract out the writing assignments, which frees up the full-time people to edit, plan content, and manage personnel and projects.

The previous chapter used the analogy of a marathon to describe a periodical's editorial and production cycle. The same applies to periodicals that are magazines.

Working for a weekly magazine is not unlike working at a weekly newspaper, with respect to its production schedule: i.e., pulling each issue together; laying out ads, graphics, and editorial content. The production week starts out steady and relatively slow, then things get incrementally crazier toward deadline, and the night before the issue is sent to the printer—in production argot, "put to bed"—people work into the wee hours of the morning.

You might imagine that working on a monthly or a bimonthly magazine would allow you a more relaxed work environment than if you worked, say, at a newspaper, but workload depends on how big (or rather, how small) the magazine staff is. You could be part of a large team or one of a half dozen people trying to pull together the whole show.

The managing editor at a magazine is responsible for making sure the ship runs smoothly, and magazine staffers have told me that having a managing editor who is less than efficient and responsible can mean longer and later hours.

Magazines, like any other periodical, come big and small, with their own pros and cons. You might enjoy working for a small magazine where you know everyone by name and, for the benefits of your professional education, can learn what everyone else does to contribute to the magazine's construction. Conversely, you may prefer working for a large

**Most Important Skills**

Most English majors I speak to who say they want to work for magazines express an interest in working on the editorial side: that's only natural. When they tell me, however, that they want to work full time for a magazine and *write* full time for a magazine, it's time to explain that most magazines freelance out their writing assignments and that magazine editorial staffers have the word "editor" in their job title. For that reason, let's address the most important skills in editing.

The greatest disservice done to English majors occurs when they are taught to be good writers but not trained to be effective editors: that is, to take a manuscript and not only scrupulously correct it for spelling, grammar, and usage, but also evaulate its strengths and weaknesses and work with the author to help revise the piece to its maximum effectiveness and impact.

Being an effective editor entails good writing skills, yes; but it also involves strong interpersonal skills and knowing how to deal and work with writers. Writers can get prickly when asked to revise their work. Not all writers are dependable enough to hand in their work on deadline, which requires project management finesse on the part of the editor. Writers can feel underpaid and underappreciated (which, as it turns out, is the main thing they have in common with editors).

If, as an editor, you have good word skills but poor interpersonal skills, you might improve the writer's work, but in the process, you might sour the relationship with the writer, and editors—for magazines, newspapers, and book publishers—are judged, in large part, by their ability to attract and retain good writing talent.

A good editor is also a good thinker, a good brainstormer, an idea person. In magazines, the editor has the critical thinking ability to know and understand the readership and meet their needs and expectations. Good editors have an ear for the tenor of the times; they can anticipate what people want to read about, and what they will want to read about five months from now; and they know how to keep their publication or their department consistent in tone, voice, and style.

In a previous chapter, I note that the only way to find out if teaching is for you and if you are for teaching is, simply, to teach: similarly, finding freelance or full-time work as an editor is the only way for you to determine if this life is for you and if you possess or can develop the skills necessary to succeed.

magazine, where it less seldom falls upon a staff member to wear more than one hat and do someone else's job. Large magazines, like large families, can also afford you a wider field of people with whom to associate or befriend. Small magazines can make for a more tightly-knit team, but with a small staff size comes less upward or lateral mobility (to say nothing of contempt bred by familiarity).

Bear in mind, too, as you apply for jobs at magazines, that magazines have a higher mortality rate than newspapers or book publishers. A common life expectancy estimate for a magazine startup is three years, and the odds for survival are not necessarily favored by having a founder who is wealthy (like John Kennedy Jr.) or a celebrity (like Rosie O'Donnell) or by having just awesomely cool content.

Granted, it's unlikely that *Time, Reader's Digest* or *Modern Maturity* is going to go belly up any time soon, but no magazine is immune from financial woes: time was, the biggest magazines in America were *The Saturday Evening Post* and *Life*. I refer you to histories for lessons in how even the mighty can fall.

Magazines can also change their focus and their style, and you may not like the makeover. *Esquire,* for example, used to publish terrific literary fiction: no longer.

The good news is that the magazine industry—especially in New York, where so many are located—can be a collegiate group, more so than newspapers. Any one person on staff at a magazine knows a dozen people who work at a dozen different magazines, because he or she has worked at a dozen magazines in the past. People who work in magazines in New York hop from one publication to another. Networking and maintaining good relationships with peers is highly valued.

And if your magazine does indeed fold, or you lose your job to downsizing, you may work for an organization which owns dozens of magazines, so new opportunities may be very close at hand.

## Where Are the Magazines?

Most major consumer magazines have their offices in New York City, an area with a high concentration of media, publishing, and broadcasting.

Not all magazines are in New York, however: Clapper Communications (publishers of *Pack-o-Fun, Crafts 'n Things,* the *Cross Stitcher,* and other magazines) is located in Des Plaines, Illinois. A type of magazine called a "regional magazine" is located, like a newspaper, in the city or state it covers: e.g., *Boston* magazine, *San Diego* magazine, *Las Vegas Life* magazine, etc.

A quick way to find magazines in your area is to visit www.crmn.org, the Web site of the City and Regional Magazine Network (CRMA). Click on

"Magazine Selector," and choose a state from the drop-down menu: the site lists magazines in that state, as well as circulation figures. Web sites such as www.journalismjobs.com list opportunities in magazines, as well as newspapers.

It is also possible for a magazine to have its editorial offices in one city and its sales offices in another city. A magazine and its parent company may have jobs all over the country. At this writing, the Web site for Reed Business Information lists job openings in New York City and Los Angeles, but also in its offices in Waltham, Massachusetts; Oak Brook, Illinois; Highlands Ranch, Colorado; and Norcross, Georgia.

So regardless of where you would end up, working at a magazine, how do you know if you belong there? As opposed, say, to a book publisher or a newspaper?

## *Magazines Versus Books*

If you take the Columbia Publishing Course, you'll find that its six-week schedule of lectures and workshops is divided in half: the first three weeks for book publishing, and the second three weeks for magazine publishing. When I took the course, one of the seminar moderators tried to help us students determine which field we were suited for—books or magazines—by parsing the difference between "book people" and "magazine people."

As you'll probably be able to guess from the following tongue-in-cheek descriptions, this fellow was a satisfied member of the magazine industry.

- Book people sit on a plane, spending the whole trip with a novel; magazine people scoop up every free periodical available on the plane and spend the trip reading, skimming, flipping pages, assimilating information.
- Book people think in terms of nine months to a year (typically how long it takes to birth a book); magazine people think in terms of what's happening now and what trends or news stories are coming down the road.
- Book people listen to National Public Radio to get a high-level sense of what's going in the world, and maybe they'll peruse the day's paper; magazine people listen to talk radio and consume

information wherever they can get it: periodicals, TV and radio, the Internet, research reports, talking to people, and more.

- Book people drink tea; magazine people are jacked up on coffee.
- Book people have a memory for history, anecdotes, principles; magazine people have a memory for stories, articles, and features that ran anywhere from last week to five years ago.
- Book people like long projects; magazine people like a quicker turnover of assignments.

Obviously, comical stereotypes such as these make "book people" out to be tweedy, intellectuals who prefer a slower pace of life and who are insulated from the outside world, while "magazine people" are made to look like more energetic, more outgoing, idea- and story-related people.

**Best Advice I Ever Got**

If you're interested in magazines, read them as you usually do: here and there, a little bit at a time, flipping pages, looking at the pictures, and enjoying yourself. If, however, you're interested in working for magazines, use your skills as an English major to analyze the magazine, to understand its mission, its personality, its strengths, and its weaknesses. Read the whole magazine, cover to cover, with a discerning eye. (See the "Try This" exercise for pointers.) Understand it as you would a novel or a poem. Doing this will help you regardless of whether you want to work in sales, editorial, or production.

Also bear in mind that magazines, catering to a particular subject matter or area of interest, are a good way for you to combine your foundational skills as an English major with your own personal expertise or interests. If, in addition to loving writing and working with words, you enjoy computers, try getting a job at a trade magazine dedicated to computers—or doll collecting, or yoga, or celebrities, or history, or what have you. Again, your specialized knowledge or expertise will stand you in good stead regardless of what job you hold at the magazine.

And as obvious it may sound, if you want to work in magazines, read magazines. There are magazines about magazines: about the industry and issues that affect it. Read magazines for story ideas, for graphic ideas, for inspiration and for education. Read, analyze, retain, and apply.

Let's just say that true words can be spoken in jest.

Or let's say you're trying to decide between newspapers and magazines.

## Magazines Versus Newspapers

A newspaper person's mind is intensely local, focused on what's happening today or this week. A magazine person, in contrast, is able to plan content farther in advance and concern himself with subject matter with a longer shelf life than today's late-breaking news story.

A newspaper can plan stories a month in advance; a monthly magazine can plan some of its content six months to a year in advance.

That state of affairs creates pros and cons for magazine staffers: on the plus side, they're allowed to think "bigger picture" and in terms of seasonal content (i.e., planning in autumn for the spring issue), but as one staffer from a celebrity magazine told me, by the time the next issue rolls out, the rock band or the celebrity couple you're writing about could be splitsville or just plain passé. The timing and framing of the content is an acquired skill and a delicate art.

You might say magazine people have their ear to the ground and their finger in the wind, while newspaper people are more concerned with the immediacy of their surroundings. A magazine can afford a writer more space and latitude to be concerned with ideas, trends, and analysis; a newspaper can certainly write about ideas and trends, but there is always the connection to the people, places, and events of the community it covers.

It's up to you, to determine which you prefer. You may get satisfaction from magazine content that identifies the "top ten mutual funds" or the "top seven secrets to drive your boyfriend wild"; you may prefer newspaper content that engages the nitty-gritty of the lives of a person, a public figure, an issue or an event.

The frequency of the publication and the length of the editorial content also influence the depth of the editing process. Obviously, daily newspapers are under a stricter time deadline than a monthly magazine, and because magazines are at liberty to run longer or more indepth features or articles, there is more time to write, rewrite, edit, and revise.

Some other key differences between magazines and newspapers:

**Magazines can move from city to city.** Let's say the magazine's editorial offices are in Boston, but the parent media company has its offices in New York: the parent company could decide to relocate the magazine to New York, and they may go a step further and relocate the magazine without relocating the people. It happens. In contrast, it's not likely the New York–based owners of the *Boston Globe* are one day going to decide to move the entire operation from Boston to Manhattan.

**There are newspaper jobs wherever you want to be.** If you're interested in relocating to the Southwest, you can find newspaper opportunities there, and if you're interested in staying put wherever you are, opportunities are local. Magazines are not as ubiquitous, and the editorial offices may be in one city while the sales and advertising offices may be in another.

**Voice.** Magazine content allows for more "voice," stylistic flair, or humor than newspaper content. Newspapers are charged with the duty to pursue and report the truth; magazines, with a narrower subject focus, may have a narrower mission, such as helping women become better mothers or helping men aged eighteen to thirty-four dress for success, and that focus can call for a more particular "voice" in the tone and tenor of the magazine content, whether it is the editorial, the ads, or the graphic look.

**Magazines are more visual.** The next time you're in transit (on a commuter train, subway, or airplane) or in a waiting room, note the difference between the way people read books and newspapers and the way they read magazines: you don't ever see someone idly flipping the pages of *War and Peace,* pausing to read for a few minutes, then flipping again. You might say people read books and newspapers, and they look at magazines. With a few exceptions (*Harper's* leaps to mind), magazines have more pictures than words. In some issues of *Vogue,* the first third of the book is ads, and once you hit the articles, there are either ads that look like articles ("advertorials" or "advertising supplements") or articles that recommend goods and services with big splashy photos.

---

**TRY THIS**

Success at working for any kind of periodical involves a close study of the periodical itself: not an idle flip-through or reading only those pieces that catch your eye, but the whole enchilada—front to back, up and down, and crossways. If the periodical in question isn't available at your local library, contact the magazine and request a press kit. See if they allow you to order individual back issues: Order a half dozen at least. If the magazine is indeed available at your local library, set yourself at a table with a stack of back issues. Read each issue and take notes:

- What common subjects or themes are addressed, issue to issue?
- What is the main purpose of the articles in the magazine: are they meant to educate, tell a story, provide opinion, give an overview of an issue, entertain, spread gossip, amuse, enlighten, inspire? Or do the articles seem incidental relative to the pictures and ads?
- Compare the subjects or topics in the first two-thirds of the magazine and those buried—I'm sorry, *positioned*—in the last third.
- Look at the contributors' bios. What are the credentials of the people writing the articles? That is, are they working professionals in the field about which they write? Are they academics, published authors, first-time writers?
- What kind of advertising does the magazine carry? What does that tell you about the magazine's readership?

If you're really up for an exercise, find the biggest wall in your living space and clear it. Take two issues of a magazine (preferably one fewer than two-hundred pages) and tear out every page. Tape each page to the wall, in succession. (You'll need two issues, obviously, so you can see every page.) Then go to work examining what you see: articles, ads, visual elements. What you're looking at is basically a "dummy" of the magazine—i.e., a schematic identifying what elements go where—that is in the editor's office. Ask some of the questions above, and see what there is to see.

One of my favorite things to do, in studying a magazine, is to note where the magazine's editorial content mentions or plugs a business—it could be a product or a service—and then look through the magazine to find an ad for that business, and note where the ad is positioned in proximity to the copy. You could do the same for announcements of art openings or performances; "staff picks" for new books, CDs and DVDs; interviews with authors or artists; and fashion pictorials that feature this or that designer. Of course, this is not to say that some magazines trade editorial coverage for advertising dollars or, far worse, endorse products or services because they received freebies from a business. It's just fun to connect the dots and see what picture emerges.

## GLOSSARY

### WHAT'S THE DIFFERENCE BETWEEN ...

Masthead

The magazine *publisher,* just like the newspaper publisher, develops an editorial and business vision for the publication, controls the budget, and deals with staffing and sales and marketing issues.

The *production director* deals with the physical production of the magazine and works with the printers and typesetters.

A *contributor editor* is someone who doesn't work at the magazine's offices, but performs editorial duties: e.g., finds new writers; edits content to be published; sifts through submissions; or generates ideas or story topics.

An *assistant editor* at a magazine handles administrative editorial work (research, proofreading, etc.) and will typically write or edit smaller features.

An *associate editor* works on longer or more high-profile editorial content and, along with the editor, represents the magazine at business or industry functions or conferences.

Terms

All magazines all periodicals, but not all periodicals are magazines.

A *periodical*—a term that sounds more medical every time you say it—is a publication with a fixed time period between issues: weekly (fifty-two times a year), monthly (twelve times a year), bimonthly (six times a year), quarterly (four times a year), semiannually (twice a year), or annually (once a year).

Strictly speaking, newspapers are periodicals, too, so you add "daily" to the list.

At the risk of further confusion, a *tabloid* is popularly understood to mean a tawdry magazine-format periodical on newsprint, but the term also refers to a size format of newspaper: i.e., a newspaper half the size of a standard newspaper, without stories about Bigfoot and Paris Hilton's dog.

And of course, people in the magazine industry refer to the edition of the magazine as "the book," as in, "If we have to run a short story this month, let's stick it in the back of the book."

The world of magazines is full of industry terms, many of which are shared with newspapers. These are some of my favorites, not because they're necessary to know as you're looking for a job, but just because I like saying them:

- **charticle**: an article or feature that is organized in the form of a chart or other graphic
- **FOB**: "front of book," or the first half of the magazine. Compare **BOB**, "back of book"
- **house organ**: a magazine that is internal to a company or organization. Compare **official organ**, the official magazine or publication of a trade or business group
- **maquette**: a layout for the magazine showing where the ads appear
- **outsert**: pre-printed material that is attached to the magazine, as in the *New Yorker*'s "cover wrap"
- **polybagging**: packaging a magazine in a plastic bag to contain anything from CDs, subscription renewal notices, supplemental publications, etc.

- **squib**: very short editorial matter, as you find in *Maxim* or *Men's Fitness*

Consult the Internet (such as articles on www.mediabistro.com) for more magazine terms, many of which are held in common with the newspaper industry and aren't as comical-sounding as the above.

### Regional Magzines

Many major metropolitan cities have an eponymous monthly magazine whose raison d'êtres are manifold: to give restaurants and night clubs a glossy place to advertise; to educate middle-aged yuppies on "The Top 10 Doctors," "The Top 20 Schools," "The Top 50 Weekend Getaways" and "The 100 Most Powerful People" in the city; to publish 50,000-word features on notorious city crime figures, the internecine soap opera of the family who owns the city's largest seafood restaurant, and apologia for why their city is a world-class city. These magazines—known as *regional magazines*—are glossy vehicles for restaurant advertising and the tourist trade. They are willing to print the city's foibles, but not its flaws (go to the city newspaper for that). Your success in working here, as with any periodical, is predicated on your understanding and acceptance of the magazine's mission in life, such as it is.

### College/University Magazines

Your alumni magazine has no news in it. That is, it only has good news, and as we all know, no news is good news. Good news for the college or university means financial support from alumni, and one doesn't get that by reporting warts, controversy, or questions to the status quo. Alumni magazines can be thought-provoking, entertaining and informative reads, but their main mission is to make alma mater look good. You may find job turnover here slow and infrequent, given a small staff and the desirability of receiving the benefits and perks of working at a university.

### Literary Journals and Magazines

Literary journals are run out of someone's dining room until a university buys them and moves the journal's operations to a dining room on campus. The staff and the founders are usually the same people, and the staff have other jobs. It's not a moneymaking enterprise: not for them, and alas, not for you.

## Q&A
## A LONG WAY FROM THE MAILROOM

The road not taken for magazine publisher Bob Fernekees was blocked by an electric typewriter.

The time is the late 1970s, and the location is St. Michael's College in Vermont: Fernekees is an undergraduate English major, and the one journalism course available has aspiring student reporters typing away at old electric machines against the clock. The instructor literally pulls the plug when the time is up.

You were graded, Fernekees remembers, on how much of your article you finished while making as few errors as possible. "I was just grappling with the technology," says Fernekees with an audible shrug, "hunting and pecking as fast as I could.... Had I been a better typist, I probably would have stuck with [journalism] a little longer."

Today, Bob Fernekees is publisher of *CRM* magazine (*CRM* stands for customer relationship management). CRM is a property of Freedom Technology Media Group (FTMG), a wholly owned subsidiary of Freedom Communications, a leading private media company. Headquartered in California, FTMG publishes twenty-seven newspapers and fifteen magazines, and it operates eight broadcast TV stations along with more than fifty Internet sites.

When you were a student, were you concerned about what you were going to do for a job after you graduated?

I was afraid to think about what to do [for a living]. If I could have done more internships or even stuck with the school newspaper or things like that ... but I didn't really take advantage of those things. There weren't that many options, and I just didn't have the drive and I especially didn't have the focus to do those things.

I had no concept of what I wanted to do or what I could do or even what these jobs entailed.

You took a job sorting mail at CBS TV (which sounds low-level) until you found out the company would foot 80 percent of the cost of postgraduate education. So you took the GMAT exam and started on a six-year path to earning your MBA in finance and marketing. What was that like?

It wasn't easy, going to school at night and returning to a dead-end job during the day. Being an English major, I had no clue what people were talking about when they were talking about business. I didn't know what a ledger was, or liabilities, or assets.

You lost your job at CBS, but then a lead came through your sister-in-law, correct?

She worked as an advertising rep for a magazine. Not only did she make more money, she seemed to be having more fun at an easier job. I sent out a thousand résumés that went unanswered, until I saw a sales opening at a trade magazine in professional film and video. I didn't get the job, but I kept after the company and when the magazine fired the person they originally hired, they gave the job to me.

The guy was sick of hearing from me, so he hired me!

You learned that sales wasn't exactly your game, though: You were fired. You were fired from your job after that, too. Didn't you become discouraged?

After getting fired so many times, I got really good at getting a job quickly!

Even though you had a family to support and a mortgage, you took a pay cut to work as a sales rep for the New York–based trade magazine consortium The Freedom Group.

By this time I knew enough about business and had worked long enough in magazines to be involved in launches, media kits, trade shows, and so on.

My boss had less experience than me. Over time, even though I was a sales rep, I knew how to do things. Publishing is one of those businesses where titles are one thing, but it's really about what you know and who you know, and that's where you get your power from, from how much you take on. You can rise up through the ranks, from ad director to associate publisher.

It sounds like magazine publishing has a great potential for mobility. And, in trade magazines, you have a great variety of magazines.

Trade publishing is huge. There are magazines for every single market niche you could want to explore. And it's fun, too.

I never would have survived in a cubicle farm, or being an analyst at IBM. I needed something that allowed me to do a lot of different things and be super-independent.

What advice would you give job applicants?

Pick up the *Standard Rates and Data* [a periodical that], in addition to listing media rates and data, lists every magazine across the country. From there, call the magazine and ask for a media kit, if you can't find a copy on the newsstand. Investigate internships, and, once in, write small pieces for the magazine as a way of building up clips.

So how do you become the publisher, the big cheese?

Most publishers come from the business side, but not always. Quite honestly, there's more money to be made on the sales side. It's not necessary to [become] a publisher, coming up through the sales side, but it is necessary to know the business aspect of it and be able to balance all the different things: editorial integrity with my favorite line, The best magazines are the ones still publishing.

CHAPTER 6

# Books (As Opposed to Literature)

In class after class, semester after semester, English majors read books. They analyze books, write about and discuss books, and celebrate and critique books—all without being told how books are made and marketed, sold and distributed, priced and purchased, warehoused and remaindered.

When the beneficiaries of standard English major curricula set themselves on the postgraduate path to becoming editors or agents, more frequently than not, they do so with an ignorance so big and so wide, you could drive a trailer truck through it sideways. Many do not know how to start out in the field or even what people in publishing do.

Yet many of the English majors I meet tell me they want to go into publishing. When I ask why, they unfailingly reply, "Well, because I love books."

That's actually the correct answer.

Not all people who love books work in book publishing, but, safe to say, all people who work in book publishing love books. That may sound excruciatingly obvious, but bear in mind that loving books is different from loving literature or loving to read. So what does it mean, to love books?

It depends, to borrow from Raymond Carver, on what we talk about when we talk about love. It's important to figure this out so you'll know if book publishing is for you, and, if so, what part of the industry you want to join.

## Do You Love Books?

If you say you love books, but what you really mean is that you love being surrounded by books, handling books, hearing about new books and recommending them, you should consider working in a bookstore or in a library.

If, however, you say you love books and among the things that really float your boat are:

- being part of a book's creation and development
- participating in the manifold and sometimes novel ways (sorry) a book is marketed and sold
- discovering or developing unknown talent
- exploring the cover and interior designs of books
- reading about the controversies, debates, or cultural changes a book can trigger
- helping create something that is both a good and a service

then you may want to consider working in book publishing.

Among book publishing people, you find an unwavering wonkish interest in how this book or that book was secured, edited, made, marketed, and sold. Book publishing people not only want to hear what a book is about, they want to know the dish, the gossip, the inside scoop: Who was the editor on that book? What was the bidding like for it? How hard of an edit was it? How many copies has it sold? How was it marketed to booksellers? What was the advance, and has the publisher recouped it? What's the author's marketing platform?

Most of us, when we're asked whether a book is good, will think of the quality of the writing—plot, characters, dialogue—and say yea or nay. To people in book publishing, the answer to the question *Is it a good book?* can involve many other questions: Is the binding, paper, print size, and packaging any good? Is the cover design for the paperback better than that of the hardcover? And when you ask if the book is good—good for whom? Its intended audience? The publisher? The author and her agent? Independent bookstores, chains, other retail outlets?

English majors learn to evaluate a book based on its literary merit; people in book publishing have a wider field of concerns. Some of those concerns may strike the ears of an English major as, well, disagreeably mercantile, shall we say. The last thing some people want to think of books as, is a business.

Listen to disgruntled authors, especially, who believe they've been given short shrift by their publisher, and you'll hear all manner of talk about how the book publishing industry is rife with people who have no love for books, and why? Because they worship the false gods of greed, profit, conglomeration, and the bottom line.

Well, before you buy in to that way of thinking, realize that people who worship money above all else are not stampeding over one another to get into the publishing industry; rather, the true disciples of Mammon are daily communicants at the altars of Wall Street and such industries as oil, pharmaceuticals, and military defense. In fact, in the amount of time required in the book publishing industry for you to graduate from editorial assistant to a position where you're starting to see real money, you could easily go to law or medical school or earn your MBA, and end up making more money in the long run.

People in the book publishing industry really do love books. They wouldn't be in the business otherwise.

## *Do You Love All Books?*

If you are an undergraduate English major, does it naturally follow that you love books?

Depends on what you mean by *books.*

As a major in English, you are exposed to and become familiar with certain kinds of books. In the classes required for your major, you become familiar with anthologies and collections of poetry; plays; essays; and short fiction; as well as novels and the occasional graphic novel. In your other classes, you become familiar with textbooks or works of nonfiction (to use a very general and unhelpful term) in the various disciplines of history, psychology, philosophy, or the sciences.

Again, that may sound obvious—until you appreciate that the kinds of books you encounter as a student are a slim fraction of the kinds of books published in America every day.

I don't know about you, but I cannot remember, in my college studies, being assigned a biography or celebrity memoir. I didn't come to class with diet books, cookbooks, or self-help books under my arm. If we read children's literature, it was those titles approved for collegiate study, such as *Alice's Adventures in Wonderland* and *Through the Looking Glass, Huck Finn,* and *The House at Pooh Corner,* not *The Berenstain Bears Bigger Book of Stories, Arthur Meets*

**Most Important Skills**

- ***Teamwork.*** The author Truman Capote once wrote that when he was a boy, he thought books were so magical and perfect that they just fell from the sky—which, I suppose, you could take to mean that they came from God. When you first become aware of books, all that is important is content. Later on, you learn that there are authors. You may then learn about editors or perhaps agents. The more you learn about book publishing, the more the mind reels at how many people are involved in making that perfect little thing that fell from heaven (or, perhaps, rose from the other direction). The ability to collaborate, cooperate, compromise, and basically play well with others is key to your success in book publishing, no matter what job you end up having.
- ***Attention to detail.*** I've heard it said that God is the details and that the devil is in the details: Whatever the case may be, the details are important in book publishing. In journalism, if your lead paragraph in today's paper misspells *accommodate*, you look like an idiot, but you can always console yourself that today's paper will be in the trash by the end of the day and a new edition will take its place tomorrow. A book with an initial print run of five thousand copies that has the word *accommodate* misspelled in its opening paragraph—or a textbook with the wrong answers, or a cookbook with a page missing—is a mistake with a little more permanence. That error will last; you won't.

*the President, Sammy the Seal* or *Go Dog, Go!* As an English major, I was not required to read mysteries, fantasy, thrillers, horror, science fiction, westerns, romance, or erotica.

Are there any English majors out there fulfilling credit hours studying coffee-table books such as *The National Enquirer: Thirty Years of Unforgettable Images*?

How about nature guides and manuals? Books on home improvement, interior design, landscaping, and gardening? Anyone taking a final exam on *How to Make Money Selling Stocks Short* or *Who Moved My Cheese?*

Let's see, what have we left out? Christian fiction? *Windows XP for Dummies*? Books on genealogy, atlases, *Proficient Motorcycling: The Ultimate Guide to*

*Riding Well*, foreign-language titles, parenting books, gay and lesbian mystery novels (not kidding), and books written by presidential dogs, cartoon characters, anarchists, rodeo stars, and God.

These are the books people buy and read, and despite what you've heard in your English classes, it doesn't mean people are stupid.

## What People Read (If They Read at All)

Prospective English majors leave the privacy of their parents' homes for the insular seclusion of the campus. So sequestered, these young men and women immerse themselves in good books—for all intents and purposes, the best books—and they are, variously, challenged by James Joyce, inspired by Virginia Woolf, stirred by Shakespeare, or confused by William Faulkner. This is normal. Doesn't everyone enjoy the classics?

Confined to the classroom, English majors have no direct experience of what most people—inhabitants of the real world—read; or rather, of the fact that most people don't read, and those who do choose books for escapism, entertainment, the comfort of familiarity, or to keep up with what everyone else is reading.

English majors are accustomed to reading books for discussion, analysis, the challenge of unfamiliarity, or to keep up with what everyone else in class is reading.

When people don't treasure or cherish what we do, we tend to think either that people are ignorant or that civilization is nearing its end-times. (We may think both, one state of affairs being contingent upon the other.) The fact that people spend more money on video games than novels, or spend more time watching TV than attending poetry readings, is somehow causally related to the earth going to hell in a handbasket.

Seldom do you encounter an individual who considers differences in taste to be morally neutral, and simply something to be tolerated because nothing can be done about it. It's much more comforting to one's own value system and ego to think everyone who would rather read *Presumed Innocent* instead of *Their Eyes Were Watching God* is an idiot.

## *Publishing, Debunked*

As an undergraduate English major myself, I thought working in book publishing meant sitting across from William Faulkner at an oak desk, helping him edit the manuscript of his next masterpiece (with cocktails at 21 afterward, of course). I knew there were other books besides novels, but my sense was that all publishing was literary in atmosphere, which meant it was full of smart and witty people who never tired of talking about novels and consorting with writers.

And because I had plenty of experience with books but no experience with the business of publishing books, I naturally concluded that books had nothing to do with business. I dutifully parroted the authorial lament that books were packaged and sold like breakfast cereal and financial concerns were ruining literature.

Not so. There proved to be many exceptions to what I thought were the rules.

There are book publishers in cities other than New York, although that is where the majority of the largest ones are. There are jobs in the book publishing industry that do not involve working directly with authors. There are jobs that do not require you to dress in tweed, drink chamomile tea, read Proust, and own a cat. There are jobs in book publishing that never require you to have contact with an author. (Some people love books more than they love authors or working with them.)

In short, the term *book publishing industry* could mean just about anything—comprising, as it does, the industries of publishing novels, anthologies, nonfiction, poetry, chapbooks, textbooks, reference books, and book-related media such as audio books, language lab recordings for foreign-language textbooks, and Web sites for book publishers.

So how do you know where to start?

## *Publishing Seminars*

A good place to start would be an adult education course—or, better, a seminar explaining how book publishing works.

The University of Denver conducts such a seminar—the Publishing Institute—for four weeks in the summer. Similarly, New York University conducts an annual Summer Publishing Institute in book, magazine, and electronic publishing. The Columbia Publishing Course, formerly the Radcliffe Publishing Course, lasts for six weeks in the summer and operates under the aegis of Columbia University.

Such seminars attract a wealth of speakers and guests from the high echelons of the industry, and the opportunity to listen to these professionals, ask them questions, and network with them is otherwise unavailable to the common man. These programs typically feature workshops or role-playing exercises in which you and your fellow students literally build a publishing house or a magazine from scratch, having your product judged by a panel of experts or tested in a mock book auction. A program may hold its own job fair at its conclusion.

One drawback to these seminars is the price. The intensive, university-sponsored programs can run you about four thousand dollars in tuition, and the program may encourage you (that is, insist) that you pay for room and board as well (which may be another couple grand), because, since you will be immersed in the program for four or six weeks, it's just plain easier on you to have a nearby place to crash after late nights in workshops or hours spent talking and networking. You may wonder if it's worth six thousand dollars to try to get your foot in the door of an industry in which an entry-level editorial assistant makes only about twenty-five thousand dollars a year in a city with an astronomical cost of living.

Another potential negative in the equation is that these programs are not a 100-percent guarantee of a job in book publishing (though the job placement rate can reach the ninetieth percentile), nor does completion of the course confer some kind of professional accreditation. You don't come out with a sheepskin saying you have your degree in book publishing.

My own opinion is this: The connections you stand to make among professionals in the field, as well as among your colleagues similarly struggling to find a job, are priceless. People may say, disparagingly or otherwise, that in the book publishing business, it's all about who you know—but the fact is, connections and networking have the same importance in any profession. While you will not be guaranteed a job by participating in the program, you may have access to an alumni network, and people in book publishing will recognize the names of these programs on your résumé. I got my first job out of college as a production editor at Houghton Mifflin, pretty much because the woman who hired me saw I had taken the Radcliffe Publishing Course, and she figured I knew a thing or two about publishing, which I could honestly say that I did.

## *Publishing, Self-Taught*

If you cannot or do not want to spend the money on a seminar, there's always the self-education route. I recommend starting with books on how to publish your own book, because in the realm of self-publishing, you are not only the author but also the editor, proofreader, press agent, marketing director, and distributor, just to name a few of your responsibilities. Further rudimentary knowledge about how the book publishing industry operates can be culled from books on how to find a good literary agent, how to be a good literary agent, what editors are looking for, how to write a good proposal, and so on.

If your city or town, like mine, holds an annual book festival, go. You'll find professionals who know the business and who likely all know each other. Buy someone a cup of bad coffee on her break and ask her about her business, how she got started, what's moving these days and what isn't, what she thinks of the current state of the publishing business, etc., then go and look at all the pretty books. Take a careful look at the covers. Look at the colors used, the position of the type, how big the title is in comparison to the author's name, and where the type is located on the cover. Look at the spine, too. This is usually the only thing you see when browsing shelved books.

Then there's the Internet. Nearly every book publisher has a Web site where you can examine their imprints, their backlists, their mission statements, and, if applicable, their holdings. And there's a host of Web sites dedicated to the latest publishing industry news and gossip. Aspiring authors may benefit from Web sites set up by aspiring authors for aspiring authors, where you can read people's thoughts on any of a hundred publishing subjects, including accounts of their firsthand experiences with marketing departments, agents and editors, and subsidiary rights and movie deals. (You can find the best publishing industry sites in appendix IV.)

You should also examine job listings in the publishing industry; you can access a mother lode at www.MediaBistro.com. See what qualifications and credentials publishers look for in a candidate. For example, if you're wondering whether you need or should get an advanced degree to work in the publishing industry, check out the requirements for the job you think you may be interested in. Not only will you gain an understanding of and appreciation for what people with that job title do, you'll learn where they typically come from. You may learn, for example, that an editor of dictionaries could stand to have a master's in linguistics, or that editors of foreign textbooks would benefit from having an advanced degree in a foreign language.

## What Makes Book Publishing Unique?

An oft-quoted observation is that book publishing is a nineteenth-century business in the twenty-first century. Several things about the business make it idiosyncratic: The price of the product is not set by the point of sale (the seller); the point of sale has the option to return unsold units of the product; and the original creator of the product (the author) can have a dickens

**The Best Advice I Ever Got**

- ***Book publishing isn't about good books.*** It's about good *ideas* for books. Recently, a friend of mine submitted his dissertation to a prominent academic publisher, but he was concerned that the manuscript still needed work. I told him not to worry, that editors see through flaws in a manuscript to the heart of its ideas, and if his ideas were good—that is, marketable and sellable—his book would be accepted for publication. It was.
- ***Books are a business.*** While it may pain the heart of an English major to think of books as *units*, that's what they are in the marketplace. The decision to publish a book is not only based on whether the book has a good idea, it's also based on how well it could sell and who is going to buy it. The latter question, who is the target audience for a book, is answered with specifics of age, gender, education, geography, background, and more. The wider the potential audience, the more likely a book will be seen as marketable.

of a time finding out how many units her creation has actually sold. Book publishing is a business of printed words that relies heavily on word of mouth, and it seems the more units the industry produces, the more people like to say that the industry is in decline.

The biggest adjustment for English majors entering book publishing will be seeing books not solely as objects to be revered, but also as units to be produced and sold. It doesn't have to be either/or, and you're likely to find within the publishing industry what Keats called *negative capability*—the ability to keep in one's mind these two seemingly opposing ideas.

Book publishing people are more comfortable with long-term assignments: It takes at least nine months to turn a manuscript into a book, and there's a lot of detail work involved. You have teams of people who all collaborate on one book: The production team delivers the book to the printer and ensures a top-notch physical product; the sales team gets the book into stores and on display; the marketing and publicity team decides how it will make readers aware of the book's existence in the stores. Editors collaborate with and play a part in all of these teams by generating company enthusiasm and support for every book and making sure everyone understands what a book's about, why it will sell, and how or why it should be promoted or publicized.

The drawback to a job in publishing might be that your work is less appreciated. *Authors* may receive kind letters from their readers, saying how much they appreciated the book, but editors and other people who work in book publishing? When was the last time you finished a book and sat down to write a note to the book's publisher that said, "Hey, thanks for publishing that! I really enjoyed it"? I'm sure people who work in book publishing enjoy congratulation from their colleagues, and maybe that's enough for them, but relative to the other professions in this book, it seems to me that book publishing people are the ones who have to pat themselves on the back the most. When the tens of thousands of decisions that go into editing and making a book turn out absolutely right, you never hear about it. Countless people across America—whose names you never know, whose faces you never see, and whose efforts often go unrewarded by plaques and prizes and honoraria—are doing their job, which is helping to make books.

## *Where Are the Jobs?*

Like many magazine publishers, most major book publishers have their editorial offices in New York City. If every book publisher were located in Manhattan, however, the island would have sunk a long time ago.

If the publisher you want to work for is in New York, then you're going to New York—unless the publisher has offices in cities other than New York. (The publisher of Harlequin romance novels, for example, has offices in New York and in Toronto.) If you want to work in book publishing and aren't particular about where you begin, you could go to New York and just try to find a job anywhere, with any publisher.

If you don't want to work in New York City, either because you're not into the big city or because the kind of publisher you want to work for isn't represented there, there are other options.

I happen to live in New England, where there is a fair concentration of colleges and universities. Many area institutions of higher learning—Harvard, Yale, MIT, Northeastern, the University of Massachusetts—have their own book publishing division, or academic press. Relative to trade publishers in New York, these academic presses are small in size and scope and publish books with a narrower, more scholarly appeal. Jobs do open up in these academic presses from time to time, so check to see if there are any such presses in your area: The online listing of the Association of American University Presses is a good place to start (aaup.uchicago.edu).

There are also independent book publishers all across the United States: Graywolf Press, Coffee House Press, and Milkweed Editions are in Minnesota; Beacon Press and Candlewick Press are in Massachusetts; Loompanics Unlimited is in Washington; and Raven Tree Press is in Wisconsin. These are but a few of the small independent publishers in existence.

Between these small presses and the corporate conglomerates are midsize publishers. Another subset is specialty publishers, which may concentrate in technical books, legal materials, or instructional books. F+W Publications, the publisher of this book, is a specialty publisher, and it is also an example of a publisher with offices in more than one non–New York location, including Ohio, Wisconsin, Colorado, Georgia, and Massachusetts.

The caveat with small publishers is the same as with any small business: The smaller the business and the fewer the employees, the fewer the job openings or opportunities. If you find a job with a small publisher, there may not be the kind of mobility within the organization you would find at a larger company. And of course, the smaller the operation, the greater the possibility it could tank one day or get bought by a larger company.

**TRY THIS**

Go to www.caderbooks.com to subscribe to Publishers Lunch, a free e-newsletter about trade publishing. This and other resources in print and on the Web will keep you posted on developments in the industry you wish to join, and help you learn its language and hot-button issues.

Go to your local bookstore and offer to take the buyer to lunch, for an informational interview. If your local bookstore is a large chain, there will be several people responsible for ordering books, in different genres; if your local bookstore is a small, indie operation, the book buyer may be the owner. Pick the buyer's brain about how books end up in the bookstore, which ones get placed "cover-out" on the shelf, which ones get discounted, and so on.

Learning how to make a book—through an art class or your local adult education center—won't exactly help you get a job, but there's much to be said for using your hands to make the product that's at the center of the industry you're trying to join. Pick your own font, design your own cover, sew your own binding: you'll see how hard it is, how fun it is, and how many decisions go into the process.

## GLOSSARY

### WHAT'S THE DIFFERENCE BETWEEN ...

Terms

An *assistant* or *associate editor* assists another editor in editorial or production duties, or the title may just indicate a lower rank or experience level.

A *developmental editor* gives vision, organization, and editorial know-how to a project. A developmental editor may consult with authors before the pen even hits the page, and can even be involved in significant content and copyediting once the project is underway.

A *managing editor* oversees editorial and production deadlines, manages and supervises staff, and ensures that everything falls into place.

An *acquisitions editor* finds new authors and/or titles—which may sound exciting, but consistently pulling geniuses out of your hat is no easy trick. This editor is keenly in tune with the marketplace, with trends and relevant data, and with the competition.

*Editorial assistant* is an entry-level administrative position vague enough in title to support any kind of writing, editing, filing, or coffee-fetching duties. While not a glamour position by any means, it is a foot in the door that can quickly lead to opportunities.

Most editorial jobs, especially those in New York, require an editor to build her own stable of authors and to develop and edit all the books she acquires. Success and continued employment depend upon those books selling. A person with this kind of responsibility could have a range of titles, including *associate editor, acquisitions editor, editor, senior editor,* or *executive editor.*

*The Elements of Style* and *The Chicago Manual of Style*?

As an English major, you may know Strunk and White's *Elements of Style*: It's the slim volume you refer to when writing papers, to try to remember everything you've forgotten about punctuation and spelling.

A style guide is a resource a publishing house or media (such as a newspaper or Web site) uses to ensure consistency in grammar, usage, spelling, punctuation, and the like. Some publishers rely on a published resource such as *The Chicago Manual of Style*, and some have developed their own idiosyncratic style guides. (Some even use both, and, more remarkably, some don't have either, which inevitably leads to mistakes, confusion, and headaches.) Be prepared to use one if you go to work in publishing or journalism, or at least ask if there is one (and if not, volunteer to assemble one yourself for your employer).

Copyediting and Proofreading?

*Proofreading* means reviewing a manuscript or document for clarity and sense and calling out errors in spelling, punctuation, and grammar. Proofreaders mark up the manuscript in colored pen or pencil and append questions or comments to the author or editor on little sticky notes in the margins.

*Copyediting* is proofreading with added attention to sentence structure, sense, style, flow, and expression. The copyeditor not only edits, but rewrites, rearranges, and reworks—and also performs needed fact-checking. This is why the copyeditor is paid more than the proofreader. Minimal copyediting is sometimes called *baseline editing*.

### Unsolicited Manuscripts and Solicited Manuscripts?

When I ask college students if they know what a slush pile is, they usually think I'm talking about a mosh pit or about something to do with beer slides. The slush pile, as a thousand other resource books (but not your English classes) will tell you, is the stack of unsolicited manuscripts received by a book or magazine publisher. Solicited manuscripts are those specifically requested by an editor. A magazine editor, for example, may write a polite letter to a writer whom she has published in the past, inviting the writer to submit new pieces for consideration for publication. (Wouldn't you love to get one of those?) That's a *solicited manuscript*. The *unsolicited* ones are from people like you and me, who send a book, article, story, or poem off to a publisher and hope for the best. The volume of unsolicited submissions compels some book publishers to refuse to receive manuscripts that have not been sent by an agent.

### Publisher and Imprint?

If you're a book *publisher* and you publish a few hundred titles a year, the answer to the question *What kinds of books do you publish?* is not always answerable in one simple sentence. To make it easier to market their books, large publishers create *imprints*, or publishers within publishers. These smaller houses specialize in certain kinds of books and cater to targeted demographics. *Writer's Market* and the Internet will help you determine which imprints belong to which publishers, and knowing the personality and direction of a publisher's imprints will help you refine your job search.

## *Q & A*
## LATE BLOOMER MAKES GOOD

Today, Joe Terry is an editor in chief at AB/Longman publishers, and he divides his time between his Boston-area home and New York. Terry's job is to supervise and manage acquisition editors, who are the people who go out and find new authors and books.

He is a self-confessed late bloomer.

After a false start in college, he says, he threw his back into working as a fisherman on Long Island, during which time he discovered that the books he read for pleasure were the same books college English majors read for assignments. This minor epiphany encouraged him to return to college and pursue his BA in English "with really no thought," he says, "as to what [he] would do with the degree once [he] graduated."

After working in book sales, Terry became an editor and now publishes textbooks. What is particularly exciting about textbook publishing, says Terry, is making something click—through the combined efforts of a textbook and teacher—for young people in high school or college ("kind of like I was," Terry confesses, "struggling or just not interested"). "That moment of transformation is what it's all about," says Terry.

It may be his sales background talking, but when Terry is asked what qualities are welcomed and advantageous in book publishing, he focuses not on intellectual or editing skills but on the need for initiative, self-starting enthusiasm, self-motivation, and self-directedness.

Your first job in publishing was as a sales rep, a position you found through a placement agency. Why sales?

It looked like a fun job. And it was the only job I could afford to take, since most entry-level jobs in editorial did not seem to pay enough to both live on and repay student loans.

How did you get your first job in sales?

I went on college campuses and pretended that I was a sales rep, for the day. I talked to a dozen professors and bookstore managers and other folks, gathering information about books, reps, what makes a good sales rep, and I wrote a report. And I had this with me when I went to my interview.

We should point out that you didn't purport to represent a book publisher; you just went ahead and did what sales reps normally do. In other words, you gave yourself the job you wanted! How did you transition out of sales into editorial?

After a short time in sales, I starting writing and submitting editorial reports, and I was promoted to editorial and sent to Boston from New York.

Why did you go into textbooks and not trade publishing?

When you publish a textbook, you can point to a specific, quantifiable need (X number of students will take a literature course this year), whereas in trade, the potential market for many books is harder to gauge, more subjective, more of the moistened finger in the wind.

Frequently, when I talk to people and they hear I work on textbooks, they assume that I'm sitting in a back room with a textbook and line-editing a book, when in reality I spend most of my days talking to teachers and writers about the joys and challenges of the classroom.

What do you enjoy most about the book publishing industry?

I think there's nothing that quite approaches the excitement and satisfaction that comes from having a conversation one day on campus, feeling that spark with a potential author, and seeing that spark of an idea eventually turn into a terrific book.

What advice would you give someone preparing for a job or internship interview?

Think about what everyone else would do, and then do something different.

## *Q & A*
## WORKING BOTH SIDES OF THE DESK

Margaret Park Bridges' experience in book publishing comprises being a published author and working as an editor for both small and big publishers. Bridges has written several children's books, including *I Love the Rain* and *Edna Elephant.*

With more than twenty years' experience in print production, eleven of which were spent as a managing editor or copyeditor in textbooks and trade books, Bridges knows of what she speaks. And fortunately, she was willing to speak with us.

When you were an undergraduate English major, did you know you wanted to go into publishing?

As an undergraduate, I had no idea what I wanted to do after school. It was only after I'd graduated and moved to New York City that I started to look for a job, which isn't a career strategy I'd advise for most people. I interviewed at publishers, literary agencies, and ad agencies. But I did do one wise thing: I found out from my college which older alumni worked in publishing, and I contacted some. One alumnus took me out to lunch and connected me with a friend at Simon & Schuster, where I ended up getting my first job: in the school and library trade sales promotion department. It was a good first job and typical of the kind of entry-level position a grad could expect. I even remember my salary, which, if you can believe it, was a mere $9,600.

What year was that?

I won't tell you the year.

Did the job have its perks?

Yes! The glamour of working near Michael Korda and running into Norman Mailer on the elevator! Later I switched to advertising and ... tried in-house art and editing departments of various businesses.

There are actually a lot of jobs out there for people who know and care about words and language.

Currently, you're a senior project editor in Houghton Mifflin's college division. What does that mean?

As a senior project editor in the college division, I'm responsible for managing and overseeing the production of specific textbook titles. Because HM is a fairly sizable publisher, there are separate divisions for college, school, and trade.

In my division, the books are assigned to many project editors, each of whom handles the hiring and management of copyeditors, proofreaders, indexers, and designers. I do a lot of troubleshooting. When a sponsoring editor accepts a manuscript (that's what sponsors do: seek out and acquire new books), a development editor may work on it a bit more (fairly big-picture editing, like restructuring, switching or removing whole sections, etc.), then it's handed over to me. I run a meeting in which the book is launched—that is, I gather all pertinent details and information about the book. Then I oversee the production of that project (which is really how the company views a book, just as an architect views designing a house as a project).

What are some of the issues you deal with day to day?

A few everyday details that I concern myself with are:

Can I get approval for the authors to see every round of proof instead of just one?

Should I delay the publication of a book in order to accommodate an editor's design preference for blue instead of purple?

What should we do if the electronic files of the book don't match the printout the author gave us?

What's most important: getting the book done on schedule, keeping the length down, or staying within budget?

Sounds like multitasking and project management skills are key. What qualities or personality traits would you say serve people well in book publishing?

As in most jobs, working well with individuals and teams serves anyone well. It is a sedentary job and at present I'd say about 80 percent of my everyday work requires e-mail. There can be a lot of little details to worry about—sometimes things the people in other industries can't believe we have to care about—so it helps to be someone who notices misplaced commas, wrong shades of red, and reversed photos.

You've worked for both small publishers and big publishers. Can you compare and contrast the two with respect to the work environment and the particular rewards and challenges?

Employees at a small publisher are expected to do more than those at a large press. This can be great if you want to learn how the company (the *house*) works and want to contribute in a substantive way and feel needed. It can also mean, however, doing a lot of little mundane chores, because there's simply no one else to do them. Hard workers are truly valued; no one gets far with a big ego by bluffing their way through a job.

Most people don't go into publishing for the salaries, which are notoriously low. They usually ... stay because they love the industry or they love books, or both. At Beacon Press and Candlewick Press, I was the managing editor (ME), but at Houghton Mifflin, the MEs are at a much higher level, supervising many project editors, whose responsibilities are more like those of the ME at those smaller presses. As an ME, I handled the details for every single book in the house, whereas now I handle only a handful of titles assigned to me. A good aspect of working in a large company is that there are a lot of coworkers to learn from and to share the workload with. A big company also has more perks for employees, such as book sales, higher salaries, technology and industry classes, tuition reimbursement, a cafeteria, good health insurance options, etc.

You've edited fiction and nonfiction. Are there differences between editing the two, or is editing editing?

First, the word *editor* has so many meanings that it's virtually meaningless on its own. There's copyediting, line editing, development editing, art editing, and the staff member who accepts a manuscript is called an acquiring editor, although she may actually not alter the text at all. To edit just means to select what to include and what to remove—and that is done at all levels of detail, whether one is looking at the forest or at each individual tree.

My experience has been in copyediting: fixing grammar, syntax, typos, and consistency. Copyediting fiction can surprisingly be more challenging than nonfiction, in that nonfiction authors, who are expected to be experts on their topics but not necessarily the best writers, are often grateful to whoever makes their prose look good. Creative writers, while usually requiring less substantive editing, often resent any changes to their writing. So it's a balance of editing judgment and diplomacy. It's usually quite important to the house to maintain good relationships with authors, as most feel almost possessive about their authors. And authors often will indeed remain with the same house for each new manuscript—as long as they feel they're treated well and appreciated.

How does being an author affect or influence your role as an editor?

After hearing people in publishing complain about working with "difficult" or even "nightmare" authors, I promised myself that, as an author myself, I would always be as diplomatic and flexible as I could be. I was gratified recently to read that my editor (the one who published my first book and accepted several thereafter) called me a dream author—easy to work with, takes constructive criticism, and comes up with revisions quickly and on time. It never pays to have an attitude—on either side of the desk.

As an author, I respect the editor's expertise about the book's needs, whether it's an editorial comment or a marketing concern. It's not an adversarial relationship—the editor truly wants the book to do as well as it possibly can. That means not only garner good reviews, but also sell well. Prima donnas are not appreciated; being polite, open-minded, and willing to learn and do whatever the job takes always makes you someone that others enjoy working with.

At the same time, it's important to pick your battles; if you really disagree with something critical, stand your ground—but be prepared to give in somewhere else. Being an author makes me appreciate as an editor how hard it is to face down the blank page and create something from nothing.

Since my title is *project editor*, however, I know that book production is, for the publisher, a project, and the company is a business that needs to make money like any other. It's not a source of subsidy for an elite club of literati.

What would you tell people who think getting into publishing is a way to advance their fortunes as a writer?

The only benefit to a would-be writer of working in publishing is that she gets to know editors personally and can literally walk into their offices to ask in person for manuscripts to be considered. That only puts them on top of the huge slush pile of anonymous submissions. It is no guarantee of acceptance. In fact, it can be downright embarrassing if the manuscript is rejected and the writer has to continue working with the editors. The book will either be good enough to sell itself or it won't. No book deemed unworthy of publication will be accepted because of friendship or sympathy.

For young people considering book publishing as a career, what would you say are the most important things to know—about the business, about the people, about anything?

Don't expect most publishing jobs to be too glamorous. Although there are certainly highly publicized examples of trade book editors who have made names for themselves by "discovering" a successful author, and who hobnob with celebrities, most work tirelessly and anonymously for meager salaries. Editors and other publishing employees tend to be very well read, however; they actually read books, as opposed to the people I worked with in advertising, who consume practically nothing other than magazines.

What is the most gratifying thing about your work?

It's gratifying at the end of a project to hold a real published book in my hand, sometimes one that includes my name in the masthead on the copyright page. Also, like any job, it feels good to be praised for hard work and smart strategies. But books are products that often last a long time, so quality is important. If the books are intended for students, then accuracy is especially critical. Even if a book is produced under budget and ahead of schedule, if it contains errors and typos, those are what last and what you'll be remembered for.

Books, often produced within about nine months, are sometimes likened to babies, and you want to be a good parent. You want to send them out into the world looking their best, so they can contribute beauty and knowledge to others.

# CHAPTER 7 Freelancing for a Living

Back in the Middle Ages, *free lances* were mercenaries not employed by or allegiant to any one individual—knights or soldiers who were free with their lance, so to speak. Just because they were professional killers, though, didn't mean they always made a killing.

The same is true today.

Whether you are writing, editing, or both, being a freelancer is a challenging enterprise. Freelancing requires constant hustle, networking, time management, and project management.

## The Upside of Freelancing

Freelancing can allow you more flexibility and freedom than a full-time office job, and can spare you a routine commute and the vicissitudes of office politics. As a freelancer, you can enjoy a variety of assignments from more than one client. You stand to save money on such expenses as new work clothes, not to mention commuter train passes, parking, and other costs associated with traveling for work. As you make and manage your own hours, working freelance can empower you to feel entrepreneurial and in control.

Depending on what kind of work you're doing (and the amount of work you're getting), you could hold a part-time job and still be a freelance writer or editor. If you don't mind work, you could hold a full-time job and do freelance editing at night and on the weekends.

You have flexibility. Calling in sick could amount to telling yourself, as you lie in bed, *I don't feel well today.* You don't have to sign a piece of paper that says your employer can terminate your services at any time, for any reason.

And the coffee at home tends to be much better than the stuff they serve in the cafeteria.

## The Downside of Freelancing

Working out of your home means living where you work. Cabin fever can set in quick.

You may not have expenses related to full-time work, but you also don't have perks—medical or health insurance topping the list. You also don't have access to training, classes, or the professional development programs an employer may offer its full-time employees gratis.

Freelance work can be feast-or-famine: One month you are scrounging for work, and the next month you receive so much work, you have to turn assignments down.

Depending on how much money you earn, working freelance will change how you do your taxes. You may have to keep track of expenses related to your home business in order to claim part of your living space as a work environment.

You have to make your own vacations. You may not receive the kinds of rewards and recognition some office people enjoy, such as the boss deciding to buy everybody pizza or to take the project team bowling.

And sometimes it can get a little lonely, staying home all day and night and not seeing anyone around the water cooler. If you have a water cooler.

## When's the Best Time to Go Freelance?

In 1991, I was two years out of college: I got fired from a magazine job and didn't see full time work for another three years. I was a freelance editor for a book publisher, a freelance reporter for a newspaper, and I was a security guard. Oh, and I worked at a coffee house, too.

Because I wasn't employed full-time, however, I got a deferment from paying my college loans. I lived with three other people, which kept my rent down, and my parents, who lived nearby, brought me food on the weekends.

Because I didn't have a mortgage or a family to support, I could undercut my freelance competition when it came to pay. I wasn't picky about assignments: You know what they say about beggars.

I ended up surviving pretty well. I felt good, like I was living by my wits. I had the energy and determination of youth, as well as the eagerness of someone who wanted to eat something for lunch besides soup. I worked hard and I made it work.

Of course, over those three years, I had no health insurance, and my gross income averaged, as I recall, $11,000, then $13,000, and then $13,500. I'll never forget the year I started freelancing, because I've never been skinnier in my life.

Many people wait to go freelance until they've worked full-time long enough in their industry to build up a hefty list of contacts and a solid track record of work. Other people build up their portfolio as freelancers and show the world how enterprising and hardworking they are.

Risk and reward may vary, but one thing is sure: It ain't easy.

## *Freelance Opportunities*

Virtually any type of work can be freelanced. The freelancer may work at home or may work on-site at the client's offices. The client may be a local newspaper, or it may be a book publisher in a different state (a publisher with the budget to overnight work to the freelancer and reimburse the freelancer for return mailing costs).

Whatever type of client you freelance for, it's a good idea to develop a network in the freelance community: I've received many an editing assignment from a too-busy freelancing friend who's referred me to his publisher.

So where do you look for freelance opportunities?

### BUSINESS OR CORPORATE CONTRACT WORK

Book publishers, hospitals and clinics, banks, public relations firms, university offices: They all need things written and things edited.

Before you send a résumé and portfolio to a business or corporation in search of contract writing or editing work, call the company's human resources department and find out if you must first go through a temp agency or a placement agency with which the business is partnered. The agency will have its own policies and procedures for you to follow in order for you to apply for jobs or get your information into its database. (If you apply online for contract work, the link will automatically direct you to the placement agency, if there is one.)

You may find that corporate freelancing pays better than freelancing for newspapers or even book publishers. The bigger the company, the deeper the pockets. Experience will reveal to you, however, whether you enjoy working for large corporations or prefer nonprofits, educational institutions, or government bodies.

Bear in mind, too, that if you do well as a contractor, you could be hired full time.

**Most Important Skills**

- ***Idea Generation.*** Reporters and writers for magazines and newspapers are under the gun to come up with ideas for hundreds of stories a year: They benefit from being big idea people. How do you get ideas? Read. Read newspapers, read magazines, read material online. Other people's ideas will inspire and motivate you, and every now and then, give you an idea to steal outright.
- ***Record-Keeping.*** Depending on how much money you spend on tools and equipment in your freelance enterprise, and how much of your home you dedicate exclusively to the operation of your freelance business, it may be to your advantage to declare these expenses on your tax forms. Keeping assiduous records of expenses, invoices, and payments can only work to your benefit.
- ***Hustle.*** Freelancing does not favor people who rest on their laurels or the seat of their pants. When you're full time, people stop by your desk and dump work into your inbox. When you're freelance, you need to scare up the work yourself, and you have only yourself to depend on.

## NEWSPAPERS

Newspapers hire freelance writers (not editors), and you are paid by the article and as cheaply as possible. Some freelance writers appear in a newspaper once; others, on a continual basis. One kind of freelance writer is a *stringer,* a person who fetches reporters quotes, information, or other material for their articles. Stringers may or may not receive a byline or credit in an article.

I encourage undergraduate and recently graduated English majors to start out thinking small. If you live in a sizable city or town, your daily newspaper won't consider hiring you as a writer until you've logged five years as a professional journalist—and even then, because their offices are open twenty-four hours a day, you may be offered the third shift.

In contrast, there may be a small Jewish newsletter two towns over whose office is an elderly man's kitchen table. He may not be able to pay you anything more than a compliment, but you may have an easier time getting a short interview or book review published there than in your city's daily.

So if you're starting out, concentrate on the community newspapers or the alternative newspapers, which are most likely weeklies.

Hint: Aspiring journalists who are fluent in a foreign language should note that there are plenty of newspapers and publications in this country printed in Spanish and Chinese. Your town newspaper may have a supplement in Russian or another language, to cater to an immigrant population.

## MAGAZINES

College students I meet who express a desire to write for magazines usually want to write for the consumer magazines they know and love (but don't necessarily read cover to cover): For the guys, it's *Maxim, Sports Illustrated,* and (on occasion) *Esquire* or *Harper's*; for the ladies, it could be anything from *Self* or *Vogue* to the *New Yorker.*

Unfortunately, just because you enjoy reading a particular magazine doesn't mean you would make a good writer for it or stand a good chance of being published there. I enjoy reading *Harper's,* but I don't have the credentials, the credibility, or the skill to write for that magazine. I also like watching *The Simpsons,* but that doesn't mean I'm in the league of people who could write for that, either.

Explore the trade magazine industry, whose editorial content is specialized to a niche audience. If you have a hobby or personal obsession, chances are there is a magazine for it. Write about what you know, because the magazine will want to know what qualifies you to write about a particular topic. Note how in magazines, at the end of an article, there are usually a few lines indicating the author's credentials as related to the article topic: *John Doe has been a ski instructor for several years; Jane Doe spends her summers rescuing animals in Oregon; Richard Roe runs a blog about jazz fusion and has contributed to several jazz magazines.*

Play to your strengths, study the magazine, follow its submission guidelines, and be persistent in the face of rejection.

By the way, magazines have freelance editors, but they are called *contributing editors,* and they are often previously published writers, ex-staffers, or high-profile writers of the magazine's own choosing.

### BOOK PUBLISHERS

Book publishers routinely freelance out copyediting and proofreading work: The freelance editing marketplace comprises full-time people who have left publishing to freelance, and individuals who try to make a go of it without having worked full time in publishing.

There is no industry standard for freelance editing rates, although twenty to twenty-five dollars an hour is not uncommon. The fee depends on the material being edited, the credentials of the freelancer, the time frame for the assignment, the level of editing work being done, and the publisher's budget for freelancers.

Possession of specialized knowledge (in computers, sciences, medicine, etc.) or fluency in a foreign language can very much work in your favor, provided you market yourself accordingly and target the appropriate publisher in your field of expertise.

## *How Do I Make Contact?*

A business or corporation may have a director of communications, of editing services, or of creative services. Call or contact this person to set up an informational interview, at which time you can discuss their needs for contract writers or editors. The director may refer you to a contract agency with whom they work, and they may ask you to provide a writing or editing sample on the premises.

A book publisher, similarly, may ask for an editing sample: Most likely, the publisher will respond to an inquiry for freelance work with an editing test, mailed to your home. If no assignments are immediately forthcoming, follow up with the editor or director of editing services with friendly e-mails or phone calls, just to let him or her know you're available and eager to work.

Newspaper and magazine editors are always interested in finding new talent: writers that have strong ideas, solid writing ability, and are reliable and consistent.

A magazine's submission guidelines are usually available on their Web site. These guidelines will explain how you contact the magazine, how long your submission should be, and whether or not you may query their interest in an idea for an article via e-mail. (There are plenty of resources on how to write an effective query or pitch: check the library, bookstore, or go online.)

Newspaper editors are receptive to ideas for articles but may be more interested in seeing a strong portfolio of clippings. It's a good idea to approach a newspaper editor with both: solid clips and good ideas. Mail your résumé and portfolio in, sending clean, clear copies of your articles. Follow up with a phone call or e-mail. The best time to contact any editor is the day or two immediately following publication of their periodical, when they are not on deadline.

**The Best Advice I Ever Got**

In a conversation I was having with a friend who is a professional cartoonist and illustrator, the name of a mutual acquaintance came up: a fellow who was also a cartoonist and whose work, I noted, appeared regularly in a certain newspaper. Candidly, I told my friend that I didn't think this guy's work was any good.

"No," my friend said, "but at least he's consistent."

That may sound like a vaudeville joke, but there is truth there, spoken in jest. As my friend explained to me, this fellow's work wouldn't win any awards—but his work was clean, submitted on time, and consistent in quality. He dealt with his clients very professionally, and because he was reliable, good enough for publication, and not terribly expensive, the newspaper would stop publishing his work only if the guy quit or was sent to jail for mail fraud.

Being professional, punctual, consistent, reliable, amiable, affordable, and otherwise low-maintenance goes a long way toward your attractiveness as a freelance writer or editor.

## What Will They Look for in My Clippings?

The editor will probably not read every word of your articles. (The readers won't, so why should the editor?) If anything, the editor will read your leads to see if you can catch his attention, and he will see how long it takes you to get to the point. He'll scan your quotes to see if they're interesting, and then, if you still have him at this point, he may read your close.

The editor will not consider you based solely on what you've done: He will, instead, consider you based on what ideas you bring to the table. An editor's value is based on how many good writers he can attract, and the writer's value is based on how many articles he writes based on good ideas. Thus, a good start is to come to an editor with ten ideas for articles. Make sure the ideas are very well-suited to that particular publication. Chances are the editor will find one or two of your ideas to be worth consideration.

If it comes down to it, offer to write an article on spec, which means for nothing. You are trying to get your foot in the door here, and if it turns out the editor doesn't want to run the piece you write, then you have a finished article to put in your portfolio and pitch to someone else.

And be a reporter: Do your homework. Research the town or city or demographic the publication serves, and read and research at least a half-dozen recent issues of the publication. A magazine publisher can send you back issues if they're not available at your library or online.

## How Much Should I Charge?

When it comes time to discuss payment, a lot of books on how to be a freelance writer or editor spill ink telling you what the industry average is in terms of dollars per inch, pennies per word, or dollars per hour. My own experience is that the editor does not give a hoot in Hades what the industry average is. He is interested in getting as much out of you as he can for as little as possible, and he will tell you what he routinely pays freelancers: e.g., forty dollars for a six-hundred-word article, or twenty dollars an hour for proofreading. Take it or leave it. It's all well and good for those how-to books to encourage you to stand your ground, negotiate, assert your worth, or whatever, but if you, as a perfect stranger, start giving the editor static over five dollars here or ten dollars there, he will tell you to beat it.

## TRY THIS

If you're interested in freelance writing, take note.

Some stories never go out of style: They're *evergreens*—or stories that can run anytime, on a theme that can be applied to just about any city or town. Editors usually reserve these stories for the slow news weeks or months, and they may be of interest to you. If you include one or two in your submitted portfolio and the editor hasn't run this kind of story already, chances are he will consider doing so—and your portfolio has a longer shelf life.

- ***Construction/destruction.*** What's slated to be torn down or built up in your city or town?
- ***Ugliest buildings.*** Do a top ten. Interview architects or architecture students.
- ***Salaries.*** Everyone always wants to know who makes what. The salaries of government officials is public information.
- ***Worst jobs.*** Find five jobs in town that no one else wants, and interview the people who currently hold them. Ask them how they ended up with the job. You may find they like it.
- ***Unsolved crimes.*** Revisit some of your city's unsolved murders, assaults, thefts, etc.
- ***By the numbers.*** Compile statistics both relevant and irrelevant about your city or town: How many police in the department? How many times have they fired their weapons in the past six months? How many manhole covers are there in town? Run numbers, and have some fun.
- ***Tourism update.*** Talk to the chamber of commerce; see how the local economy is helped or hurt by tourism or the lack thereof.
- ***Budgets.*** Do your firefighters, police, teachers, DPW workers, or EMTs have enough money to do their jobs? Where are cuts being made, and why? What's the effect on the community? How do people feel about it, and what do they suggest the town do about it?
- ***Armed forces recruitment.*** Talk to local recruiters and see how well and by what means they're meeting their quotas. Talk to new enlistees—get some human stories.

- ***Charity.*** Who gives? Talk to the local charities and see how they're doing. Find out who the biggest philanthropists in town are.
- ***First house to hit $1 million.*** If you live in a modest neighborhood or town, find out who has the first house to be listed for $1 million or more. If a house has already hit $1 million, make it $2 million.
- ***24-hour town.*** Stay up all night and patrol the town to see who's awake and doing what, rather like on the show *Insomniac* on Comedy Central. Photographers love this story because it gives them the chance to take a lot of artsy nighttime shots.

As you brainstorm more stories, bear in mind that no matter what day or season it is, people always like to read about taxes, real estate, schools, environmental issues, crime, budget talks, local heroes, youth sports, test scores, doctors, government pork, and the squirrel that shows up every morning at the local bakery to be fed a piece of muffin.

## GLOSSARY

### WHAT'S THE DIFFERENCE BETWEEN …

Consultant and Contractor?

These terms not only describe your status as a worker; they have a legal dimension and an economic dimension. Basically, the difference is in your relationship with the employer and how you pay your taxes.

A *contractor* is a freelancer. When you stay at home and proofread the manuscript of a book for a publisher, you are a contractor. You're an independent worker or vendor, and the employer can terminate the relationship whenever it likes.

If you go through an employment agency (temp agency, placement agency), and you work on-site for a company or organization, you can still be a contractor—but you are also an employee of that company or organization: You have a supervisor; you're subject to the same rules and regulations as employees; and you may receive the same benefits. You are still, however, a contractor.

The term *consultant* could refer to a self-employed person or to an employee of an organization. A consultant consults: They are experts who sit down with clients and offer them guidance and counsel, or who help people develop strategies, plans, programs—any number of things.

Consulting and contracting are not synonymous; when you have hammered out the particulars of your functional relationship with an employer—expectations, guidelines, financial and legal arrangements—then you can call yourself by the right name.

## Q&A
## WORKING THE BUSINESS OF FREELANCE BUSINESS WORK

William Donovan, whom we last heard from in chapter four, runs his own writing and editing consulting firm for businesses. Whatever a business's communications department needs—newsletters, brochures, marketing material, articles, sales collateral—Donovan is there for hire. Having worked in business and journalism, he says he enjoys being his own boss and the excitement of finding new assignments.

How do you find opportunities as a freelance writer for business? Networking, following changes in the industry, temp agencies, or something else?

You need to market yourself in many ways. Perhaps the most common mistake freelance writers make is not putting enough effort into marketing. There's a reason why successful companies devote big portions of their budget to marketing and PR. It works. I look at marketing in terms of my time and money. Networking is one very important approach, because people are more inclined to hire you if they know you as a person first. Leveraging contacts is another way to open doors. If you contact an editor or marketing director and you're able to drop a name of someone they know, it helps. Direct mail can be effective if it's done with some planning.

Many writers and editors wait to go freelance until they've worked full time long enough to build up a fat index of contacts. Would you recommend that route, or is not strictly necessary?

It helps having a lot of contacts, but more importantly you need to gain the experience that comes from working full time at a newspaper or magazine. When you're in a service industry, you're selling your expertise. You need to develop those skills working with experienced editors, working on a variety of stories, and working among other writers with whom you can exchange ideas and just talk shop. You get that in a full-time job.

Explain the difference between writing for business and the kind of academic writing that undergraduate English majors are familiar with.

The difference has to do with the audience. In college, your professors *have* to read your work—regardless of its quality—so that they can apply a grade. In business, you want readers to stay with you, so you need to hold them. The writing has to be quick, engaging, and informative.

Is freelancing kind of like being a door-to-door salesperson? That is, do you have to be able to deal with lots of people telling you "not interested"? Explain a few of the biggest challenges, being a freelancer, and how you deal with them.

Many people incorporate some cold-calling into their marketing and so they regularly have to deal with rejection. But that happens to people in any profession and speaks to the broader challenges of freelancing. You aren't just a writer. You're also in charge of marketing and sales and you need to apply as much thought to those responsibilities as you do to the core discipline of your business.

How do you determine what to charge people for your services, especially in a competitive environment in which other people could just undercut your fees? Or is it more of a matter of the client telling you what they've budgeted for?

Sometimes the client tells you what they pay and then you have to determine if, on an hourly basis, the project is worth your time. I try to work with people who can afford the fees I charge. There are price choppers out there, but at some point clients realize you get what you pay for.

How do you think an undergraduate English major could go about building a portfolio of clips for business writing? Or would journalistic writing samples, for example, be acceptable as representative of a person's ability?

Newspaper and magazine clips should give a hint of how well people write. But college students should also think about the type of writing they want to do. If they want to write ad copy and branding material, they could also try for internship work at ad agencies or PR firms. If they're more interested in longer pieces, newspaper and magazine clips would tell a prospective employer if they have the skills to write for their business.

## Q&A
### FINDING MISS MAGAZINE

As I was writing this book, the wisdom of reading as much as possible for idea generation and making contacts was brought home when I came across, in the *New York Times Sunday Magazine,* a short local-cuisine feature about Wisconsin cheese curds. Despite the fact that my Wisconsin-born wife is lactose intolerant, I read the piece to her at the dinner table, and we both got a kick out of it. When my wife asked me who the author was, I told her it was someone named Louisa Kamps.

She nearly did a spit-take with her soy milk. "I rode the school bus with Louisa Kamps!"

And wouldn't you know, this woman—who has written for the *New Yorker,* the *New York Times, Food & Wine,* and Salon.com—was a Literature and Society major.

**You've held a number of titles in your magazine work: editorial assistant, freelancer, staff writer, and contributing writer. Can you briefly describe how one job led to another?**

I never went to journalism school, so I consider the training I received on the job as an editorial assistant an invaluable first step in my career. As an assistant—a position I held at three different magazines [the *New Yorker, ARTnews,* and *Blitz,* a now-defunct London arts and culture magazine], I learned a great deal about the operation of magazines (how they run, who does what), as well as writing and editing.

I made a point to read every revision of every story, and by paying close attention to the work writers and editors do together, I began to understand how important style and mechanics are to clear, captivating writing. As an assistant, I also began submitting short pieces [150–1000 words] to some of the editors I worked with, and, after many failed attempts, eventually the editors began publishing my stories.

Later, as a freelance writer, I used the clips I'd accumulated as an editorial assistant to get more assignments. When my portfolio was well-rounded enough to demonstrate that I could handle a range of subjects, I was able to get two staff writing/editing positions: one at *Elle*, and another at *Mirabella* (*Elle*'s now-defunct sister publication). When I finally decided I wanted solely to write, I left the staff positions and became a contributing writer to both magazines. So, there's a step-by-step progression there.

Is freelance writing for magazines an endeavor you can successfully break into, on your own, without first working full time?

While I'm sure some have done so, to my mind, it would have been difficult (if not impossible) for me to launch a freelance writing career without first having worked on staff at several magazines. Having written for each magazine I worked at and developed relationships with many editors (some of whom have moved on to other magazines and, kindly, gotten me started writing for these places), I was able to count on enough work to make a living by the time I went freelance. My experience is only my experience, but I do believe it helped me to have built up a track record and relationships with various editors before I went freelance.

Is there such a thing as magazine-style writing, and if so, how is it different from the kind of academic writing to which English majors are accustomed?

There's a great deal of common ground in academic writing and journalism. What's common in both is that the writer has a thesis and uses examples to support that thesis. Tone is probably what differs more. A magazine writer needs to be a careful student of the publication she's writing for, in order to understand the audience and how the magazine in the main strives to communicate to its audience. At the same time—and here's the tricky part—the magazine writer also needs (if she wants to continue working) to tell stories in a way that no one else can: with voice, perceptions, humor, and maybe even wisdom that's inimitably hers.

Several of the magazine people I've interviewed recommend that young job applicants get their foot in the door either through an internship or a job in sales. Do you agree? Could you comment on what would help someone applying to either a full-time job or an internship at a magazine stand out?

Writing clips—even from college newspapers or a hometown daily—would be a great help to anyone trying to secure a job on the editorial side of a magazine, and it never hurts to attach them to a résumé. An entry-level position will not necessarily include writing (though it would be great if it did, and anyone interested in writing should make sure a prospective employer would at least be open to hearing her story pitches). But writing samples can demonstrate your sensitivity to language, and convey where your interests lie, to an employer in a very impressive way.

I'm all for internships on the editorial side. You can learn a great deal from filing and photocopying, as long as you pay attention to (that is, take time to read) the material you're handling. But because most magazines' editorial and business departments are kept separate (physically and figuratively), taking a job in sales, if you'd rather be a writer or editor, could be frustrating.

Is being a staff writer at a large consumer magazine as glamorous as it sounds?

A lot of magazines host cocktail parties and launches for special issues these days, with varying degrees of fanfare and extravagance. Of course, it's fun, when you're invited, to go and gawk and socialize with colleagues, but the work of writing itself, at least as I experienced it, is hardly glamorous at all.

These days, mostly it's just me, at home at my desk in sweats, batting the cat away from the computer.

# CHAPTER 8 *Going Corporate*

Every business, from the smallest entrepreneurial venture to the global giant, needs to communicate: internally, to its employees; and externally, to its customers, prospective customers, investors, the media, federal and state regulators, shareholders, and more.

A hot dog vendor makes a sign—"2 dogs 2 bucks"—and thus communicates externally. At a business of fifty people, the human resources department circulates a package of benefits information and thus communicates internally. Departments within an organization need to communicate with each other: Legal and compliance needs to communicate with product development, and product development needs to communicate with marketing.

Hospitals need to communicate; so do universities. Companies that manufacture missile systems need to communicate, as do companies that make chocolate bars. Large companies, like small ones, issue memos and letters, pamphlets and brochures, advertising and direct mail marketing materials. They may even have their own internal newspaper, magazine, or newsletter.

The above information is evident to anyone working in the business world, but it's likely to be news to English majors (either in college or freshly out) who think that teaching or publishing are their only career options. Moreover, English majors resigned to the belief that they will never command an annual salary higher than $27,000 may be surprised and encouraged to know that some businesses consider communication important enough to multiply that figure to hire good writers and communicators.

And good writers and good communicators do not always come in the same package.

## The Difference Between Writers and Communicators

If you had asked me the difference between writers and communicators when I was an undergraduate English major, I would have said that writers major in English and communicators major in communication. Not so.

To parse the difference between writing and communicating, consider:

- Writers know a lot of words. Communicators know which word to use when, how, and why.
- Writers know what to write. Communicators put value on how written content is relayed, the manner in which it is presented, in what format, and how frequently.
- Writers express themselves through words. Communicators may express themselves through words accompanied by pictures, music, charts and diagrams, and interactive media.

**Most Important Skills**

- ***Interpersonal skills.*** In the 1980s, there was a popular TV drama called *thirtysomething*. In one episode, a character named Elliot flies out to the West Coast for a job interview at a stereotypically laid-back company. As Elliot's host shows him around, introductions are made to a copywriter: a bearded, bedraggled hippie type who is sitting in his cubicle staring at a pencil. The copywriter is enthusiastically heralded as the Wallace Stevens of copywriting, or some such praise. Eliot extends his hand, but the copywriter doesn't look up from his intense, artistic trance. He just mutters, "Leave me alone." The host laughs and takes a confused Elliot aside, assuring him that the copywriter is a genius and a great guy, really. When I saw that on TV, I said to myself, *I want to be that guy: brilliant and bedraggled, left alone to compose, and unburdened by the need to engage other people with professional niceties.*

  I'm here to tell you, this approach doesn't work out in real life. It's just like elementary school: You could earn number ones all down the column concerning your ability and intelligence, but if you don't play well with others, you'll get a three, and it'll bring down your average.

- ***Adaptability.*** Companies are like little countries—each has its own mores. If you visit a country for an extended period of time, you need to learn these mores and abide by them, even if they strike you as silly. A thumbs-up gesture in America could mean quite the opposite in another country, and a minor lapse in etiquette (discarding gum on the sidewalk) could get you arrested. Call it unjust or ridiculous, but that's the way it is.

  I knew a woman in a very conservative company who told me she could never survive in one of those offices where people wear jeans every day and bring in their dogs and have volleyball parties on Friday: It wouldn't suit her, she wouldn't feel comfortable. We see those dog-and-volleyball offices on TV and think, *What an awesome place to work*, but for all you know, it's *so* informal that the office is lacking in professional behavior, courtesy, and respect.

  Find the country where you can adapt and where you feel most comfortable, because if you keep tossing gum on the sidewalk, you could end up being deported and having your passport revoked, regardless of how brilliant you are.

- ***End-user thinking.*** As an undergraduate English major writing papers about novels and plays, the end user of your writing was a professor. (In actual fact, it may have been a teaching fellow to whom the professor delegated paper grading duties, but that's beside the point.) Regardless of the class, and regardless of the topic, you wrote for that professorial reader.

  Depending on what kind of professional writing you end up doing—marketing, advertising, corporate training—you will need to adapt your writing style to different end users. The fact that you write differently for different readers may itself be a new concept for you.

  Think about the way you speak. Naturally, you speak differently to different people. When speaking to your mother, you don't use the same vocabulary as when speaking with your friends. You don't use the same tone, speaking to your professor, that you use with the person at the DMV. Your voice remains the same; it's still you talking. But sometimes without even having to think about it, you alter your tone, your word choice, your inflection, and even the pitch of your voice, depending on what you're saying and the person to whom you're speaking.

- Writers—especially creative writers—are often told to write to please themselves or to be guided by dictates of The Craft. Communicators seek to achieve comprehension, understanding, retention, and often action on the part of their audience, and those considerations dictate what they write and how it's presented.

Writing, naturally, is a form of communication, but the kind of writing English majors do as part of their education—analytic essays, written to fulfill the requirements of an assignment and earn a good grade—is narrower in its set of concerns than writing and communicating done for business. An English major whose writing ability is versatile can learn and adapt to writing for the various needs a business or large organization may have.

## *Business Needs in the Corporate World*

Good writing and effective communication is of interest to just about every department within a corporation, from human resources to information systems. The better you understand the infrastructure of an organization and its departments' various needs, the better you can determine whether or not you have the knowledge and skills to meet those needs. What follows are major categories in which good writers and communicators may find work—or, as we say in the corporate world, "add value."

### TRAINING, EDUCATION, AND LEARNING

Ideally, everyone in an organization, from the person just hired to the twenty-year veteran, is in a continuous state of learning: The former is learning the ropes, and the latter is learning new skills or information in order to advance or to position herself for her next assignment or job.

A company, then, needs people to write, edit, format, and package training, from hour-long online tutorials to week-long seminar courses. Training and education comes in all manner of media and format: e-mails, kits, meetings-in-a-box, lectures, CDs and DVDs, slide presentations, one-page documents, and hundred-page papers.

Additionally, employees need to be told about and taught about every new product or service a company develops. Employees dealing with customers need to be told what to say about it and how to present it.

Finally, a company teaches and trains people to be better managers; better members of a team; or simply compliant with rules, regulations, and laws about behavior—everything from safety to sexual harassment to handling confidential company information.

A company may have a department dedicated solely to developing training and related communication, or it may engage an outside firm to develop and administer training. A company may, in fact, do both. In seeking out opportunities in this area, you might do an informational interview with a company and ask about opportunities internal to the organization and about what outside vendors the company uses to teach and train.

## DEVELOPMENT AND ADVANCEMENT

An organization's revenue is not always based solely on people buying its goods or services. Nonprofits, for example, rely on grants and private donations; similarly, colleges and universities rely on gifts, grants, and investments.

The development office (or advancement office) is charged with cultivating this revenue, and the campaigns to do so can be sophisticated, involving both internal and external communication. This office works with publicity, marketing, media relations, and in the case of a college, the alumni association and the office of the president.

## INTERNAL PUBLICATIONS

Large organizations often use quarterly bulletins or a monthly newspaper or newsletter to communicate information to employees:

- a profile of a new vice president
- coverage of a recent conference or seminar
- a message from the CEO or president, outlining a vision for the coming quarter
- personality profiles of people within the organization
- notices about company celebrations, contests, etc.

As if it were any surprise, the news a company publishes internally is more sunny and celebratory than investigative and revealing. But it is a necessary and often welcome form of communication. No company wants its sole internal communication to be gossip.

## SPEECH WRITING

The higher up someone is in an organization, the less time she has to sit down and craft her own speeches, addresses, or remarks. So she enlists other people to do it for her.

On a regular basis, senior company executives sign their names to—or, rather, have the digital file of their scanned signature appended to—communications that they did not write. They also, as the occasion demands, stand up in front of their employees and read words they have seen only recently.

Every word from a VIP in a large organization is listened to and interpreted very closely; therefore the VIP requires a message that's note-perfect and carefully controlled. (VIPs may fall victim to their own extemporaneous and spontaneous speech, as when Harvard University president Larry Summers decided to be provocative in a gathering about the sciences and suggested that a disparity between the number of women and men working in the sciences was perhaps attributable to nature. I can guarantee you that the communications department of Harvard did not burn the midnight oil crafting those sentences to get them just right. If President Summers had stuck to a script, the cost to Harvard would have amounted to far less than the price that was ultimately paid.)

## RESEARCH

Companies and organizations conduct research as a part of the goods or services they provide, to stay competitive, and to provide information to their customers. A nonprofit organization may apply for and receive a research-based grant; a for-profit company may research market trends and activity for its investors.

Here's where you come in: As an English major, you can apply your abilities in researching information, acquiring information, synthesizing or ordering information, and delivering that information to its intended audience. Your job may simply be to put research into language the intended audience can understand. You might also apply writing and editing skills to relay that research into articles, brochure content, presentations, advertising, and more.

If a company cannot hire you for its own research staff, it may work with an outside research firm that could use an English major.

## Me? Corporate?

You may be saying to yourself, *I couldn't work in the [banking, insurance, pharmaceutical, investment industry] because I don't know the first thing about that industry. I was an English major!*

Ignorance of a particular industry does not preclude your getting a communications-related job in that industry. For one thing, companies are in the business of training their people. They can train you, too, either in a formal educational setting or via a mentoring relationship. Moreover, depending on who you're communicating with, ignorance may actually be a boon.

Let's take for example the world of finance, something about which English majors aren't likely to know a whole lot. Now, a financial firm needs to communicate to its customers and prospective customers (or *prospects*), and they also need to train employees to answer customer questions or perform services for the customer.

The firm is interested in making finance, for both groups, so easy to understand that an elementary school child could grasp it. In addressing these groups, the firm must rely on simple, clear language—as opposed to jargon, technical terms, and sophisticated constructs.

If your job is to make things plain for the trainee or the customer, then your ignorance of the industry could work in your favor: In crafting communications, you will consistently be asking, *What does that mean?* or *Can we state that more simply or in terms the average person can understand?*

If you are a quick study, so much the better.

## What Makes Business Writing Unique

A charming prejudice one picks up after decades of studying literature in school is that literary writing, as the highest form of human expression, requires the most talent and ability, and that advertising and marketing materials, technical writing, speech writing, and correspondence are far lesser forms for people of lesser ability. We know this to be true because our English profes-

**The Best Advice I Ever Got**

To some ears, the very word *corporate* sounds negative, especially if you qualify it with *typical*, as in *typical corporate behavior*.

Some advice about corporateness: If you interpret the term *corporate* negatively, understand that corporateness is a set of behaviors found in people, not a set of laws forming the foundation of a building or an enterprise.

Companies and organizations are not selfish, greedy, heartless, childish, petty, uncommunicative, insecure, or shallow. *People* are. If you connect any of the preceding adjectives to what you think of as typical corporate behavior, remember that behavior is ascribable to individuals—commonly, the same individuals who try to excuse bad behavior by assigning it, abstractly, to the company: *That's just the way things are here*, or *I agree it's unfair, but that's just our culture* or *Hey, welcome to big business, stop whining*.

Not all corporations or large organizations fit the stereotypes you find in Dilbert or the movie *Office Space*. A parody, however, bears some resemblance to its real-life subject, such as when you find people who use words like *value-add*, *uptick*, and *messaging takeaway* with a straight face.

A good friend of mine who works in journalism once confessed to me that he could never do what I do: work in corporate communications. He wouldn't last, he said. In his newsroom, he explained, people knew what they were supposed to do (the same thing, issue to issue), there was very little middle management, and salaries were so low that if something went wrong, no one really cared all that much.

If there's one thing that makes corporate communications different, it's the corporate structure: Day after day, hour to hour, you're cheek by jowl with managers, vice presidents, senior vice presidents, team project leaders, associate managers, and more titles, titles, titles. You move through power and politics like a fish negotiates the current, and that can be a job in and of itself.

Weird thing about power: A lot of people want it (if only so that someone else won't lord power over them), but few, in my experience, handle it with grace, a sense of fair play, compassion, and understanding. Often, people promoted to positions of power are secretly so uncertain about their ability to manage that power that all their emotional and psychological baggage comes spilling out.

Ironically, the bigger and more powerful a company gets, the more likely it is that its concern over image and reputation will become pathological: This can foster an internal culture of fear that is especially hard on creative types. In the culture of fear, employees are obsessively concerned with how things look or appear; employees and managers may even state, with a straight face, that appearance is more important than reality. The work becomes less about the end user and more about pleasing one's superiors, and this is lethal to imagination, humor, and a spirit of fun.

Now, this scenario can be found just as easily in a college, high school, newsroom, or publisher's office as it can be found in a bank, a hospital, or an insurance company. Wherever you interview, formally or informally, talk to the people there, look at what they're wearing, and notice how they decorate their cubes. If you ask them flat out if the company supports creativity and imagination, press them for examples.

The trick for you, as a job applicant, is to find the right home for your sensibilities and temperament, as well as for your talents and abilities, whether it is a West Coast computer business that is cool with your wearing jeans five days a week or a financial firm that is most definitely not cool with your wearing jeans, even on Fridays. Naturally, the landscape is full of places in between.

sors tell us so, and conveniently, there were no copywriters, speech writers, or grant writers on the faculty to contradict them.

Business writing, for lack of a better term, requires no small amount of skill and talent; indeed, there is no reason to believe that true excellence in business writing requires any less ability and creativity than excellence in writing a poem or a short story.

Of course, we could debate this assertion in the faculty lounge all day and night. What we can agree on—one would hope—is the neutral statement that each form of writing has its own unique challenges, with business writing being no exception.

So let's review a few challenges of business writing.

## WRITING FOR OTHER PEOPLE

A curious feature of corporate communications is that you may find yourself putting words into other people's mouths, as when you write a letter or invent quotes for someone else. To look at it another way, someone else gets credit for your writing.

Let's say that you're writing a letter for an executive. You receive from her a general idea or some bullet points as to what she wants to say, you spend time and energy composing the letter and, after edits come back, a final version is approved and distributed to the audience—and the words belong to someone else. There's a suspension of ego that needs to take place in the creative person crafting the words.

If you're coming to corporate communications from, say, journalism, there may also have to be a suspension of what you formerly thought of as acceptable practices. For example, if you're writing an article about an executive for your company's internal newspaper, it wouldn't be uncommon for you to invent quotes for that person, submit the quotes to the person for approval or revision, and then place the quotes in the article as if the words came extemporaneously and glibly out of the executive's mouth.

Not exactly the Chicago school of journalism. But then, you're not in Chicago anymore.

## WRITING FOR PEOPLE WHO CAN'T WRITE

In my first week working in corporate communications, I met with a client—that is, someone for whom I would be performing a corporate communicative service—and listened to him explain that he wanted to develop an internal two-page newsletter.

"Tim, I really need your help on this one, because I've got as much creativity as this can of [diet cola]," he said, gesturing to his morning caffeine fix. (I won't mention the brand of diet cola, for fear of incurring litigious wrath.)

I laughed, not only because I thought his self-effacing remark funny, but also because I felt flattered. This person made me feel like my talents were needed and appreciated. Always a nice thing.

This is one side of the sword's edge when you're an English major in corporate communications. The business world is full of very bright, very skilled individuals—some truly visionary in their thinking—who cannot, for the life of them, put a sentence together. It makes you feel good to have a skill they don't.

Now, before you take that fact as cause and license to feel superior to people earning six figures to your five, consider that English majors are often very bright, very skilled individuals who cannot, for the life of them, understand municipal tax codes, insurance policies, or even the difference between a stock and a bond.

I wrote and pulled together that newsletter for this client, and his expressed satisfaction was, to say the least, effusive: He virtually considered me a genius for being able to whip something up so quickly and for sounding so good on the page. I was flattered when asked to perform the task; I did the work; the work was simple; and the client was thrilled to pieces.

As you would expect, it's more routine to write something, submit it to a superior, and have it returned with corrections, edits, and suggestions for revision. The other side of the sword is when you get copious edits back from someone who wasn't supposed to know anything about writing. On occasion, you may find that the suggestions for revision say pretty much the same thing (if not exactly the same thing) you originally wrote or that sentences unimportant to the overall message of the piece have been tinkered with and retooled. You may submit a third or fourth version of the piece, only to have the person you're writing for come back with new edits having to do with commas and the capitalization of a word that, outside of the corporate environment, is not capitalized.

If this happens, it's possible that you are in the presence of someone who needs to feel important and knowledgeable: hence the hailstorm of red pencil marks over locutions or linguistic details of no consequence. The person for whom you are writing may feel the need to convince herself that she does indeed know something about writing. This means you, the hired writer, must incorporate into something you wrote the byproducts of someone else's insecurity and need to control.

People are funny. A person who jokingly says that she cannot write may never be able to confess it in a serious tone of voice. Few people have the security of self to admit a deficiency such as that. After all, most people have been writing since they were old enough to hold a pencil. They may be, in other respects, quite accomplished and intelligent. They may be the head of the company, for Pete's sake, but that doesn't make it any easier to admit that they need help putting words together on the page.

Corporate communications sometimes requires a degree and caliber of interpersonal skills not found in journalism or other kinds of professional, contracted writing. You may find, at the outset or in time, that you take to those skills handily; or, you may consider it, to put a polite phrasing on it, not your cup of tea.

## The Corn Nut Conundrum

If you are a capable writer and effective communicator, you could, no doubt, walk into any organization—regardless of whether they sell lug nuts or corn nuts—and write their memos, develop their newsletters, manage their Web site content, or craft their marketing materials. You may even be recompensed handsomely for it. And if the content of what you're writing doesn't exactly feed your soul or even float your boat, chances are you could fake it and still turn out good work.

There are, however, at least two problems with this picture.

Let's say you work for the corn nut company. You will be writing for and working alongside people for whom corn nuts are life. These people may dedicate sixty to eighty hours a week working on, thinking about, and worrying over corn nuts. They may travel the country, bleary-eyed from stopovers and inferior hotels, all for corn nuts. They may be compelled to elevate the importance of corn nuts in their own minds, if only to justify spending so much time and energy on corn nuts instead of on their loved ones and children—if indeed they have decided to take time and space in their lives away from corn nuts for a family, because such time is time taken away from corn nuts.

Now, if you are not as dedicated to corn nuts as these people, they will smell it on you. They may envy you for it or they may resent you for it or they may do both, and despite your abilities in writing and communication, they may not want you around in the long run. They may suspect (and quite rightly) that you are only working in a corn nut company for the paycheck, which naturally calls into question your loyalty and devotion to the company and your colleagues (and corn nuts).

The second problem has to do with those times when, after working on your novel or reading selections of Rilke, you lie awake at night and think to yourself, *What am I doing? For crying out loud, I'm writing about corn nuts for a living.* Feelings of fraudulence can open a Pandora's box, releasing guilt, anger, resentment, isolation, loneliness, and a dozen other demons.

This is not to say that you cannot build a successful career in the corn nut company. It's only to remind you that no matter what you do, if your heart isn't in it, it will show up in your writing, in your work, and in your attitude around the office.

Choose the company or organization that fits you. There's no point in wearing a jacket from Armani if the sleeves are two inches too short.

## TRY THIS

### Practice Adaptability

Think of something you know how to do: change the oil in your car, plant a vegetable garden, buy the right present for someone, or have fun in San Francisco on a hundred dollars a day—anything. Now think of three people: a close friend, a family member, and an absolute stranger. In six hundred words or less, write an instructional article or essay on your chosen topic, and rewrite it for each different audience. Note how you need to change your tone, your word choice, and the way you explain a process.

### (Re)Do It Yourself

The next time you:

- receive a letter that tries to get you to take out or renew a subscription to a magazine, read it over, study it, and understand how it's trying to get you to do what it wants you to do. Then sit down and try to rewrite the letter, adding your own style or taking an approach you think would be more effective.
- listen to a speech by a politician or public figure, try to obtain a copy of the speech online. Then sit down and rewrite the speech yourself, staying faithful to the speaker's voice and style.
- see a commercial or an ad for a product or service you like, sit down and craft your own ad for it.

# GLOSSARY

## WHAT'S THE DIFFERENCE BETWEEN ...

The one thing I learned as an English major that proved the most helpful when I was working in the corporate world was the following quote from T. S. Eliot's play *The Cocktail Party*:

> Half of the harm that is done in this world is due to people who want to feel important. They don't mean to harm—but the harm does not interest them. Or they do not see it. Or they justify it because they are absorbed in the endless struggle to think well of themselves.

To apply this observation to the business world and the language it uses: Most people in business don't mean to sound like robots, but using boardroom buzzwords is part of their struggle to feel important and think well of themselves. I worked in a department whose mission was clear, concise communication—and *still*, one found the following abuses of language.

**action item (n.)** something to do. *We identified several action items for today, leaving some to actionize tomorrow.*

**actionize (v.)** do.

**bucket (n.)** a parameter of thought or content. *Which bucket does this project come under?* or *Tim, you're a loose cannon: That's the just the bucket I've put you in.*

**deliverable (n.)** content to be communicated or delivered. *Does this deliverable belong in your bucket?*

**delta (n.)** challenge or obstacle. *The pros of this plan are clear: the deltas are less so.* (Remember: always use *challenge* or *delta* instead of the more negative-sounding *con* or *downside.*)

**disconnect (n.)** an instance of discontinuity. *There's a disconnect between our mission statement and these action items.*

**drive (v.)** to manage a project or assignment. *Who's driving that action item?*

**face time (n.)** interaction in person. *Bill sure is getting a lot of face time with the chairman this month! Think he's going to get promoted?*

**fast-track (v.)** do something quickly. *We need to fast-track this deliverable for Tuesday.*

**going forward (adv.)** from here on in; moving forward. *Going forward, we will fast-track all deliverables into this bucket.*

**incent (v.)** to motivate or inspire someone. *Our marketing collateral isn't incenting our customers.* (Always *incent* someone to do something, as opposed to simply telling them or asking them to do it.)

**learning (n.)** a lesson or instructional message. *The vice president imparted several key learnings in his biquarterly e-mail.*

**matrix (n.)** a chart. *Our team has developed this matrix showing our progress this year.*

**messaging (n.)** a message. *Key messagings delivered through the newsletter were . . .*

**metric (n.)** any method of measurement. *What metrics are we using to help maximize our effectiveness?*

**next steps (n., pl.)** what we will do until our next meeting. *Let's target next steps on this initiative.*

**off-line (adv.)** one-on-one, or in private. *Let's talk about that off-line, when the meeting is over.*

## *Q & A*
## SOY ENGLISH MAJOR. ¿AHORA QUÉ?

Back when I worked in journalism, I wrote a book column and some book reviews. My job gave me the opportunity to help out some colleagues of mine from the MFA program at the University of Michigan; whenever I could, I wanted to give some press to MFA alumni who were getting published.

But keeping in touch wasn't always easy. I found that in order to track down one of my colleagues, I had to look overseas: An inventive fiction writer named Nancy Strauss was alive and well and working in Spain. This Cincinnati native had left the United States for Europe, she told me, not long after we graduated from the MFA program in 1996.

Nancy, how did you end up in Europe? Is that where all the jobs are, for English majors?

After I graduated from the MFA program, my priority was to find a job that would leave me the mornings free to write fiction. So the obvious option was teaching. And in Europe, I thought, I would be able to do that while learning languages at the same time, so that I could also explore the option of translation work.

Through my wonderful Czech professor at the University of Michigan, I found a job teaching English classes in a small town in the Czech Republic.

What level of teaching did you think would leave your mornings free?

I was teaching English as a foreign language in a Czech high school—actually schools taught out of the same facility. During my first semester there, I was teaching all day, but for the following year, I made an agreement with the principal to schedule my classes beginning late in the mornings on most days.

How did you apply for that position?

I sent a CV and exchanged some letters—I made all arrangements from Michigan.

And then you left the Czech Republic for Spain. What was in Spain?

I went to Madrid initially to research a novel I was writing at the time, which involved Americans in the Spanish Civil War. I thought it would be useful for this project to live in Spain for a while. The novel fell apart, but by then I had already started researching jobs and become excited about the idea of moving here, so I came anyway.

I have been in Madrid for eight years now.

You must be pretty fluent by now. Did you know Spanish prior to arriving there?

I didn't speak the language at all when I arrived, but I'll tell you it's a lot easier to learn than Czech. When I'm nervous, I lose my Spanish almost entirely; on the other hand, when I'm angry, it improves, and I start talking really fast.

I'll try not to upset you in this interview. Now, did you pick up teaching work in Madrid?

I found a job teaching English at a language academy.

How'd you find it?

When I was still in the Czech Republic, I accessed the Madrid yellow pages online and sent CVs to every language academy listed. I think I sent out about 140 CVs.

Wow. You mentioned that you originally wanted to explore doing translation work. That's what you're doing now, correct?

Well, my work has to do with translations: I am managing the translations and member communications department in a company that runs online survey projects.

How did you end up there?

I heard about a position in this company four years ago through a former teaching colleague. At the time, it was still a start-up office; I was originally hired to answer e-mails in English, and the director was flexible about letting me work a late schedule, leaving the mornings free for writing. The company has grown very rapidly since then, and my work there has become much more interesting.

Could you explain in a little more detail about what you do?

My company has a number of shopping and survey Web sites in various countries. When people register to be members of the Web sites, they can opt-in to be invited to paid online surveys. Then, let's say, for example, that a market research institute wants to interview five thousand French and Italian women between the ages of twenty and thirty who own mobile telephones: We would send a survey on the client's behalf to our members who have this profile.

What my department does is to write or check all texts and communications sent to our members: preparing the survey invitations, translating the questionnaire when necessary, testing the programmed questionnaire, answering e-mails about surveys or membership, providing content for newsletters and other campaigns to keep members active and returning to the Web sites.

I am the department coordinator, so my job includes hiring and managing the team, setting up the work processes we use, etc.

Any other Americans there?

In my office, I am currently the only American. However, my company, which was German-based, has just merged with an American company.

Any English majors?

I'm really not sure, sorry. I don't know very much about the people working in our U.S. offices.

Nancy, how well do you think your degree in English helped you in your job search?

A degree in English may have been reassuring to employers when I was looking for an English-teaching job, but to be honest, I don't think it has been an enormous asset on my CV. For the kind of work I am currently doing, I would be better off with business credentials.

Anything you wished you had studied while you were an undergraduate?

The Spanish language.

You came to the MFA program straight out of college, right?

Yes, that's right, I went straight out of college.

A lot of English majors I talk to ask me if that's the way to go, or whether it's better to wait. What do you think?

I don't regret having done it that way, although in some respects, I would have gotten more out of the program if I had been older; for example, at the time, I felt very shy about talking to faculty—I think I still felt like a teenager talking to adults—and if I had gone later, I would have taken better advantage of the opportunities to meet and talk to writers whom I still admire.

Do you think the MFA served you in any way?

I think the MFA has been very valuable to me personally and for my writing. When looking for a job, I also appreciated the teaching experience I was able to get through my MFA fellowship. However, the degree requires some explaining in Europe, where university programs in creative writing are far less common than in the United States.

## Q&A
### MAKE YOURSELF AVAILABLE

British prime minister Benjamin Disraeli once remarked, "If I want to read a good book, I'll write one."

Tom Campbell, senior writer for Fidelity Investments in Boston, may just as well say that if he wanted a good job, he'd write one.

Campbell, thirty-nine, exemplifies the vocational philosophy of starting your next job before someone hires you for it. When Campbell graduated from college in 1987 with a double major in English and economics, his first media-related job was an entry-level position as a sales assistant for *Rhode Island Monthly,* the one consumer magazine based in his tiny native state. Then twenty-three, Campbell describes his responsibilities as being "the guy in the office who all the other sales reps called in to"—not exactly what he went to college for, but it was a start. And an opportunity.

How did you go from answering the phone at *Rhode Island Monthly* to being a writer?

I put my name in whenever there was some small minor editorial work that needed to be developed. One monthly department was called something like "Neighbors"—these half-page profiles of prominent Rhode Islanders, usually in either the arts or politics. I also wrote advertorial features for *Rhode Island Monthly* on subjects such as condominiums, home improvement, and secondary education, and within about six months on the job, my writing was in almost every issue of the magazine.

Were you that industrious as an undergraduate English major?

I was way, way too complacent. It's a fairly common thing among people who are twenty and twenty-one years old. You think the opportunities are going to come to you, as opposed to your having to go out and get them.

You were originally an economics major as an undergraduate, but you switched to English, correct?

Even then [in the mid-1980s], people would say that English is not a great major for getting a job, so with that in mind, I kept the econ, but then I found that it's not so hot a major either. It doesn't really give you any clearer path as to where to go. And the econ was just a grind, whereas the English courses were a pleasure. In college, I was very much into the whole liberal arts thing, and was barely thinking about marketing myself once I got out.

A referral from a friend led to a job at Hasbro, the Rhode Island–based manufacturer of Mr. Potato Head and G.I. Joe. There, you transitioned to writing brochures, catalogs, packaging copy, and other marketing materials. Was that a hard transition?

To be honest, it's not a hugely challenging style, once you get the hang of it. I stayed on at Hasbro for eight years, during which time I branched out and got into writing executive communications: letters, memos, and speeches. Eventually I became a de facto member of the executive communications team. Whenever they needed something substantial and their resources were stretched thin, they would call me and I would work it into my schedule.

Another referral from a friend got you an interview with Fidelity Investments in Boston, which needed a senior staff writer to handle internal communications to the company's representatives and, most of all, write executive communications. What's it like, writing for presidents and vice-presidents?

Fortunately, most of the executives I work for are pretty good writers themselves. That's definitely not always the case, but it is here [at Fidelity]. Their feedback tends not to be overbearing, and is usually quite constructive.

What's the most gratifying part of your job?

Without question, the most rewarding aspect is when I can write something substantial—say, a business update for the company president; say, about two thousand words long. Something that the president of the business looked at, made very few edits on, and thought was a good piece of work. Then it goes out, he gets great feedback on it, and we both look good. It's very rewarding to see that go out to the whole company, even though it wasn't visible as my work.

What advice would you give undergraduate English majors, or those just starting out in the workforce?

You have to insinuate yourself: Take the initiative, make yourself available, and seek out opportunities to do the kind of work you want to be doing next. I also regret not using more of the resources available at college: the career center, the alumni network, and internships.

On the side, you also write creatively: a manuscript about one of your favorite jazz performers and more than one screenplay in your drawer. You can do both—write for business during the day and write for pleasure in your free time?

The creative and the professional writing are two different worlds. As a writer, I do have my own style, and that, for the most part, is not evident in the stuff I write in my everyday job. That writing needs to be straightforward and fluent—there is definitely an art to it—but not necessarily stylish.

And if that screenplay hits big?

In the split that exists for all writers between the creative and the purely professional, I'd say on the purely professional side I feel like I've got a pretty good gig with Fidelity, and I'd like to develop that and see where it goes.

## Q & A

### WHEN LITERARY GUYS GET TECHNICAL

John Warner is the editor of McSweeney's Internet Tendency and the co-author of *My First Presidentiary,* a fictional scrapbook by George W. Bush. When Warner is not putting his MFA from McNeese State University to work by getting his fiction published in *Zoetrope* and *The Mississippi Review,* he is getting his humor published in *Modern Humorist* and *McSweeney's,* among other publications. His latest book, *Fondling Your Muse,* is a humorous approach to writing advice.

So naturally, I spoke to him about technical writing.

Can you explain why, after majoring in rhetoric as an undergraduate, you thought the only thing you could do was go to law school?

Basically, it was all I knew. My father was a lawyer, my older brother had gone to law school right after college, and I thought I probably had the right skills to do relatively well. The profession can be lucrative and, despite the ubiquitous lawyer jokes, enjoys high status. The problem was that I didn't have any specific desire to actually be a lawyer. My interest in writing had been stoked in college, but I was convinced that creative writing was a dead end financially. My friends who majored in engineering or business had specific companies coming to recruit them, but I don't remember anyone beating down the door for the rhetoric majors. To be fair, I didn't spend that much time knocking on doors either.

After college, you worked as a paralegal. Would you recommend that job as one option for English majors unsure about what they want to do?

I wouldn't necessarily recommend the job, per se. It can be a lot of scut work with some pretty grueling hours at times, but as a young person just out of college, it allowed me to pay my bills with a little left over, ease into being an adult, and buy some time to figure out what I wanted to do. I'd recommend new graduates to not freak out about trying to find a job that's going to be their lifelong career. Just get something where you earn enough money, have benefits, and get some kind of real-world experience. Being a paralegal worked for me.

Did you know what technical writing was before you found a job in it? Tell us how you broke into the field and, once in it, how you advanced yourself.

I went to work for a marketing research firm not knowing anything about marketing research or the kinds of writing demands in the field. I broke in through a series of connections that eventually led to an interview and an offer for a spot at the bottom of the totem pole. Once there, the company was very good about giving people opportunities to prove they could do other, more advanced work. There was a lot of on-the-job mentoring if you were willing to learn. I tend to be intellectually curious and that was rewarded with more work and more responsibility.

My writing skills were in high demand because they were somewhat rare, particularly among the younger (under forty years of age) employees. Some of the brilliant strategists couldn't necessarily express their thoughts effectively in something like a proposal or project report, or, often, they were too busy managing projects and clients to have the time to work a document over. Some of them actually called me Shakespeare because they'd bring stuff to me to read and rework. Advancing in any job was essentially just a matter of demonstrating competence. Good companies still do reward that.

When you applied for a job in technical writing, how did you present yourself? In other words, were there particular skills, abilities, or experiences you advanced to argue for your suitability as a candidate?

Unfortunately, I presented myself poorly because I was ignorant of how my skills intersected with the company's needs. In fact, in an interview with the founder of the company, he tore apart my résumé and even some of my answers to his questions. I ended up walking home from the interview along the Chicago lakefront (about four miles) contemplating plunging into the icy waters of Lake Michigan.

Fortunately, the founder of the company saw more in me than I saw in myself, and he gave me a chance. I think that I waited to cry until I got out of the office probably weighed in my favor.

I think the primary skill he saw in me was the ability to think critically. I'd been trained to read quickly and take in and then summarize or analyze information. Technical writing is applied writing that relies on this particular skill. In every occasion there is a problem to be solved utilizing communication, and I'd been trained to identify and then solve that problem.

What kind of people were you working with, in terms of background and personality?

There was really a wide variety of people with any number of different education backgrounds or personality types. The biggest thing is that every project involved a huge amount of teamwork and coordination, which again made the ability to effectively communicate key. Some of the people were PhDs or MBAs with years of experience in research and survey methodology, something I knew nothing about when I started. Others had worked their way up in the company by starting as a phone interviewer and advancing to the position of project manager or department head. Most of the people came from business, marketing, or sociology backgrounds, but because there was a lot of on-the-job training, they'd take a shot at anybody who seemed like they could contribute to the team.

Like any place, the personalities varied, but in general it was a place where people liked to have fun, but also took a lot of pride in the work and maintaining the company's good reputation.

What was the greatest challenge about the job (or the field), in terms of your job duties or responsibilities?

I think one of the biggest adjustments people experience coming out of school is orienting to the pace of the professional world. The nine-to-five job doesn't really exist, and naptime is a thing of the past. My average days were 8:00 to 6:30 and I often had to work longer hours than that. When people first start their jobs, they often worry that they'll have nothing to do, but once they're rolling, they'll find that they almost always have too much to do. There are no natural pauses like a spring or summer break, and you're expected to be at least somewhat available on vacation (which you'll never take anyway because you're too busy). You always owe someone something and that can be hard to grapple with.

The other big struggle is not having a teacher telling you what to do and how to do it all the time. As great as my particular firm was at mentoring, they still expected me to do a lot of self-teaching and working through issues for myself. If you're not comfortable with spending time casting about blindly, the work would be unbelievably stressful. You just need to get comfortable with knowing that eventually, things will become clear.

**Today you're teaching technical writing at South Carolina's Clemson University. What exactly are you teaching, in terms of skills or assignments?**

The course, as developed by the English Department, is designed to mirror the kinds of situations students will find when they enter the workplace. For example, their major assignment is a ten-week-long group project where they're expected to find a client that has a need for technical writing, assess that need, and then produce the appropriate document. We're trying to teach them to be proactive and curious, and most importantly (to my mind), how to work effectively in groups—something they get very little instruction in at the college level. Work is just an endless series of group projects, and the sooner they get so they can work effectively and efficiently with others, the better.

I take great pains to model the instruction along the lines of what's expected of them in the "real world," including the threat of firing (dropping) them from the class if they're absent three times. I think the students appreciate that the university has made a concerted effort to provide them with the kind of experience that they'll benefit from in the workplace.

**In retrospect, what might you have done differently, as an undergraduate, to help advance your career path?**

I honestly wouldn't change much, but that doesn't mean that I recommend people follow the same path. I was never worried about my career path per se, because I think it's a mistake to look too far into the future. I've had three "careers" already, and there may be more on the horizon. To fret about finding a first job that you can stick with forever is a recipe for unhappiness. I just need a job, not a career path.

I think the key is to try to find work that is interesting and stimulating, and worry about money and advancement later. If you have a college degree and can work hard and play well with others, you'll do fine. You might not retire at thirty, but if you're working toward finding a career that keeps you engaged, you're not counting the moments to retirement anyway. My wish for myself would have been to spend more time investigating possible areas of employment before I left college. In the end, I'm doing what I should, but I may have taken a less circuitous route.

I truly love my jobs, and I think that's the most you can hope for. Even though the Joneses may have more money, I've seen that Jones looks like an extra from *Night of the Living Dead* on his way in to work. In the end, if all else fails, marry rich.

**You're in touch with undergraduates constantly, in your line of work. How prepared or informed about their career plans do they seem to you?**

A lot of it depends on what they're majoring in. Students in engineering or applied sciences often have done some kind of co-op work or internships during college, which has really helped them gain knowledge of and experience in the workplace. Others—often the liberal arts majors—have no clue. As universities continue to emphasize training over education, I think the liberal arts majors will be marginalized even further.

For the most part, students gather around the poles: Either you have a direct path and focus, or you're totally lost. I was part of the latter group.

**Often, when we give people career advice, there's an emphasis on planning, preparation, organized thinking, and the like. Using your own career, can you speak to the importance or role of chance or serendipity?**

You can't overestimate being in the right place at the right time, which can be largely a matter of luck. This has happened to me over and over again in my professional career as well as with my writing and editing. Many times, opportunities have just found me.

In reality, though, just about everyone will have a bit of lagniappe fall their way at some point in their lives, and the key is to seize the moment when it's presented. If you're too focused on what's next, you won't spend enough time thinking about what's in front of you, and your work and performance will suffer. By and large, good work gets rewarded and noticed. That doesn't mean that slackers don't progress up the ladder as well, but that's a kind of pure luck that most of us can't hope for.

# CHAPTER 9 *Other Options*

No doubt your major is important to you. It may even be close to your heart, and for good reason: You chose it.

As children, we don't choose which elementary school we attend, and as teenagers, our preference for private or public schooling seldom abrogates the state of our parents' finances. From kindergarten to high school, we do not choose our teachers (or, we select from the few choices), and, apart from token classroom gestures in which students are invited to help shape the curriculum, the books we buy and the subjects on which we are tested are chosen and determined for us.

Subsequently, some of us were (or are) matriculants at the college of our choice, but, really, the college chose us more than the other way around. Then, once we got to college, we were allowed to make one of the few genuine choices of our education, which we'll be paying off for a while.

Regardless of your major, however, remember: Your major is not you. Nor is your future determined or limited by your major. If it were, every politician would have majored in political science.

At certain points in your life—and not just when you're fresh out of college—you may have to look for work outside your field, outside your comfort zone, and outside your expectations of yourself.

And guess what: You might find what you're looking for, out there.

Let's take a quick look at some fields and professions that might not top your list, but are worth consideration.

## [RADIO]

Radio stations need writers, editors and editorial-based project managers like any other form of media; bear in mind, however, that these people work behind the scenes of on-air broadcast, which is a world invisible to you as you rock out to the radio in your car or dorm room. The reality of working in that world, while gratifying, may be less romantic or cool than you imagine.

**Good for people who:** have terrific flexibility for working hours (especially weekends and traditional vacation times); jacks-of-all-trades who are willing to do what's needed, as needed; quick studies; those with a tolerance for equipment failure.

**How to break in:** Obviously, if you're still an undergraduate, seek out opportunities at your college radio station. If you're a graduate, contact other radio stations for internship or volunteer work, and work as much as you can for nothing. A degree in broadcasting or communications may be preferred (but not strictly required) for the radio station to hire you. If you're not interested in being an on-air personality, there are plenty of other jobs: The production director, for example, often writes and develops commercials and promotional spots.

**Upside:** Once you're in, if you show initiative and a desire to learn everything about the station's operations, you could be given more responsibilities. If you have the time and the stamina, you could work your way up through your own self-education. There are also plenty of broadcasting schools that offer part-time and nighttime training and education.

If you're looking for a way to freelance for a radio station, think about writing for on-air personalities who need jokes, fake commercials, and other humorous spots. If you're good at humor writing, you might pitch a portfolio of such material as a freelance path into the station.

**Downside:** You will be competing with a thousand other people who want to work in radio because they think it would be easy and/or cool. It will be a challenge to make your case to the program director, who is one busy beaver with very little time and patience. The PD may tell you that consolidation in the radio industry has eliminated many job opportunities.

If you get in the door through a willingness to work for very little and to do as much as possible, this strategy could work against you: You could get stuck being the unpaid volunteer who does everything. Even if you do get a paid job, you're not looking at a big salary. As you're getting established, having a second source of income will be helpful—especially if you're shelling out money for broadcasting school.

**Bottom line:** Job availability and salary ranges are determined by a radio station's location and market size. Also, in case you haven't noticed by watching competitive battles between broadcasting conglomerates and satellite radio, the radio industry is in constant flux.

## [TELEVISION]

Television, like radio, has a seductively romantic appeal: the news, drama, commercials, comedy, sitcoms and serials just seem to flow through the cathode ray tube, finished, polished and complete. It's a big industry, with opportunities on the local and national level, on network and on cable, for people who want a high profile and folks who don't mind being one of the tens of thousands of employees whose names you'll never know.

**Good for people who:** work well under deadline; don't mind climbing the ladder slowly; can tolerate rejection; and can collaborate creatively.

**How to break in:** Like radio, television is a foot-in-the-door industry. On the local TV level, you'll be calling the news director or production manager of your local TV station to ask about internships and volunteer opportunities. Also investigate your local community cable access channel for education, training, and work opportunities. Network and cable television, obviously, constitute a bigger playing field, but require relocation to New York or California—and even then, you're looking at either assistant-level or low-level production work to start: e.g., helping out a producer with administrative duties or reading through the endless influx of scripts. Contacts made through a workshop or training program may help you break in. Several networks have talent development and scholarship programs.

If you want to write scripts for television, be forewarned that the odds against having your unagented, unsolicited script noticed by a studio or production company are greater than the odds against having your unagented, unsolicited short story published in the *New Yorker*. Writers are hired and contracted by studios and production companies. You may have luck getting a position as a writer's assistant. Writer's assistants perform low-level administrative duties, during which time the more enterprising candidates will learn the business, make contacts, write on spec, and keep at it.

**Upside:** It is absolutely necessary for you to learn how the entire industry works. Doing so will expose you to a variety of jobs, responsibilities, and opportunities you may not have considered or known about. The financial rewards are great for people who make it. Salaries for staff writing positions average $70,000, and development deals (contracts to develop one idea) can pay in the millions.

**Downside:** Fierce competition and a start-at-the-bottom hierarchical structure will test your mettle, patience, and that other thing you need—talent. Writers for network television shows work long hours throughout the year. Not only must you understand the industry from a production standpoint, you need to learn the legal end of matters from the standpoint of writers' unions and guilds.

At any level, more opportunities are available in the technical and production aspects of the business. The creation of a television program is a highly collaborative enterprise, which is to say that your beginnings in the industry are not assisted by your being an inflexible prima donna.

You've seen TV shows that last for a few weeks and get canceled. That's a lot of people getting axed. It's not just low-quality shows that get the axe: Consider the fate of a critically acclaimed but unwatched show like *My So-Called Life*. You need to be comfortable with the potential for failure.

**Bottom line:** Television is creative, stimulating work in a highly competitive environment. You cannot thrive without networking. Vicissitudes in public taste influence your job future—for example, if the public decides it likes reality TV more than scripted shows, then lots of writers are out of work. Success is predicated overall on knowledge, ability, contacts, and tenacity.

## [MARKETING]

Marketing (not the same as advertising) is a general term that refers to communication concerning goods, services, or ideas. Marketing involves strategic planning, development of collateral across all types of media, pricing, distribution, media planning, and public relations.

**Good for people who:** are highly creative and are not only good writers and editors, but are able to present their ideas effectively; can persuade and influence people; have project management ability; can think strategically and tactically; have good interpersonal skills for dealing with sales reps, account managers, clients, etc.

**How to break in:** Courses, tutorials, workshops, and other educational opportunities can give you an overview of the industry and help you start to make contacts. Project management jobs usually require several years' experience in the marketing field.

Build your own abilities, knowledge, and enthusiasms: Seek out marketing jobs in industries to which you take a shine.

Come to the table with evidence of your creativity and personality. I once applied for a marketing-related job at an art school's continuing education department by coming up with my own marketing campaign packaged in a PowerPoint presentation with artwork and photos, a slogan, and a strategy for rollout. Take a shot at a project yourself, and show your prospective employer that you can do what you want to do.

**Upside:** The industry likes a liberal arts background with specialized knowledge, as well as creative people strong in idea generation and presentation skills; stimulating work; variety of assignments.

**Downside:** Hours can be long (expect more than forty hours a week); travel often required; intensely competitive field.

## [ADVERTISING]

Advertising is one component of marketing: It involves the development of the ad itself (for print, broadcast, etc.), the positioning of the ad, and consideration of how the ad fits in with a larger ad campaign. You see all around you the manifold ways in which ads are presented and positioned: It's not just developing a five-by-seven spot in a newspaper.

**Good for people who:** live in California or New York, where the industry is strongly represented; are effective team workers; are creative idea generators; have a technical or computer background; and can implement innovative ways to deliver advertising.

**How to break in:** As with marketing, being a liberal arts major is a good foundation, but it must be matched with training and experience in a niche market, a specialized skill, or a particular industry. Appreciate that advertising isn't just about coming up with a catchy jingle or catch phrase: There are jobs in event planning, project management, strategic development, public relations, sales, production, and more.

**Upside:** Innovations in advertising strategy not only make for a highly creative environment but also for an ever-broadening area of opportunity (such as mining the advertising potential of new technological advancements). You would be working in a strong teamwork environment. Ad agencies can be large corporations or a two-person office (more than half of the jobs in this field are with offices of fewer than fifty people), so you will be able to find the office size that works for you.

**Downside:** When accounts get lost, so might you: The loss of one major account could translate into one hundred or more people being laid off. There's a lot of money at stake in advertising, and where there's more money, there's more pressure.

## [TECHNICAL WRITING]

Technical writing is a broad term that describes a wide spectrum of writing activities—basically, writing for business or technical purposes. This could mean developing instructional brochures for a toy company, research reports for a marketing firm, or proposals for a nonprofit. You could find a technical-writing job in the industries of computers, science, law, medicine, finance, and more.

**Good for people who:** can translate sophisticated or complex ideas into plain language; have a command of the mechanics of writing and editing (sentence structure, grammar, usage); can adapt their writing style to suit a specialized audience. Your candidacy is enhanced if you possess knowledge of authoring software or programs that incorporate visuals into text or publish text to the Internet.

**How to break in:** College students should seek out internships. Contract or temporary technical-writing assignments are a good foot in the door and could lead to full-time positions. As with marketing, seek out industries you think you might work well in, and interview with the editorial services director, the head copywriter, or the communications department.

**Upside:** Businesses put a high premium on effective communication, and the larger the business, the more opportunities and the higher the salaries. You're bound to find people on a technical-writing staff who are business by day and creative by night, so if you're an artiste worried about being alone in a corporate environment, you needn't be.

**Downside:** Writing or editing for a technical or business audience may be drier work than you might like. You need to have the willingness to learn an industry and the ability to find satisfaction in working the communications end of that industry.

## [PUBLIC RELATIONS]

Public relations is a blanket term for the profession of acting as an intermediary between an organization (business, government, school, nonprofit) and the public. PR people advocate for their clients, craft and deliver their message, and provide information to the public and to the media.

**Good for people who:** can research and synthesize information into a clear, concise, memorable message; are creative "idea people"; have outstanding project management and interpersonal skills.

**How to break in:** Develop a writing portfolio that exhibits versatility, creativity, and effective communication skills. No particular educational background is necessary for public relations work, but proven expertise and knowledge of a particular industry will help you secure a PR position within a given company.

**Upside:** Public relations is a large field with innumerable opportunities for people with writing, editing, and creative ability. In the area of writing/editing alone, you could be working on speeches, press releases, newsletters, op-ed pieces, and more. You'll never be short of work. As competition increases for the public's eyeballs and attention spans, companies and organizations need more creative and innovative ways to communicate their message and interact with the public.

**Downside:** Writing and editing ability must be matched with excellent project management and interpersonal skills, knowledge of the business, and an outgoing personality. Not just anyone will fit the bill. Entry-level salaries can hover around low to mid-twenties. PR firms tend to be full of very busy people.

## [PUBLIC AFFAIRS]

What makes public affairs slightly different from public relations is that the former deals with the efforts of institutions, organizations, and the government to effect social or legislative change; and the latter represents a product, service, or idea to specific groups or the general public. Organizations of all kinds, sizes, and shapes have a relationship with the public. In some areas, this relationship involves issues of policy or the foundation of law.

A financial institution, for example, will have a public affairs office or department; in addition, it may engage the services of an independent public affairs firm. For-profit and nonprofit organizations alike have needs in public affairs. An environmental nonprofit group, for example, would have someone working in public affairs to effect changes in pollution laws or industrial policies.

**Good for people who:** have a background or interest in law, public policy, or government; can communicate effectively and have the ability to persuade and influence people.

**How to break in:** If you're applying to a company with an internal public affairs department, it helps to show experience or expertise in a field related to the company's business, be it medicine, finance, or technology.

**Upside:** You don't necessarily need a degree in public relations or communications to get a job in this field. If you're applying for a job with a large company's public affairs department, an internal training program may be available.

**Downside:** Writing and editing ability must be matched by knowledge of and interest in law, public policy, and government.

## ALUMNI AFFAIRS/ADVANCEMENT OFFICE

The advancement office at your college or university is charged with the very important ask of securing financial resources for the school. Typically, the advancement office comprises the offices of alumni affairs, alumni giving, and public affairs.

The alumni giving office deals with alumni fund-raising, donations, gifts, endowments, and the like. Alumni affairs deals more broadly with the relationship between the school and its alumni; it hosts events for alumni (such as homecoming), coordinates educational programs for alumni, maintains alumni records, and so on.

Jobs in these offices could include speech writing; writing or editing for the alumni magazine; coordinating special programs involving alumni; media relations; and more, depending on the size of the college or university.

**Good for people who:** work well in an academic environment; understand or appreciate the needs of the university, with respect to raising money or cultivating a strong relationship with its alumni; prefer a more community-based working environment as opposed to, say, a large anonymous corporation.

**How to break in:** Your own college or university is a good place to start: you're already familiar with the environment and, one hopes, you have some contacts with alumni or administration. If you're a writer, submit a feature article to your alumni magazine and start making contacts via that avenue. Volunteer at a college and university and make an in-road that way.

**Upside:** Always great benefits, working for a university: access to its facilities; tuition reimbursement programs; a tight-knit community; and prestige. Colleges seldom go out of business.

**Downside:** Despite their giant endowments, universities tend not to pay writers and editors Wall Street salaries; they try to balance out low salaries with the allure of good benefits.

## [THE U.S. MILITARY]

Every branch of the United States military employs people in media and public affairs: The military employs about two thousand broadcast journalists and news writers alone. The military has its own internal publications and communications, and needs people to handle its external communications as well.

**Good for people who:** obviously, are open to considering a career in the military. Your best bet, here, is to talk to people who have served in the military to understand the *sui generis* culture and environment of military service. It's not just a question of skill: It's also a question of character, temperament, willingness to sacrifice, and an interest not just in being a news writer or broadcast journalist, but being a news writer/journalist for the military.

**How to break in:** Visit to your local military recruitment office and discuss what's involved in enlisting in the military.

**Upside:** You don't need to be able to do a thousand push-ups to perform news writing duties for the military. The armed services provide initial training for these positions, and as anyone who has served in the military can tell you, the military is a great place to acquire technical skills, and you may get the opportunity to travel.

**Downside:** The location given for these positions is "worldwide," which means you need to be willing to relocate.

## NONPROFITS

A nonprofit (or not-for-profit) entity is a noncommercial venture, in either the public or private interest, whose primary purpose is not the enrichment of its founders, owners, and staff. There are nonprofits in a wide variety of fields: the arts, medicine, religion, politics, education, and more.

Just because an organization doesn't pursue profit doesn't mean it doesn't take in revenue. Nonprofits operate under exclusive laws governing how they accept donations, how they pay taxes, and how they finance their programs.

**Good for people who:** are more interested in the public mission of the nonprofit itself than in the personal accumulation of wealth; are changing their vocational focus and want to enhance a portfolio or gain new skills and experience.

**How to break in:** Nonprofits are always interested in attracting talented people. A volunteer opportunity may give you the experience necessary to secure a full-time position—either at the nonprofit itself or at a for-profit organization.

**Upside:** Your enthusiasm and dedication may compensate for lack of experience. Nonprofits tend to be small organizations, but not always—charitable foundations, for example, can be large. Staff camaraderie and cohesion tend to be higher, not only because of the size of the organization, but because everyone has a sense of being there because of a higher calling or mission.

**Downside:** Salaries at nonprofits are not as big as at for-profits. There may not be the same opportunities for advancement at a nonprofit, and although people who work at a nonprofit may feel empowered by their organization's mission—saving the world, if in just a small way—there may be a sense of frustration at trying to save the world with limited resources, a low salary, and not as much help as you need.

## Q & A
### SPEECH, SPEECH!

Jacque Goddard Snyder took her English major into a thirteen-year career in radio and television news: She's done everything from working as a DJ for a big-band music station to being a morning news anchor in Bangor, Maine, to working as a news director for several radio stations in New England. In 1994, she was hired as press secretary to Mayor Thomas M. Menino of Boston, Massachusetts, and five years later, she began writing speeches for Angela Menino, the mayor's wife.

Jacque, how many speeches do you write for Angela Menino, and what kinds of speeches does she give?

The number of speeches per month has varied from two to six. The type of speech has varied from a congratulatory speech in presenting an award to being the key speaker at a conference for Boston teenage girls.

Last month, some of the speeches I wrote were welcome remarks for the first lady of Rwanda; a speech about domestic violence prevention to a group called the Asian Task Force Against Domestic Violence; remarks for the planting of a rose bush in memory of the former Boston parks and recreation commissioner; fundraising breakfast remarks for Dress for Success, a program that helps low-income women in obtaining employment; and a Mother's Day speech for a senior citizens' lunch.

What's the process like?

We are notified that Angela needs to make a speech—sometimes we get several months' notice, sometimes we get one day. I contact the group and get information about the event, who will be attending, what the group would like Angela to say. I speak with Angela about what she would like to include in the speech, and usually, each speech has two to three drafts. Sometimes, the drafts are given to the group for fact-checking, sometimes the drafts are given to a city hall official to see if any information needs to be added (if the remarks are to include the Mayor's policies).

What occasioned the transition from press secretary to speech writing?

I began to write speeches for Angela Menino in 1999, when my son was born and I could no longer continue in the position of press secretary to the mayor.

How did you adjust, given the change in responsibilities?

Speech writing for Mrs. Menino was a natural transition. I knew the Menino family well. I was familiar with the mayor's positions and had experience attending the events the Meninos often spoke at. I was familiar with the mayor's and Angela's styles of speech and with their sense of humor.

As the mayor's press secretary, I occasionally had to write a quick speech for the mayor during a time of crisis when the speech-writing office was closed. For example, late one night, a well-known community activist and prosecutor was murdered. A news conference was scheduled within the hour, so I wrote a text for the mayor to read.

You make it sound pretty easy. Are you drawing on standard language for a particular type of text, or are you coming up with something unique each time?

Some speech-writing books would suggest having generic speech formats for common occasions, such as for award presentations, for fundraising events, or for general welcoming remarks. I feel these generic formats sound *too* generic. I think every crowd is different, so therefore the remarks should always be different. The best speeches are personalized. The best speeches make reference to people in the audience or to their experiences. It can be difficult to personalize speeches.

So how do you do it?

The speech writer needs to have direct contact with the speaker: no intermediary! The writer needs to hear from the speaker, in the speaker's words, what should be included in the speech. The writer can then sense how much passion is involved. The writer can then sense what the speaker wants to emphasize. More than one conversation with the speaker is usually required.

Do you attend all the events you write for?

The speech writer should be present when the speech is delivered. When you are present, you can see what lines worked with the crowd and which did not. When you are there, you can determine what sentences might have given the speaker some trouble delivering. You will then be better able to write the next speech.

I imagine your experience as a reporter and news editor comes into play when you're writing for a specific event.

Yes. The speech writer should do his or her own phone-calling and research. As the writer, you know how many facts are needed to support an idea, and an assistant may not. For example, in writing welcoming remarks for the first lady of Rwanda, I researched Rwanda and the country's civil war. We did not need to include that information in Angela's speech, but the information helped me set the tone for the remarks and helped set the stage for a paragraph emphasizing Angela's admiration for what the first lady had been through.

Were your undergraduate studies as an English major at all helpful to you in your career?

I believe my educational and career background has been a tremendous help in speech writing. My BA in English from Holy Cross meant I learned a great deal about critical reading and writing. Thirteen years as a radio and television reporter taught me how to write "for the ear"—that is, I had to write stories that would be heard and not read. Being a broadcast reporter also helped me work efficiently on quick deadlines and gather information from many sources. And finally, because I worked for five years as press secretary to the mayor, I was exposed to every event imaginable and all varieties of people.

What happens to you when Mayor Menino is no longer in office?

I feel that speech writers will always be able to find employment. Many dignitaries, officials, and community leaders have to speak constantly.

They are short on time. They need writers to help with their speeches. I think I could easily get another job as a speech writer if the Menino family no longer needed my help. I would call several nonprofit groups and perhaps offer to write remarks for all speakers at their yearly fundraiser. Perhaps I would call several politicians and offer to work on a pay-per-speech basis.

Jacque, what part of your job gives you the most satisfaction?

The most satisfying part of my job is having a speech well received.

What, to you, is *well received*?

This would mean that the audience laughs when they are supposed to and people pay attention to the remarks. Generally, if I have done my job well, the speaker is comfortable and enthusiastic in delivering the remarks.

Challenges?

The biggest challenge in my job is getting information from people. Many people who plan events don't know what I need. They are in a hurry and try to dismiss me with such phrases as, *She can just say something like she said last year,* or *She can say whatever she likes, she knows the group.*

Isn't that true, though? She could just say the same thing as last year.

Even if Angela speaks at the Boys & Girls Club fundraiser every spring, her remarks need to be different each year. The speech may change because in the last year, the club may have introduced new programs, the club may have just suffered through a scandal, or a club member may have just been cited by the White House for some wonderful outreach work. If I can get these relevant personal details in the speech, the speech will go over well.

And then comes the part where the speaker thanks her speech writer, right?

Only you and the speaker know that a great speech was written by you! At the event, the speaker will be congratulated for a terrific speech and you will be in the shadows. That's fine with me, since I know it's my job to make her look and sound good.

## *Q & A*
## ENGLISH MAJOR HOLDS THE MAYO

If you ask Amos Kirmisch, fifty-nine, if he knew what he wanted to do with his major in English once he graduated college, he'll tell you that he knew he wanted to write.

He ended up making good on those words, working for sixteen years at the Cleveland *Plain Dealer* before moving on to public relations and marketing work at IBM and Brodeur Worldwide of Boston. At Brodeur, Kirmisch ran a Web development division, working in the high-tech and health-care sectors, and today, he is Web manager at the Mayo Clinic in Minnesota, overseeing a staff of writers, editors, and content developers for one of Mayo's main Web portals.

In your career, you've written for a variety of audiences and in a multitude of media. What particular challenges are posed by writing or developing content for the Web?

The hardest thing is to divorce the Web from paper. The truth is that it is a software application and you need to start thinking about interactions with the audience and multimedia as well. The Web gives your audience an opportunity to interact with the software and the information: That means you are conversing with people. That's fundamentally different from just writing something that is going to be consumed by someone anonymously.

You've worked for a newspaper, a corporation, a public relations/marketing firm, and now for an academic medical center. Can you compare and contrast these different working environments? Does each favor a particular personality or temperament?

You're right when you say these are different working environments that require different behaviors. Let me take them one at a time.

When I worked for newspapers—in the late 1960s through the mid-1980s—hard-nosed reporting was in. Remember, in the early 1970s, a couple of reporters at the *Washington Post* pushed a president out of office for, as it turned out, really being a crook. This kind of reporting requires people who are willing to be dogged and tenacious—people who are willing to dig to get the facts and then are willing to stand behind those facts regardless of the consequences. Sometimes the consequences can be very difficult, even if the articles are absolutely on target and correct. Much of the work is one individual doing the job of reporting over weeks and months. Sometimes this work pays off with compelling stories that can make a real difference; sometimes it is frustrating because the facts are just out of reach.

Working for a corporation is all about developing strategies, marketing, messaging, and tactics. It is less about writing and more about marketing. After all, you are trying to sell something. I experienced a big transition when I switched from reporting to working for a Fortune-100 company. I had been used to working largely on my own developing stories, and suddenly I was part of an international team dedicated to marketing. There were new rules about what could and couldn't be done and there was a totally different way to look at the world. After all, I had been a reporter for a long time, and my perspective was always that the glass was half empty. Suddenly, that was not the issue. In fact, what I wanted was to tell the world that the glass was full and that its contents were not only worth drinking but worth paying for.

The transition from corporate marketing communications to a PR/marketing firm was not as dramatic as moving from journalism to corporate communications. The big change had to do with being personally responsible for generating revenue and being billable on an hourly basis. There was also the need to please clients, meet their needs, and keep them as happy customers. The fact is that working for an agency turns you into a consultant. The client expectation is that you are an expert and will provide insights and advice worth that big hourly fee they are paying.

Working for an academic medical center is again a big change. It requires collaboration, consensus-building, and a willingness to compromise. Many decisions are made by committees. There's a whole art form to this process that requires some on-the-job training. It may take more time and effort to reach consensus, but along the way the ideas and suggestions of those involved in the consensus-building are likely to result in a better decision and better end-product. There is a dramatic difference between this environment and that of a hard-nosed reporter.

You spent almost two decades in print journalism, and yet now, as Web manager for the Mayo Clinic, you're publishing cutting-edge news and reaching a wider audience. What's the lesson there for English majors looking for places to apply their skills?

I believe that being an English major is about learning to think and communicate. Those skills have served me very well, allowing me to always find new and interesting challenges. The nature of communications is changing dramatically. People are connected in ways that were never possible before. The network has made people in India as close as people in the next office. It's a new world full of opportunity. It's just a matter of identifying those opportunities.

You note that one of your editors can manage about sixty projects at any given time. Is the development of project management skills the key to advancement in writing and editing jobs?

Project management is certainly a skill that is well worth acquiring. Today, people can become certified project managers, and this is a skill that can lead to an outstanding career. In addition, I think it is well worthwhile to build expertise in a specialty or two: Health care and science writing require specialization in science and medicine. To write about technology requires an understanding of computer science and the technology industry.

I believe in continuous learning. I've tried to add skills by taking classes on different topics throughout my career. When I first began working in corporate communications, I took a series of short seminars on all kinds of PR-related topics like producing video news releases and audio news releases, speech writing, event planning, and so on. As my interest in computers grew, I started taking programming classes. These have made it possible for me to have a real conversation with engineers who have the deep insights about where technology is going.

You graduated from college in 1968, and one of your sons graduated college recently with an English major. What differences do you see in the job market for English majors, and has anything remained the same?

Much has changed. When I graduated from college, having a college degree guaranteed you a job. Today, college degrees are more common, and more people are getting advanced degrees. If I were in college today, I would be considering an advanced degree to complement my undergraduate English degree to make me more attractive in the marketplace.

What hasn't changed is communications. There will always be a need for people who can communicate and can do it well.

It appears your career path has consistently applied your skills in writing and editing and has been guided by your personal interest in computers and technology. Is that, fundamentally, the approach to take in looking for a job—use your foundational skills, be guided by your interests and passions in life?

I think it is very important to find the things you are passionate about and pursue them. Working for a living isn't an awful lot of fun unless you are fully engaged.

## *Q & A*

### CREDIT FOR THE EDIT

English major Drew McNaughton has a way with words; and thus, he made his way into an internship with a major Midwestern investment firm. In 2000, acting on a tip from a friend, McNaughton sent the CFO of Barrington Research in Chicago, Illinois, a letter of intent that basically admitted his lack of experience in and knowledge of the financial industry.

In McNaughton's case, candor and charm may have played a role in securing a position editing and writing research reports—or perhaps there's a place, after all, in the business world for people who majored in English.

Today, McNaughton, who also obtained his MFA from the University of Montana, is the site coordinator for the elementary and middle school after-school programs in Montpelier, Vermont.

What exactly did you say in this infamous letter of intent?

My letter of intent was an open disclosure of my lack of familiarity with the financial world. I think the phrasing was something like: *I know finance in the most microeconomic sense—such as balancing a checkbook. To date, however, my knowledge of the greater machine (stock trading, bearer bonds, bear and bull markets) is mostly limited to the realm of inference, movies, and the like.*

I did some pandering to the allure of finance, and expressed my eagerness to broaden my educational experience beyond that of the sometimes impractical liberal arts. I was being honest when I said I had an interest in learning a new way of thinking, but I was kind of lying when I said things like, *To me, the elegance of economic patterning mirrors that of many higher studies, including poetry, physics, and biology.*

It must have gone over well: You got the job.

During the first callback, I was surprised to hear how much of an impact the letter had made on the CFO, who responded with eagerness at my desire to enter into such a foreign field of employment.

Over the phone, scheduling an official interview, he mostly asked questions about the way in which I learned things (doing vs. instruction) and a brief rundown of the computer programs I'd have to get familiar with. Knowing Excel, FrontPage, and PowerPoint helped me a great deal, even though my familiarity with these programs was tangential and thin.

Copyediting research reports may strike some people's ears as work that's a little dry. Can you explain your duties and responsibilities, and was there a creative element to your work?

It is dry, yes. But the important thing to remember is that the reports written by economics majors in the office were fields of jargon. The same report has a much higher readability potential once a little soul is thrown in.

Day-to-day activities were routine but varied. I always had about two reports to clean up (about four pages each), which took up the morning. I did a lot of talking with the author of the report, asking what certain acronyms meant, and in the process I learned that when the authors explained things to me in layman's language, the information came out in a more palatable form. I took that idea and applied it to the reports. Luckily, the president of the company appreciated the stylistic changes.

In the afternoon, most of my time was spent doing research, which meant mostly online investigations of company investments, company leader profiles, and strategy. Almost all of this research could be done from the Web site of the company being reported on, and I sometimes called them up directly with questions.

What skills or abilities did you bring to that job, as an English major?

I had the ability to read past the obfuscatory, jargon-laden reporting of accountants, and the ability to see what they wanted to say, in plain terms. I had the background in understanding how to compress language for quick message delivery, and the creative capacity to play with a message until it became enjoyable to read.

Most of the time, the people reading these reports were stuffy investors or the minions of stuffy investors. They want the facts, plain and simple. What I was able to bring to the table was the ability to deliver these facts in a digestible—even enjoyable—format. Investors liked being able to use the reports for customers who didn't work in finance, because the reports were in plain English. This was a big divorce from the traditional model, in which the reports were written not for the public, but for the closed circle of those who understood all the investment banker acronyms and terminology.

How did you transition from editing reports to writing them? Was that an easy transition?

Often my edits of the reports were massive: I rewrote entire sections. The CFO and vice president of the company was my supervisor, and he knew that I had the ability to rewrite these sections successfully. Since I was already doing the research the reports were based on, he experimented by letting me put that research in report form before sending it to him. That was, in essence, what writing the reports was: Do the research, write out what you find for others, print.

After the experimental report proved passable, I was given some others to write by myself. Obviously, the name attached to the report was someone with the letters *CPA* after it, but I was the one writing them. All of my reports were added to and augmented with graphs and data charts whose creation I had nothing to do with.

Did you understand what all the charts meant? Did you have to?

No. I had never held a job like this before in my life. I didn't know anything about accounting, about investing. But I did fine: I found it to be enjoyable—even a little lucrative, as internships go. All the previous summers I'd worked either guiding rafting, climbing, or hiking trips, or working back in my home state of Vermont as a construction grunt.

What was the biggest challenge in the position, with respect to writing or editing?

The biggest challenge was holding back on cutting out material. Because of my lack of familiarity with the concepts being discussed in the reports, I wanted to just cut out the stuff I didn't understand. I got told that certain cuts I made were cuts of necessary material, and once I knew why the information was important, it became a lot easier to incorporate. Another big challenge was keeping the reports brief.

**How did the internship affect your perception of what kinds of opportunities were available to you as an English major?**

One day on my lunch break I was talking with someone from the office, who was asking about my major in college. They didn't understand what I was going to do with an English/creative writing degree. I said, "Well, maybe I'll do what you do."

If you have a degree in English, you'd better have an interest in a lot of different things if you want to use it, because using your degree means more than getting a job with a bunch of people who went to school for the same thing you did.

English majors are the chameleons of the job market. We're able to put on hard hats, chef hats, toupees and ties, and we can take on the responsibilities that each job has for us.

I once wrote a twenty-five-page paper about Gertrude Stein and her ability to adhere to cyclical time as the temporal meter of her short works. If I can do that, investment research is a cakewalk.

# CHAPTER 10 Avoiding a Major Mistake

Of all the questions I'm asked about the major in English, there is one I dread: *If you could do it all over again—knowing then what you know now—would you major in English?*

The answer is yes and no.

Yes, because I profited from studying literature. As highfalutin as it sounds, I believe that literature is the royal road to understanding the human condition. Nothing in life goes unaddressed in novels, stories, poems, and plays, and what's more, the material of literature contains history, philosophy, theology, psychology, and other subjects I studied in college: hence my belief in the study of literature across the curriculum. For someone to go through four years of college and be exposed to literature only through an English class is nothing short of criminal.

And no, because while I hesitate to say I made a "major mistake" as an undergraduate, there are some things I know and believe now that I didn't know or believe then and that would have made me think twice about the way I approached my education. For example, if I could do it over, I would have either minored or double-majored in education or communications. I would have taken advantage of a program my college offered to earn a BA and MA in four years, and I certainly would have sought out more internships.

It's not that I think the major in English isn't a good program of study, it's just that I don't think it's enough, and I don't think the program I took was organized particularly well—or maybe it's just that there are a few things I wish I had been told.

Let's start with what the traditional major in English is all about.

## *Academic Boot Camp*

Allowing for differences across thousands of colleges and universities across America, we can agree, generally, on what the standard English major curriculum does: broaden the students' knowledge of literature; deepen an appreciation for that literature; and cultivate an ability to read, analyze, discuss, and critique that literature.

Fundamentally, the English major cultivates two skills: reading comprehension and writing. One English major I interviewed for this book would add critical thinking, and I would agree, but I would qualify it as *literary* critical thinking and argue that you can learn critical thinking just as easily in a physics or philosophy class. For four years, an English major reads books (not just *any* books, mind you) and writes papers about them. Read, rinse, and repeat.

The papers English majors write are, frankly, book reports. They show the teacher that the student has indeed read the book and can discuss the book's meaning and its relevance or importance in and of itself or in relation to other books or other ideas.

Now, what to do with all those papers? You cannot get them published in the *Atlantic Monthly* or in your local newspaper, and not just because there is insufficient public interest in your ruminations on John Dryden. It's because the analytic, academic paragraphs that English majors are trained to write provide practice for one thing, and one thing only: writing a much longer analytic academic paper called a thesis or dissertation. Apart from developing a handful of basic composition skills—and, hopefully, a deepened appreciation for literature—those college papers have no other application.

If they did, you wouldn't have thrown them all into the trash.

If the undergraduate major in English prepares you for anything, it's the master's degree in English, in which you continue to read a lot of books and write papers about them. This degree, in turn, prepares you for the PhD in English, which prepares you to embark on a life in academia as a professor, where you'll teach undergraduate English majors how to prepare for their master's degree, and so on and so on.

The standard BA in English, therefore, is a form of academic boot camp: It ensures the university English department another generation of graduate students and teaching fellows. The majority of undergraduates with a BA in English do not go on to earn a PhD—so why teach them as if they will? Why give them year after year of literary analysis, requiring them to write five- to seven-page papers of literary criticism when, after graduation, so few of them will ever write in this form again?

Were the faculty of the English department interested in producing something other than another generation of graduate students and teaching fellows, they would devote a significant portion of their curriculum to courses on book publishing, journalism and print media, corporate communications, technical writing, and/or copywriting. Why do they not do this?

## *Those Who Don't Know, Don't Teach*

The primary reason not to teach something is that you don't know enough about it. While it is true that English department faculty may have some experience in journalism (from publishing articles in magazines or journals) or in publishing (from authoring books or editing a literary magazine), or even in corporate communications (from writing memos and letters), few have long-term working experience in those professions. Why should they have experience? They're grown-up undergraduate English majors, the product of a career in academics, not of a career in newspapers or technical writing or editing.

You rarely hear the administrative explanation, *Well, we don't teach those topics owing to our ignorance and inexperience*; what you hear more often is, *We don't teach that because it's not worth teaching* or *That's not what college is for*. This is the old education-versus-training argument.

In *Genius*, the 1992 biography of American physicist Richard Feynman, author James Gleick writes:

> Feynman himself, halfway through his freshman year ... confronted his own department chairman with the classic question about mathematics: What is it good for? He got the classic answer: If you have to ask, you are in the wrong field. Mathematics seemed suited only for teaching mathematics.

There is a prevailing attitude that higher learning and training for the real world should be kept separate.

As you can tell from James Gleick's anecdote, the problem doesn't begin and end with the English department. A professional writer I interviewed for this book—a fellow with pretty serious credentials—told me that not long ago he returned to his alma mater's communications department, offering to teach a course in business reporting. The head of the department declined, explaining, "We're really more about theory here."

How nice. I wonder how many of the students would as readily dismiss time spent under the instruction of a professional writer so they could load up on more theory.

Even the arts are subject to this point of view. In August 2004, the *Village Voice Education Supplement* ran an article about a business-of-art curriculum developed by New York artists for art school students who were clueless about how to design a portfolio or negotiate the gallery scene. Again, the guardians at the gate of academe were skeptical about the introduction of this course of study: An individual from a respected art school summed up the academics' concern—that this business-of-art program sounded suspiciously like training, as opposed to teaching (as if, somehow, to train is not to teach, and vice versa). Besides, sniffed another art professor, the introduction of "this sort of class" could "push out other skill-based classes"—as if designing a portfolio or getting your work in galleries was not a skill.

The MFA program in creative writing I attended, its many merits aside, tended to invite as speakers not editors, agents, or publishers, but mid-list literary authors who would do us the very great honor of reading from their latest volume. When I asked why the program didn't spend more time (that is, any time) on the business end of writing, I was told that doing so would distract students from writing and take time away from The Craft.

Of course, even for successful artists, time spent on business takes away from time spent on composition, just as time spent eating apples takes away from time spent eating Snickers bars—but that doesn't mean it's impossible or unimportant to develop a balanced diet.

In its penultimate edition of the year, the *New York Times Sunday Magazine* publishes an alphabetical list of the year's vanguard ideas, trends, and innovations: In 2004, one such idea was "Employable Liberal Arts Major, The," as if *employable* and *liberal arts major* were theretofore mutually exclusive. Noting that a handful of high-profile American universities was offering undergraduate liberal arts majors either special programs in networking or credit hours in vocational training, the article squeezed in the requisite dissenting opinion—that of Amherst College president Anthony Marx, who tut-tutted, "To dilute the power of the liberal arts with premature professionalism will deprive our society of the thoughtful leadership it needs." Indeed, noted Marx, if students were to head in any direction, they needed to "go deeper into the liberal arts."

Apparently, just as one would be loathe to dilute chardonnay with tap water, one would not want to adulterate the developing minds of youth with the malignant influence of professionalism.

One could take issue with the notion that our society needs the thoughtful leadership of liberal arts majors (after all, election results clearly indicate society is interested more in the moral resoluteness of multimillionaires); but instead, consider Marx's use of the word *premature.*

Safe to say that all parties concerned—students, parents, educators, administrators—hope that young adults, upon graduating college, will enter the professional world: Is it premature to prepare them for the professional world *before* they actually enter it? Which would we rather risk: premature professionalism before our students graduate or immature professionalism after they graduate?

The argument that colleges and universities are not trade or vocational schools is not new. Louis Franklin Snow, in the "Modern Reform" chapter of his 1907 book *The College Curriculum in the United States,* had this to say:

> [To] look upon college merely as a trade school, or to consider it wholly as a preparation for a single sphere of subsequent activity, is to degrade its function and distort its purpose. In the college course much can be learned which will be directly serviceable in the minutiae of the future profession. Much can be taught with the conscious notion of giving what will be directly helpful and inspiring in future years. But the main purpose of the college curriculum is not to develop, incubator fashion, so many embryo doctors, ministers, lawyers, or teachers, but to train men and women in citizenship in the largest and freest manner possible. The college curriculum is broad, systematically developed, and instinct with the life of the American people. It finds

> place for the classics, and also for the modern literatures; for mathematics and the sciences, and also for history, for economics, and for the accurate and thorough acquaintance with the English language.

Well, all right. The goal of the liberal arts, so the argument goes, is not to train a person for a job but to produce a well-rounded, cultivated individual.

I went to a liberal arts college, but I cannot say I emerged a well-rounded individual. My college, for example, did not teach me to be an oenophile or an epicure. I wasn't taught to be an equestrian or a ballroom dancer, nor did I ever take (or even see offered) courses in elocution, etiquette, or fashion. There was not even a music appreciation requirement at my liberal arts school, and music was one of the original liberal arts! I did not have to take a course in art history or appreciation (though I elected to), and I did not have to learn or play a sport such as tennis, golf, or skeet shooting.

I suspect any cultivated, well-rounded individual would sooner consider the above activities more the hallmark of well-roundedness than a course in psychology or geology.

I would also suggest (and I think Mom and Dad would agree) that a course preparing English majors for careers in book publishing has more inherent value than a course in deconstructing *The Simpsons*, or a media studies course that delivers the big news bulletin that advertising presents a misleading portrait of human life.

The heart of the problem is not just with what courses are offered, however. It runs deeper than that.

## The Yawning Chasm

When I was an undergraduate, one of my favorite professors wrote a letter to the editor of the student newspaper lamenting the "yawning chasm" between student housing and the intellectual life of the college. That term stuck to the poor man like glue.

To redeem that term, I use it here to describe the separation between a college's departments of English, education, and communications. The perception, commonly, goes something like this: The major in education is for people who want to teach at any level leading up to college; the major in English is for people who want to teach English on the college level; and the major in communications is for people who want to go into broadcasting or journalism. Nothing, of course, could be further from the truth, because in every department one finds young people who are considering becoming teachers, reporters, professors, writers, and editors.

It's high time these three departments—English, education, and communication—sat down at the same table and shared resources in earnest: combining their course offerings, partnering in curricular development, teaching classes together, and helping students see the fundamental connections and subtle differences between their offerings and goals.

Of course, English majors in colleges and universities across America today enjoy some freedom to customize their course load, even with an eye toward preparing themselves vocationally for the postgraduate world. In addition to their required English literature courses, they could elect to take a practicum in journalism; a survey course of the history of media in the United States; a course from the library sciences department in the history of the book and the printed word; and various other courses from the departments of education and communications. They could major in English and minor in education or double-major in English and communications.

There are a few problems, however.

The college or university may not offer courses in contemporary media, the history of the printed word, and journalism. If the college does offer a practicum in journalism, it is likely that the school enlists a professional journalist to teach one or two sections of such a class for one semester, limiting the pool of beneficiary students to somewhere between thirty and forty people; or, the class fills up quickly with majors in communications.

Next problem: Speaking for myself, the main reason I never looked into classes in the education and communications departments is that I thought of them as wholly separate entities, separated from the English department by an ocean of thought. *Why would I want to take classes in those departments,* I reasoned, *when there are plenty of classes to choose from in the English department?*

What is more, not all students double-major; they don't think to do so or wish to do so. A conventional double major may comprise a bigger course load than a student is willing or able to undertake. Plus, not all incoming first-year students are possessed of the kind of prescience to craft a vocationally directed curriculum for themselves, and even if their faculty advisors are available to give them time and counsel, the advisors themselves may advise against it.

How do we address these problems?

## Welcome to Platonic College

I find that there are two kinds of people who sing the praises of the English major the most: English majors who are secure in a job, and non–English majors who are secure in a job. It's very easy when you've got a good job—especially one that puts an English major's talents to use—to talk about how flexible and versatile and tremendously valuable is the major in English.

I suspect that this enthusiasm is not shared by English majors working as security guards or in an industry they dislike.

If young people find it challenging to translate the major in English into a job, could it be that the problem is not with the young person or with the job market exclusively, but with the English major curriculum?

Let's play "Plato's *Republic*." Let's imagine a Platonic College with our own English major curriculum: one that addresses some of the questions above and, most importantly, obviates the posing of this book's titular question.

Picture our graduating English majors: bright young faces, all smiles in rented caps and gowns. Aren't they something? We have no way of knowing what professions these young men and women will enter, and by and large, they themselves do not know. In all likelihood, each will hold a number of different jobs, perhaps completely unrelated to the chosen undergraduate major.

One thing, however, we do know: The majority of them will not pursue an advanced degree—in English or in anything else. Never mind going to graduate school—three-quarters of American adults, on average, haven't completed four years of college. (According to U.S. census statistics for 2003, the percentage of Americans over the age of twenty-five who had earned a bachelor's degree was at an all-time high of 27.)

So as we think about our curriculum, let us keep this fact in mind—not necessarily at the forefront of our minds, but in mind nevertheless. Let us not give our English majors a curriculum founded exclusively on literary analysis, a course of study suited only to proto-PhDs. Let their career-academic teachers not look at our young matriculants and say *Let us make them in our own image.*

Defenders of intellectual pursuit for its own sake may argue that our English majors should focus on reading and studying literature because such an activity broadens the mind and nourishes the soul. This may be true, but working among the poor also broadens the mind, and yoga nourishes the soul—but we don't, as a consequence, offer college courses in those things.

We want to graduate people who know how to make their way in the world: that is, to apply the knowledge and skills they have acquired in school to the world after school, to advantage and benefit.

All of us advance our fortunes and the welfare of others through work. The world of work consumes at least half of our waking hours, week to week. As we develop our curriculum for our English majors, surely we can devote half a mind to considerations of the world of work. Let us make a leap of faith that the world of the mind will not be torn asunder if we start making allowances for the world of work and a so-called practical application of knowledge.

And please note that I don't mean to say we should divide Platonic College into academic and vocational schools. Such a division would do anything but ensure that every student received some real-world training. My high school in Warwick, Rhode Island, was so divided, with two buildings side by side: the vocational technical school and the main high school building. That arrangement laid literal foundations for a tidy social division between the students following a college prep program and the "voc tech" kids who took classes like wood shop and metal shop in order (as the college prep kids believed) to fulfill their destiny as carpenters, electricians, and grease monkeys. The common perception was of a white-collar building and a blue-collar building: the pristine world of the mind separate from the world of dirty fingernails. (Granted, there was a bridge between the two buildings, but it was worn more by the feet of voc tech kids walking to and from the main high school building to take their required academic courses than by college prep kids investigating the voc tech offerings. Voc tech kids had to take English and history in order to graduate, but the college prep kids certainly didn't have to take wood shop.) It's time to end the perception that practical training has no place in institutions of higher learning.

## *English? Check. Useful Knowledge? Check.*

When I was an undergraduate in the late 1980s, my English major curricular requirements were organized in a checklist: I had to take two pre-1800 literature courses, two pre-1900 literature courses, one course in the novel, one course in poetry, and so on. Obviously, not every incoming English major could take the same courses in the same order, so I was at liberty to take whatever I wanted, in any order, so long as the items on my list was all checked off in four years.

There was a problem, however. Imagine you go to a travel agency and you tell the agent that you have a set amount of time—let's say three weeks instead of four years—to visit Europe.

There's a lot to see in Europe: more than you could possibly see in three weeks or even four years. Not to worry, though: The agent has a checklist.

Great. You take out some loans and pay the agent, oh, about $110,000, and off you go.

You spend two days in London, one day in Budapest, then it's over to Berlin for three and a half days, with stops in Alsace-Lorraine, Baden, and Madrid; in quick succession, you visit Rome, then Venice, then back to Germany, over to Portugal, and finally, the Czech Republic. Time's running out, so you spend one- to two-day intervals in Hamburg, Milan, Bilbao, Athens, and Bucharest—not forgetting, of course, to swing by Vienna, Palermo, Monaco, Palermo again, and finally Brussels. Everybody knows a trip to Europe isn't complete without visiting Brussels.

So then you fly back to America, stagger off the plane, and your friend who collects you at the airport says, "So! What do you know about Europe?"

"Uhhhhh ..."

Ten years go by and you're still paying off the trip to Europe. Someone asks you what you learned in your time in Europe.

"Uhhhhh ..."

Sound familiar?

Instead of persuading undergraduate English majors to buy into the fallacy that a checklist approach to English literature adds up to an education, let's borrow a page from the travel agency and organize our courses into package tours: organized, structured, carefully chosen, and thematic routes through otherwise difficult-to-navigate territory.

If you go to a real travel agency with a desire to visit Europe, you have the option of choosing from a walking tour of Europe; a tour of European churches and cathedrals; a food and wine tour of Europe; a lover's tour of Europe; a literary tour of Europe; and on and on.

Let students arriving at Platonic College be greeted with a choice of "package tours" of course offerings, each designed along a particular theme. If students elect to go with a package route, chances favor their emerging as cultivated people, and what's better, they'll have an understanding of the direction of their education, what it's for and what it's all about—and best of all, what they paid and sacrificed for. And they can still say that they've seen Europe.

If you're not interested in pursuing a career in teaching literature on the college level, it scarcely matters what literature courses you take. I obediently fulfilled my checklist requirements of two pre-1900 courses and two pre-1800 courses and so on, but somehow I managed to graduate never having studied Homer, Ovid, Virgil, Chaucer, Goethe, Molière, Voltaire, Hardy, Dante, Tolstoy, Pushkin, Montaigne, or Shakespeare. I still got a diploma welcoming me to the company of educated men and women. I was still exposed to great literature and developed an appreciation for it.

Let students pick and choose literature courses as they may, or let them choose from a host of thematic "package tours" that guide them along, lending continuity and coherence to their studies. For students not interested in careers as college professors, literature will still comprise half the course load, and students would still enjoy exposure to great literature and, by dint of their teachers' efforts, develop an appreciation and appetite for literature.

Meanwhile, how do we best accommodate those students who know (or think, or suspect, or imagine) that they want to become English teachers? Not just English professors—English *teachers*.

If we can have programs called pre-med and pre-law, there is no reason why we cannot have a program called pre-teach: a tailored course of study for those students who wish to pursue careers in teaching on any level, from kindergarten to graduate school.

At Platonic College, let the belief stand that if you concentrate in a particular field—English, history, math, science—you should graduate from college prepared to teach it. If the national complaint is that we are hiring teachers who have insufficient training and insufficient teaching skills, let's correct the problem in college, the last stop most young people make in their higher education.

This would benefit even those students who plan to continue their education. Pre-teach English majors who pursue postgraduate degrees will likely act as teaching assistants and teaching fellows while doing so. So while they are still undergraduates, let's establish undergraduate-level teaching fellowships, teaching mentoring programs, and teaching volunteer opportunities. That is, let us give them teaching experience *before* graduate school so that, as fellows, they don't have to start teaching 100-level English department courses with no experience, no pedagogical knowledge, and no credentials.

And who will be the travel agents for the students?

College faculty have enough demands on their time and energy to be curricular advisors to undergraduates, so let's unburden them. If a high school can find money for guidance counselors, surely a college or university can: people trained in vocational guidance whose sole purpose is to counsel undergraduates as they formulate and develop postgraduate professional goals. The public school I attended mandated at least one meeting with a guidance counselor prior to graduation, to discuss postgraduate plans. Colleges and universities should do the same.

## What Our English Majors Should Know, Generally

Throughout this book, we've examined the particular skills or traits that would help you in certain jobs. There are fundamental skills, however, that are applicable and serviceable across a spectrum of jobs: Let's address a few as we think about planning our curriculum for Platonic College (or, as undergraduate readers of this book think about planning their own education).

## STORYTELLING

The *Wall Street Journal* reported in 2004 that what MBA recruiters *really* want is someone who knows how to put words together. In the September 22 article—"How to Get Hired," by Ronald Alsop—investment banker Darren Whissen of Ladera Ranch, California, was quoted as saying, "No matter how strong one's financial model is, if one cannot write a logical, compelling story, then investors are going to look elsewhere. And in my business, that means death."

Journalists, grant writers, marketing and advertising people, and more: They are fundamentally tellers of stories, big and small.

English majors, ordinarily, spend four years reading stories, analyzing stories, discussing stories, and writing papers about stories. Let us, in our Platonic College, teach them how to tell stories.

In May 2004, CBS broadcast a tribute to Don Hewitt, the producer of *60 Minutes*, and the show was appropriately titled "Tell Me a Story." Should you decide to go into journalism—in print, on TV, or on the radio; as a writer, an editor, a producer, or a publisher—success will be largely predicated on your ability to tell a story.

Should you decide to become a writer of grants, success will again be predicated on your ability to tell a story. You will be telling a story to convince and persuade someone that your organization deserves money and support.

Should you decide to go into business—as entrepreneur or employee—there will also be a teller of stories. Where I work, at Fidelity Investments in Boston, Fidelity Personal Investments president Jeff Carney has often repeated the phrase "We've got a great story to tell"—that is, our success as a business depends on our ability to articulate to our customers and prospects the story of our organization: how we built our reputation and our success, what values we hold dear, what we can do for the customer, and what our plans are for the future.

In politics, candidates for elected office must tell a story to the electorate: the story of who they are, where they stand on the issues, and where they will take the country. The people who work and campaign for the candidate must compose and tell and retell that story. We know all too well the story of candidates who never successfully tell their story—they lose, end of story.

Before we jump to the conclusion that an undergraduate creative writing workshop would solve this problem, I would suggest that depending on who teaches such a class, telling a story may not be the top aesthetic priority. (A higher premium may be placed on voice, style, linguistic pyrotechnics, or conformity to the professor's personal aesthetic.) Surely, there are readers of magazines that regularly publish fiction who find themselves going months on end before coming across a story: an entertaining or engaging narrative with interesting characters and a beginning, middle, and end.

Literary pyrotechnics and postmodern theory are all well and good, but deep down, people never lose the nurtured response to *Once upon a time,* and they respond to it in the boardroom and on the sales floor and in the living room in front of the television and in the voting booth just as strongly as they did in the nursery rocking chair, when an adult led them through beginning, middle, and end.

Our students deserve to have this skill. It will serve them all throughout their lives, and the first place it will serve them after graduating from college is in the job interview, when they will need to tell the story of themselves!

If there is at least one person in your life who is a good storyteller—not a gossiper, or an anecdote teller, or a standup comedian, but a storyteller—think about that person: What does her storytelling ability suggest about her? She has a good memory; she has an eye for detail; she is an organized thinker; she is sensitive to inflection, pacing, building suspense, and keeping her audience entertained; she knows where to embellish and where to ground a story in cold reality; she projects confidence, authority, and intelligence.

Contrast that person with the idiot who can't tell a good joke. You know this person. She starts a joke half a dozen times, apologizes and backpedals, and ten minutes later, the funny story has as much life as a limp balloon.

No: Storytelling is a rare and valuable ability, and it can be taught. The ability to tell a story is not a mystical power encoded into the genes of a select few. Everyone can learn how to tell a story.

## PROOFREADING AND COPYEDITING

If an adult education center can conduct a seminar or workshop in proofreading and copyediting, Platonic College can do the same.

If there is one complaint common to every high school and college teacher I have known, it's that papers and essays come in from students chock-full of errors in spelling, punctuation, grammar, and usage. Some diligent and tireless teachers take the time to circle and underline every one of these errors and then get on with the business of the paper's theme, argument, and so on; other teachers figure this is knowledge their students should have mastered by the ninth grade, and they have neither the time nor the patience to remind them about subject–verb agreement or the difference between a colon and a semicolon.

What if—in addition to their classes in English, history, and the sciences—our students at Platonic College took a language lab every semester? A class that would continue throughout their education, a class in which they would edit, revise, and improve their writing from every other class and workshop? That one class could be where our students go to retool their writing, learn editing skills, and bring this knowledge back to all their other classes. Making the class a requirement and a natural part of their education may even help inculcate the idea that much about writing is rewriting.

How much better off would our students in English be if they thought of themselves as word doctors and language experts and not just accomplished readers of great novels and poems? How much better prepared would they be for the working world if they left college having mastered the art of editing, revising, and rewriting a piece of writing—their own, or someone else's?

## MIMICRY

One of my favorite scenes in *Citizen Kane* is when Charles Foster Kane, publisher of the *Enquirer*, comes into the newsroom to find his friend, drama critic Jedediah Leland, unconscious from drink with a deadline looming: the review of Kane's wife in that night's opera performance. Kane sits down and types the rest of the review exactly as his friend would have written it. That is understood to mean that Kane writes as negative a review as Leland would have written, but I like to think that Kane was good enough of a writer to know how to be a good mimic and write in Leland's voice.

If you're going to be a journalist, you need to know how to alter your writing style for sports readers, news readers, arts readers, and obituary readers. If you're going to pursue work in corporate communications, you may be writing letters and memos for several different executives, which will require shifting from one style to another and back again. If you get a job at an ad agency or a marketing firm, you'll need to tailor writing style and expression for any number of targeted audiences.

What you need to be, in order to be considered a truly capable writer, is a linguistic mimic or chameleon. Naturally, over time, you'll develop your own individual style, which is fine for your own writing—but in the workplace, you may have to write for a wide variety of audiences, for a wide variety of purposes. What a shame it would be if, after four years, all English majors knew how to do was write in a dry, academic style for an audience of one, their professor.

## What Our English Majors Should Know, Specifically

How much better equipped for the postgraduate world our English majors will be if they have the opportunity to take:

- a course in how to proofread and copyedit a manuscript, using *The Chicago Manual of Style* and editing marks standard to the publishing industry
- a course in how to write, for a newspaper or magazine, a short news article; an investigative news article; an arts or lifestyle feature; an interview; an op-ed; a sports article; an arts or restaurant review; and a long research piece
- a course in how to start your own magazine, newspaper, newsletter, literary journal, or other small periodical
- a course in how to write and edit a grant proposal
- a course in technical writing
- a course in writing business letters, memos, and other corporate communications
- a course in writing speeches and presentations
- a course in how to make a book and restore an old or damaged one

- a course in how books are marketed, publicized, advertised, and sold
- a course in how to teach a class in English composition
- a course in how to use knowledge of a foreign language and perform translations of a variety of communications
- a course in how to organize, write, and present a marketing campaign for a variety of products and services

If you ask an English major today what *English* refers to, chances are she will say "English literature." She'd be correct, insofar as all the literature on the syllabus is *in* English: If English majors study Homer, Virgil, Dostoevsky, Márquez, Voltaire, Goethe, or the Holy Bible, they are not asked to read these texts in the original. *English literature* could mean literature originally written in English by native English-speakers, but then what about Salman Rushdie or Joseph Conrad, non-native English speakers who elected to write in English? It's kind of a mouthful for college graduates to say that they majored in literature written in or otherwise translated into English.

The *English* in *English major* should mean more than this. It should mean an in-depth study of the English language itself. Surely, English majors can sacrifice a little time spent with Homer or Dryden so that they may learn:

- the origins and development of the English language
- linguistics and phonetics
- the history of printing, from Gutenberg to desktop publishing
- the history of the book
- typography and book design
- library science

That I graduated from a college with a major in English never having studied Chaucer and Shakespeare is a state of affairs I can manage to forgive myself for; but that I graduated from a Catholic college with a major in English never learning the name William Caxton is a fact far more unbelievable. Somehow, as a fresh college graduate, I thought of myself as a book person, and yet I could not have identified the first book published in America. I had never heard of the Book of Kells. I didn't know my verso from my recto.

Of course, for the college or university to be able to teach these skills and subjects on a sufficient scale to accommodate the interests of thousands of students, they would need to hire faculty outside the realms of PhD-level academia.

## What Matters

I know of no English majors who were informed, as first-year students, that if they had no plans to pursue postgraduate studies or a career in academics, it scarcely mattered what literature courses they took.

Come to think of it, I don't know anyone who was told that it scarcely mattered where you did your undergraduate studies in English. Some people, of course, would go so far as to say it doesn't matter what you major in, period. I know a professional book editor who majored in journalism, a full-time writer for a business magazine who majored in psychology, and a Peace Corps English teacher who majored in biology.

So what matters? At Platonic College, what matters is that young people are aware and are informed of their options. What matters is that they understand what the possibilities are, with their studies. What matters is that the college is proactively there for the students: to counsel, to advise, to coach, to train, and to provide students with a map when they leave, so that they're not standing three feet past the front gates of the college, asking themselves, *Now what?*

## Valedictory Thoughts

English, huh?

Well.

Good for you.

Pretty important subject, English. One would hope that by the time you graduate from college, you would have an appreciation for just how important English is.

For example: according to statistics compiled by the British Council, an international education and culture organization:

- by the year 2000, an estimated one billion people on Earth were learning English
- speakers of English as a second language likely outnumber those who speak it as a first language

- one out of four people on Earth speak English to varying levels of competence

*The Story of English,* the companion to the PBS series of the same name, reports:

> Three-quarters of the world's mail, and its telexes and cables, are in English. So are more than half the world's technical and scientific periodicals. ... It ... is the ecumenical language of the World Council of Churches. Five of the largest broadcasting companies in the world (CBS, NBC, ABC, BBC, CBC) transmit in English to audiences that can exceed one hundred million.

Bursts of technological innovation have introduced to people of all ages not only new machines, new computer tools, and new gadgets, but also an attendant avalanche of new words, terms, and phrases to learn and use. And when we are being spoken to—by a doctor, a mechanic, a tech support person, or a teenager—and we do not understand what is being said, we always say the same thing: *Once more, please: in English.*

We come into the world without speech (the word *infant* is from the Latin for "incapable of speech"), and before we have mastered basic motor skills, we are encouraged, enticed, and impressed into a relationship with words. We are not in the world more than thirty seconds before someone starts interacting with us with language. Even before we are expected to speak, we are taught to call objects and people by their correct name; we are prompted by an adult's slow, exaggerated mouth movements to pronounce words correctly and speak them distinctly; we are coached to match words to things and back again; and, if we are fortunate, we are told and are read stories, stories, and more stories.

How to speak, how to write, how to read—these skills we are taught well before we are introduced to two plus two, photosynthesis, or the identity of the individual buried in Grant's Tomb. Throughout our schooling, we are continually tested on our vocabulary, our ability to comprehend and answer questions about what we read, and our ability to write; and even though some colleges and universities claim to downplay the importance of the SAT, they certainly will never downplay the importance of the essay applicants must write.

Language, writing, communication, education, expression, information: All these things relate synergistically to one another. An education in English should reinforce that message in class after class.

As your job search begins, your education in English only continues as you see everything that you can do with your knowledge, skills, and abilities.

You're an English major—now what?

Now you know.

# APPENDIX I Best Job Hunting Advice I Ever Got

## Get the Word Out

If you are looking for work, don't keep it to yourself. Notify your friends, family, neighbors, alumni of your college, and even your softball teammates or people at your church or synagogue: You are looking for a job or are interested in a job change. Word travels fast among people who love you (not as fast as among people who dislike you, but still pretty fast). More job opportunities come via word of mouth than you realize. If you're unemployed, it's okay to feel embarrassed. (I've been there—more than once.) You need to get over your embarrassment, because unemployment happens to everyone and to the best. CEOs are asked to leave the very companies they founded, and talented people are laid off every day. But be discreet about letting coworkers know you're looking for a new job: Do not appear disgruntled or bitter about your job; rather, make the case that you are seeking bigger challenges and new opportunities. Be positive. When you put it that way, even your own supervisor may help you in your job search. Choose your words carefully, and choose carefully to whom you direct those words.

## Be Creative

All through your education, your major defined what classes you took, what books you read, and probably even who you hung out with—but when you are thinking about work, remember that *your major does not define who you are or what job you are best suited for*. If the only schoolteachers were people who majored in English or education, the teaching profession would be in far more serious need than it already is. The same goes for publishing and journalism: People from all kinds of educational and professional backgrounds find work there. So don't lock yourself in to an assumption that as an English major, you should be working in this or that field, or at this or that job. Be open-minded and be creative. How? One way is to . . .

## *Think Skills and Abilities*

All through your education, you had to remember facts, figures, statistics, names, dates, and excerpts from poems. In the workplace, you may find that, as important as information is, skills and abilities often trump information. Put another way: When something goes kerflooey in the office, people will not necessarily go to the person with the right job title or even to the person who knows *what* to do: They go to the person with the skills and abilities to remedy the situation. Evaluate yourself in terms of skills and abilities, and if you have an idea as to what jobs you might be interested in, find out what skills and abilities people in those jobs possess.

**Different skills, different résumés.** As you gain job experience, skills, and abilities, develop and maintain several different versions of your résumé, each of which speaks to a particular skill set or expertise.

**Job titles are (mostly) meaningless.** I once asked a professional magazine writer to help me understand the difference between associate editor, deputy editor, assistant editor, managing editor, editor in chief, and so on. Laughing, he said these titles were there mostly to establish the order of people's names on the masthead. So when you are scanning job listings in cyberspace or in print, don't breeze over an opportunity because the job title sounds too intimidating or too obscure or doesn't fit your preconceived notions of what you want to do for a living. Dig deeper to learn about job duties and responsibilities, and consider how your skills and abilities can meet those responsibilities.

## *Always Be Thinking of Your Next Play*

The lousiest chess players think only one move at a time; with practice, you learn to think several moves ahead. Take the job that will help you get to the job you ultimately want. If you cannot do that, pursue the training, education, and experience that will help you transition into the job you want.

Classroom learning doesn't stop once you graduate from college. Professionals are in a continual state of training and education. The nice thing is, if you work for a university or for a large corporation, your employer may pay for or help defray the cost of professional development.

## *Happiness First, Salary Second*

When you're fresh out of college, the first question you want to ask in an interview is *How much does the job pay?* It's a reasonable question, but you should also consider how much the job is going to cost. The job may end up costing you more than it pays you: It may cost you your weekends, your sleep, and very quickly, your happiness and your sanity. And if you think that an extra one thousand or ten will make up for that cost, I wish you luck. Don't judge a job by its salary alone. People take pay cuts all the time to get the job they need or to transition toward the job they ultimately want.

## *Keep an Eye Out and Your Options Open*

When you get a decent job, your natural instinct is to relax. *Whew! I made it!* The fact is, people with ambition and vision are always keeping an eye out for opportunity and are keeping their options open for where that opportunity might come from. Some may call it bad taste or unprofessional to be looking for a job when you already have a job. All I can say to that is don't use your computer at work to surf Monster.com: People don't cotton to this, I've found. Do an Internet search from home, from your library, or from your local career center.

## *Finally, Thank You*

Tired of giving books as gifts to English majors? Try something that works equally well for men and women: simple, professional-looking, personalized stationery or note cards. Whenever you interview, formally or informally, write a thank-you in longhand. Sending a note takes more time and effort than shooting off an e-mail to clog someone's inbox. You will always need more note cards because there is always someone new to thank.

# APPENDIX II Writing Your Résumé

Happily, there is no shortage of reference material in your local bookstore, library, and career center on how to construct an effective résumé. Because your résumé will grow, evolve, and change for different job applications, it's more suitable to our purposes here to think in terms of résumé-writing principles to follow instead of résumé models to imitate. When you apply for a job, your prospective employer wants the answer to four questions.

## Who Are You?

Lead with a two- to three-line description of yourself, emphasizing major strengths and skills. Be professional—this isn't copy for a personal ad. Imagine an employer describing you in one sentence: e.g., *Writer with experience and training in technical writing, strong interpersonal and team management skills, seeking position in project management.* Focus on the tangible (skills or abilities) and leave the intangibles (your winning personality) for the in-person interview.

## What Can You Do?

Follow with bullet points identifying your areas of expertise or competencies: writing or editing; management skills; or what software programs you know. There are many kinds of technical writers, for example; you need to identify the particular strengths and skills that set you apart.

## What Have You Done?

Anyone can list work experience chronologically. Consider, instead, organizing your experience thematically:

- writing experience
- editing experience
- project management experience
- leadership experience

In organizing this section and writing its content, play to your strengths and to what you think the employer will be looking for in a candidate.

When you identify the various jobs you've held, list your job description and your basic duties, calling out specific projects or initiatives. Identify professional development (classes, workshops, certification programs you took), any awards or honors you received, and any committees or task forces of which you were a member. Don't just describe the position: The person reading your résumé knows what a technical writer does. Rather, describe the job as *you* held it and what *you* did as a performer of the job.

## What Makes You Different?

This is not so much a feature of your résumé as an attribute of your résumé as a whole. For example, don't leave out volunteer experience on the argument that it's not paid work experience. If you developed skills or abilities that distinguish you as a candidate and have relevance to a prospective employer, by all means include them on your résumé.

Often what makes you different is the difference you make. Note specific improvements you made while at a certain job. Quantify, quantify. Perhaps sales went up 15 percent during your tenure or as a result of an initiative you worked on. Show the prospective employer what makes you different.

Finally, no résumé should be longer than two pages: Ideally, you should print on both sides of the paper so that the person receiving it has one convenient page.

And solicit feedback on what you've written. There is absolutely no reason to be shy about showing your résumé to your co-workers or even to your supervisor, provided you do so by saying, "I'm updating my résumé, and I was wondering if you could offer me feedback on its effectiveness, particularly with respect to the work I have been doing in this position." You may find that people are eager and interested to offer helpful criticism and pointers.

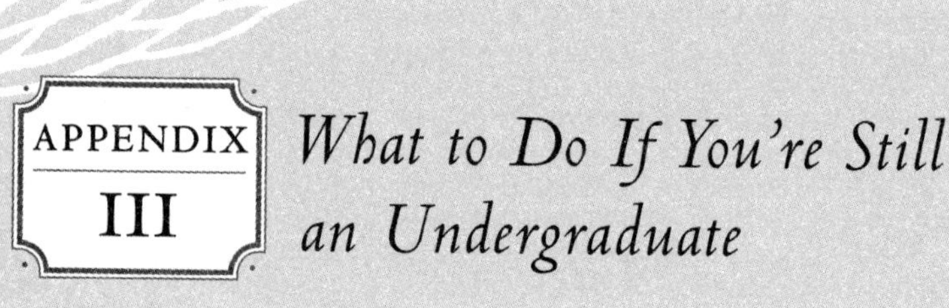

# APPENDIX III What to Do If You're Still an Undergraduate

If you're reading this book and still have at least a year left to your college education, good for you: You're in an excellent position to prepare for the world after graduation.

## Classes

I managed to finish the requirements for my English major by my junior year, and it never occurred to me to apply all those electives and remaining credit hours toward preparing for life after graduation. Consider taking elective classes outside the English department—in education or communications, particularly. Learn how the publishing industry works; take a class in technical writing, journalism writing, or creative nonfiction; explore library sciences or a class in translation.

Unless you take a job at a university after you graduate, you will never again have this kind of access to information, education, and resources.

## Internships

Every English major I interviewed for this book who didn't pursue internships as an undergraduate expressed regret for not doing so—and this, from people who are comfortably established in their chosen field.

Internships not only help you get your foot in the door of an industry, they expose you to the adult world of work. Summers spent asking people if they want fries with that may help pay your tuition, but they don't prepare you for a white-collar office environment. An internship is simply a good idea, regardless of your major.

Start with your college's career center. Ask your friends if they've heard of interesting internship opportunities. Of course, the Internet is a good tool: Companies may list internship information on their career/employment/jobs page.

Two things are true of practically any internship you apply to. First, the competition is likely to be rigorous. Identify those strengths and attributes that help you stand apart. Second, your success in achieving an internship is predicated on the amount of research you do about the company in question and how well you can present to the interviewer what you have to offer, what you hope to learn, what experience you are interested in having, and how good of a match you and the company make.

## Write, Write, Write

Regardless of what you do with your English major, it's to your advantage to write for an undergraduate periodical, be it the university-recognized student newspaper or a student publication produced by a budding Citizen Kane. Getting published in college periodicals is not only one of the better measures English majors can take to enhance their résumé, it is also one of the easiest—you may never again encounter a smoother and more supportive route to publication.

Put aside consideration of whether you wish to pursue a postgraduate career in journalism—the ability to write well has relevance and application in a variety of jobs. Even if you are applying for a non-journalism job, having an article or feature published in a periodical shows the prospective employer that you possess the initiative to get published, that you have experienced the editing and revision process, and that a third party has deemed your writing fit to print. It's better to have recent clips (from your junior and senior year) than that hundred-word CD review you wrote that one time freshman year, after which you didn't do squat. Editors like fresh copy; they want to see what you can do now. Diversify your clips as much as possible, to show your versatility.

And remember: Writing that sex advice column may have been fun, but good luck using it in your portfolio when you apply for a job in corporate communications.

## Volunteer

You may belong to a club or a student organization that, from time to time, must communicate externally: to the Dean's office, to its membership, to internal publications like the student newspaper or alumni magazine. Make yourself available and get involved in writing copy and communications for your group. You're also in close proximity to several administrative branches of the college—development, alumni association, etc.—that have their own communications manager. Schedule an informational interview with this person and try to pick up some portfolio work (either writing or editing) on spec. People may not always say yes to someone who offers to work for free, but they may say yes more often than they say no.

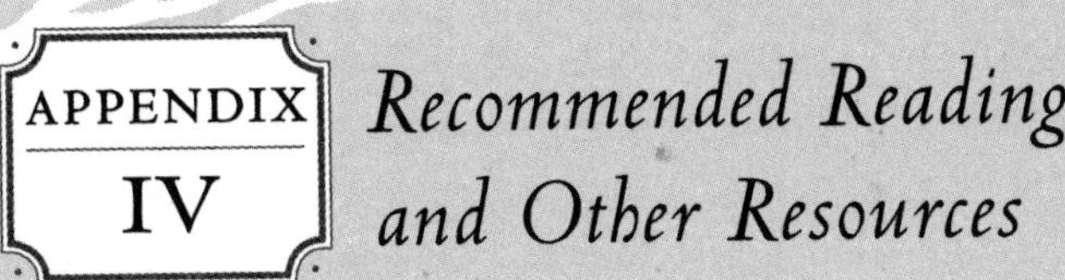

# APPENDIX IV Recommended Reading and Other Resources

## Books

*How to Be Your Own Literary Agent: An Insider's Guide to Getting Your Book Published* by Richard Curtis (Houghton Mifflin, 2003). Whether you want to be a published author or want to work with one (as an editor or an agent), Curtis's book is a handy primer to how the publishing industry works.

*At Random: The Reminiscences of Bennett Cerf* by Bennett Cerf (Random House, 2002) and *Another Life: A Memoir of Other People* by Michael Korda (Random House, 1999). In these two books, editors of Random House tell tales of the trade. Their memoirs are filled with wit, panache, colorful anecdotes, and a behind-the-scenes look at what exactly editors do. Cerf skillfully manages to balance praise of his authors with one or two incriminating details: The whole book is worth reading for the anecdote about James Joyce getting drunk and fighting with his wife. Korda's book contains similarly astonishing accounts of Jacqueline Susann and Harold Robbins. The primary reason for reading these books, however, is to see what life is like inside a large book publisher.

*Ms. Moffett's First Year: Becoming a Teacher in America* by Abby Goodnough (Public Affairs, 2004). The New York City Teaching Fellows program recruited non-education professionals to teach in that city's disadvantaged public schools. You could look to the book for insight into the teaching profession and be scared witless by what you read; but remember that one individual's travails in one particular classroom in one particular school are not representative of the profession as a whole. Goodnough tends to focus more on the challenges of teaching than its very deep, sometimes ineffable rewards, but on the whole, the book is an accessible and compellingly written account of a woman's entry into the teaching profession.

*How to Lose Friends & Alienate People* by Toby Young (De Capo Press, 2003). A young and unabashedly starstruck British expatriate gets a job working and writing for *Vanity Fair* magazine. Young may lay on the self-deprecation a bit thick, but his book is a comical and edifying read, even if not every anecdote is 100-percent true. Young is only as good as his last clipping and most recent idea: Watch how both get shot down regularly.

*Writing for Story: Craft Secrets of Dramatic Nonfiction by a Two-Time Pulitzer Prize Winner* by Jon Franklin (Plume, 1994). English majors accustomed to writing according to an outline or a formula will cotton to Franklin's book, which sets out principles of structuring a nonfiction piece. Franklin's background is in journalism, and he shows how elements of a fiction story (conflict, climax, resolution) can be effectively applied to nonfiction.

*Lincoln at Gettysburg: The Words That Remade America* by Gary Wills (Simon & Schuster, 1993). What better way to understand the structure, power, and impact of a good speech than to study one of the greatest American speeches ever delivered? Pulitzer Prize–winning author Gary Wills examines how President Lincoln's brief memorial remarks followed models and principles of ancient writers. An edifying and inspiring read for aspiring speech writers, underscoring the value of word choice and eloquence.

## Online Resources

As plentiful as the information on the World Wide Web is, bear in mind that the portion of the Web relevant to your job search is a haphazard combination of an encyclopedia, the want ads, bulletin boards, and blogs. Web pages and paper lists don't hire people: People hire people. So, in addition to doing research in print and online, meet some people. The more people you meet, the more contacts you make; the more contacts you make, the more you are in touch with people in the loop; and the more people like that you know, the more you hear about opportunities and future openings.

**www.bls.gov** The site for the Bureau of Labor Statistics within the U.S. Department of Labor. The annual Occupational Outlook Handbook (whose online component is searchable alphabetically, by industry) gives you information on what a job is, what the market is currently like, what people in the job do, what the salaries are like, and more.

**www.indeed.com** A comprehensive job search engine, searching hundreds of job listings across the World Wide Web.

**www.about.com/careers** In the careers section of About.com, you can find articles giving you the low-down on how to break into, train for, and get jobs in particular fields.

**www.higheredjobs.com** This site lists opportunities in administration as well as in teaching. **Your State's Teachers' Union** may have a Web site listing employment and educational opportunities along with news about major issues affecting educators and administrators in your state.

**www.volunteerinternational.org** The Web site of the International Volunteer Programs Association, a nonprofit organization through which you can find teaching opportunities abroad.

**www.teachforamerica.org** If you're a recent college graduate, the Teach For America program can connect you to two-year teaching opportunities across the country.

**www.peacecorps.gov** Teaching may be "the toughest job you'll ever love." Consider doing it abroad through the people who coined that phrase.

**www.newspapers.com** A serviceable search engine to give you an overview of publications in your area. Search an advertised ten thousand newspapers nationwide by state and by specialty. The site also includes an employment search section and links to international newspapers.

**www.journalismjobs.com** A job site for media professionals that handily categorizes job postings in magazines, TV/radio, trade publications, nonprofits, newspapers, and more.

**www.magazine.org** The Web site of Magazine Publishers of America. Read about the latest industry news and trends and see their careers section for job and internship listings.

**www.writejobs.com** This site lists opportunities in media, publishing, technical writing, and medical writing.

**www.bookjobs.com** Lists job opportunities and internships in the book publishing industry.

**www.mediabistro.com** A site for industry news and links, also featuring an advanced search engine for jobs for editors, journalists, and others.

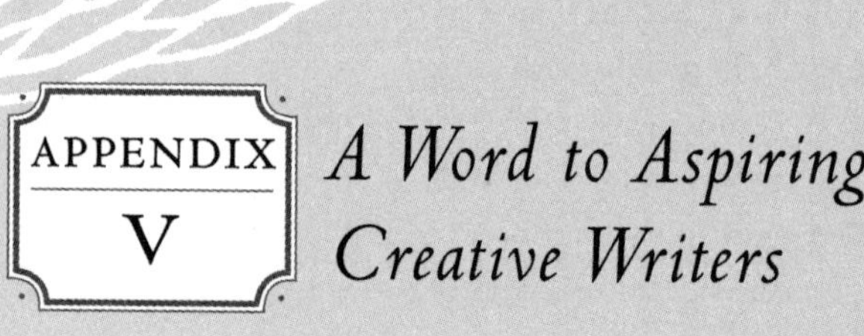

# APPENDIX V A Word to Aspiring Creative Writers

As I noted in this book's introduction, many undergraduate English majors I meet have yet to be disabused of the romantic notion that they can make a decent living after graduation writing short stories, novels, criticism, plays, and the occasional poem.

I was one such romantic. As an undergraduate, I was convinced I would write my generation's *In Our Time.* Once I made my mark with that breakout book, it would be smooth sailing: Novel would follow novel, success would follow success, and there would be regular speaking engagements, appearances on *The Tonight Show* and NPR, and a future cast in autumnal tones of gold, orange, and yellow.

It's entirely possible that you could make a living by writing novels. It's highly unlikely that you could do so by writing the kinds of novels typically assigned in English classes.

This appendix does not mean to discourage you from writing creatively. Rather, in the spirit of the rest of this book, the information is presented to spare the reader some shock, surprise, disappointment, and frustration—all of which would discourage you from writing in the first place.

## Money

The one—and arguably, the only—connection between books and money that all undergraduate English majors know is how much books cost: from the dog-eared poetry anthology they buy secondhand for their lit survey class to the new hardcover physics textbook costing twice or three times as much.

As for *why* books cost what they do—how much money it takes to make a book, how much money authors get paid to write books, and what the publishers' return on their investment is—this is another kettle of fish, and it's not what they teach you in English class. They should.

All you see of fame and fortune are the toys and perks: You never see the tax returns, the bills, the loans against future earnings, the profit-and-loss statements, or the bottom line. If you're an aspiring musician, you may become awed by hip-hop or rock stars bedecked in jewelry and other accoutrements of wealth; you're never told that joining a band is one of the least lucrative decisions a musician or singer can make. Similarly, when you read about twenty-four-year-olds or anonymous middle-aged moms landing six-figure book deals, the natural assumption is that this pot of gold can be yours, too.

Of course, it can. So can the lottery jackpot or a bolt of lightning. The reason those mammoth deals get so much press (at least within the literary world) is because they happen so rarely.

Let's crunch some numbers.

According to a study by the National Endowment for the Arts, the average total annual earnings for a U.S. author in 1989 was $23,335. At that time, the NEA calculated that female authors in the U.S. made fifty-two cents on every dollar earned by male authors. Remember that these are average earnings, so they're elevated by the inclusion of mega-authors such as Stephen King and Danielle Steel. Now, twenty-three grand may seem like a lot of money (slightly less than a year of your college tuition), but if, in your postgraduate life, you elect to rent a one-bedroom in San Francisco, New York, or even Boston, $23,000 is chicken feed.

So you get your first novel published, and it costs, in hardcover, $24.95. The bookstore gets $11.73 and pays $13.22 to your publisher. You, the author, usually get 15 percent of retail (or, possibly, of the $13.22), of which 15 percent goes to your agent (assuming you have one), leaving you $3.18 for every book sold, before taxes.

Let's say your novel sells a very respectable ten thousand copies. You get $31,800, right? Wrong. You only earn royalties after you pay back your advance, which, let's say, was $5,000. You net $26,800, minus taxes, personal expenses in promoting your book, etc.

Call it $25,000.

Now imagine you worked on your novel eight hours a day, every single day, to finish in two years (a completely unbelievable scenario, I know). At that net, over two years, you paid yourself about $4.28 an hour to write your book, at an annual salary of $12,500.

Of course, your novel may not sell enough copies to pay back your advance. No matter; you incur no loss (you get to keep the advance), but you make no gain.

In early 2005, a European Web site for enthusiasts and writers of science fiction and fantasy (www.SFCrowsnest.com) surveyed seventy-one writers in those genres and approximated the median advance for first novels in the science fiction genre to be $5,000, the same amount for first novels in the fantasy genre.

I remind you that more people read science fiction and fantasy than literary novels.

Royalties are traditionally paid twice a year in the form of a check, which the publisher does not necessarily overnight to the author. I would not recommend postponing payment of your utilities bill until that biannual check shows up in your mailbox.

If your book does not pay the bills, perhaps you might earn your keep from short stories. Didn't John Cheever do that?

## Short Stories

The market for short fiction—which helped support writers in the 1930s, 1940s, and 1950s—doesn't exist anymore.

Today, a handful of U.S. magazines pay a couple of thousand bucks for a short story, and to have short fiction published in more than one of these magazines in the course of a calendar year is a privilege reserved for Ernest Hemingway, should he rise from the grave. Even if you do pull it off and, say, earn a total of $6,000, about half of that will be eaten in taxes.

The fiction editor of the *Atlantic Monthly*, C. Michael Curtis, once told me that whenever they make fiction the cover story, that issue is sure to bomb on the newsstand. *Harper's* usually notes on the cover, in one line near the bottom, who has written that issue's short story, but the announcement is never prominent.

In the spring of 2005, the *Atlantic Monthly* announced that fiction would appear only on its Web site and in an annual summer newsstand-only issue. I subscribe to *GQ*, and although I haven't seen a formal announcement that it has given up on fiction, I haven't seen a short story in its pages for years.

Given how focused the *Atlantic* is on politics and culture, and how geared *GQ* and *Esquire* are to the urban male market of eighteen- to thirty-five-year-olds, it vexes the mind to determine what short fiction is doing in those magazines in the first place, besides fulfilling a legacy. Ditto for *Playboy*, which used to publish heavyweight fiction routinely. Back then, men wore hats and charcoal gray ties instead of baggy shorts and backward-facing baseball caps.

If you want a working definition of irony, look no further than the fact that all across America, MFA programs charge students thousands of dollars to learn how to write in a form that, successfully published, will scarcely earn them enough money to pay back the tuition.

This MFA focus on short stories makes sense for the program: It's easier for a group of people to critique a self-contained, twelve-page narrative every week than it is for them to critique chapter ten from someone's novel one week and chapter three from someone else's the following week.

But so few magazines pay a substantial amount for fiction; so many magazines pay next to nothing; so many are choked with unsolicited fiction submissions (making the odds astronomical against being discovered); and short fiction sells so poorly relative to novels, one wonders why anyone writes short stories at all.

Of course, people do, and if you want to write short stories, by all means do so. And if you want to write sonnets, play the glass harmonica, or learn Sanskrit, knock yourself out. But you ain't gonna pay the bills with that stuff.

## Why Doesn't Someone Tell Me These Things?

Not only does nobody want to be the bearer of bad news, nobody wants to be the bearer of news that people could interpret to be bad news.

One argument has it that if you give high school and college students an unadulterated look at the literary marketplace for short stories or literary novels, you will be breaking hearts and discouraging nascent writers left and right. The counter-argument posits that this is a good thing, because then, young people would discover new reasons to write creatively—reasons that have nothing to do with remuneration.

Your professors, if they have any experience having a book published, could give you the inside scoop, but most of them won't.

Why not?

Well, book-writing faculty are not characteristically keen on telling their students how little money they make from their pen. First, such a thing is hard to do without indulging in self-pity or succumbing to a fit of vindictive rage. Second, an American instinct equates low profits with poor quality. Third, teachers may see their role vis-à-vis their students as inspirational (or at least constructively critical), which would make telling a young dreamer the sobering truth about making a living from literature akin to cutting out his heart and tossing it in the trash.

Instead, writers tell their aspirant audiences that they must feel a burning desire to write because one has a hard time rationalizing doing it for the sake of profit.

## Books by the Bagful

When I was an undergraduate, I delighted in quoting one of my favorite authors, Flannery O'Connor, who said that you could make plenty of money by your writing provided you wrote badly enough. This, of course, is another facile, blanket dismissal of other people's success. No surprise, though, that an undergraduate English major should cheer O'Connor's sentiment, because the bias sets in early for students of literature, that within the walls of the classroom we read "great books," while outside these walls, the masses read bestsellers, potboilers, hack work, or, generally, that form dreaded and dismissed in all MFA programs of creative writing, genre fiction (mysteries, suspense, romance, science fiction, westerns, thrillers).

But then again, as English majors, you're studying literature, not books. You're in a small, closed environment, where everyone is reading the same book or the same kind of book.

Not like the outside world.

One summer during college, I worked in a local library—a modest operation housed in a former armory building. It was a cushy job: My most formidable task was opening the window that was always stuck. I worked with two women who could have starred in *Arsenic and Old Lace*. It was nice, the two women told me, to have a man around the house.

Anyway, most of our patrons were women aged forty to sixty, and several of them would come in once or twice a month with a paper shopping bag— one of the bigger bags, with plastic handles. They would go over to the rack of romance paperbacks and fill up. They would literally check out what looked like a hundred books every two weeks. You would think oranges were on sale for a dime a dozen.

Of course, my inner literary snob was poised to dismiss these women as ignorant hausfraus who wasted their lives and minds reading third-rate pabulum. Fat lot I knew: I was nineteen and thought I would be Ernest Hemingway (without the alcoholism, divorces, and eventual insanity).

When you're an English major, you read books to study them, reflect on them, discuss them critically, and have your soul nurtured by them. After four years of doing this, it can be a bit of a shock to discover that most people outside the college walls do not read books for this purpose. Most people, if they read books at all, read to be entertained and to escape what is often the soul-crushing routine of work.

A very intelligent woman I know—well-read, earned a master's in Spanish at an Ivy League university, works in publishing—recently told me that she was giving up on literary novels for the time being because she's tired of reading about other people's woes. She has quite enough going on in her life, thank you, without using up what little free time she has to read four hundred pages of dysfunction, psychological dread, and the pain of oddball protagonists. To people like this woman, Harry Potter is a breath of fresh air, a welcome relief from insular, suburban melodramas about academics and their relationship problems.

What people read (or do not read) is a neutral set of facts—facts you are not told as an English major. What you do with those facts—ignore them, change your writing style, use them to fuel your snobbery—is your business.

## Success

As an aspiring writer, I assumed for a long time that once publication came, everything would change: I'd have money; I'd start hanging out with brilliant, erudite people; I'd go to parties in New York; I'd never have to work at a job ever again.

Wishful thinking.

The central myth of success is that once you achieve whatever landmark you prize (publication in *Harper's*, your first book contract, a positive review in the *New York Times*), your life will change and all will be right with the world. Your defining moment of success—whatever you think means that you've arrived or that you're a real writer—is an imaginary way of validating yourself and what you're doing. You don't trust your own self to validate your writing, so you hope something external—some event or third party—will do it for you and thus let you know that you have what it takes or that you're not wasting your time.

Maybe you're waiting for a respectful compliment from an emotionally withholding professor, or an unreservedly enthusiastic book review, or notice that your book has sold through its first printing. None of these things will do for you what you hope they will.

(Hold on a moment, I'm going to strike my gong again. . . .)

What you say you want is rarely ever what you want. Rather, what you want is what you imagine will be the inevitable result of getting what you say you want. Aspiring writers, then, may say they want to be published to critical acclaim, but truly what they want is the feeling of confidence and self-esteem they imagine will result when they obtain that coveted prize.

There are easier and more immediate ways of cultivating confidence, if that's what you want. There are easier ways than getting a book published to become famous, or rich, or satisfied, or happy, or wise.

It's no wonder college students dream of becoming authors: They're living in an environment where authors get respect and attention. Many of the campus speakers are authors, and not a few of the faculty are authors (and are expected to be authors, as part of their job). In college, people care about books, about learning, and about the craft of writing. There, it's good to be an author.

Once you get out into the wider world, though, you realize that the author's cred drops precipitously. Authors don't fill seats; they don't command revenue. President Bill Clinton may have golfed with Walter Mosley, and President George W. Bush may have had Vaclav Havel over to the White House, but neither president probably asked the author for advice about anything. Authors don't represent power or large blocs of voters; they can't command or influence large influxes of funding. You can have access to power without having power yourself, but poets and authors have no power beyond that of the pen, which, contrary to what you've heard, is not more powerful than the sword.

## Now What?

In 2005, Lulu.com, a Web site for writers, reported that the average age of writers who topped the hardcover fiction section of the *New York Times* bestseller list from 1995 to 2004 was 50.5 years: evidence, claimed Web site owner Bob Young, that middle age is "the optimum age to write a bestseller."

Well, maybe, if you conveniently rule out innumerable other factors influencing who appears on the bestseller list. For example, if we tally the gender of bestselling authors, we might deduce that being female is the optimum gender to write a bestseller.

A useful kernel of truth, however, resides in Lulu.com's findings: As an aspiring writer in your twenties, you watch by the sidelines and all you see are young hotshots scoring big with their first novel. John Updike was published in the *New Yorker* in his early twenties, and similarly, Jonathan Safran Foer made the scene early.

A couple of things: Few people remember how fast or how early you did something. What most people remember is how *well* you did something. And just because you hit it early doesn't mean you're going to write a second book worth reading or even write a second book at all. When was the last time you heard someone in a bookstore say, "Can you point me toward the books by people aged twenty-seven to thirty-six? 'Cause that's who I always like to read."

The United States of America is a country that worships the young and adores the wunderkind, whether he is an author, an actor, or an athlete. Hit it big while you're still very young and it can be a challenge to shake off the label of Boy Wonder. Fail to deliver the goods as time goes by, and all you'll be is Aging Boy Wonder.

One more thing: Your undergraduate creative writing teacher will probably never tell you this, but if you're twenty or twenty-one years old, you're a *kid*. A couple of years ago, you were a *teenager*. You're probably not married; hopefully you don't already have children; and unless you grew up poor, were fire-bombed out of your village, or had to work in a sweatshop, the well of experience from which you can draw for creative writing is shallow.

What can you do now? Give yourself a break, and give yourself some time. Spend your twenties and thirties reading and writing, traveling and living, soaking stuff up and taking notes. Give yourself something to write about. You may find that you only start doing your best work when you write to have fun and please yourself.

Get your heart broken. Get your nose broken. Wander the earth.

Why not get a job, while you're at it?

And relax. You're an English major.

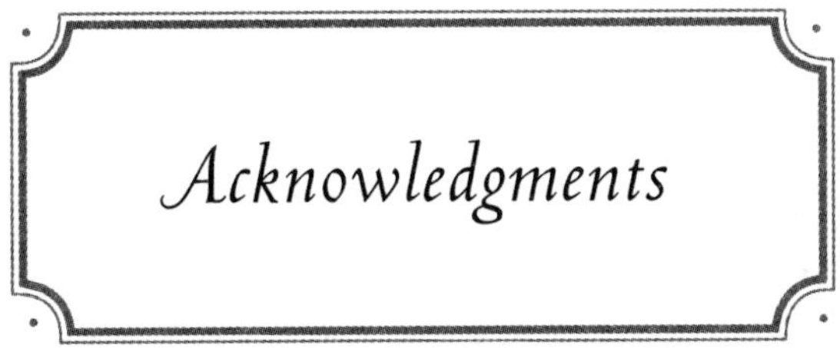

# *Acknowledgments*

First and foremost, thanks are due to the Boston College Arts Council—specifically to Cathi Fournier and Chair Jeffrey Howe—for organizing the college's annual "Career Night for the Arts," the event that sparked the genesis of this book.

Thanks are also due to my English teachers. I had several good ones—at Boston College and in the public school system of Warwick, Rhode Island—but as you might expect, there is one teacher above all: Richard Fucci, my eleventh-grade English instructor. Mr. Fucci once returned to me the worst assignment grade I ever got in English class, with a left-handed compliment: "Mr. Lemire ... we both know you can do better than this." The man had only to say it to me once for me to say it to myself the rest of my life.

Thanks are also due to my editor, Jane Friedman, whose keen judgment and vision shaped this book; the staff of F+W and its imprint Writer's Digest Books; copyeditor Nicole Klungle; to the interview subjects who lent their experience to this book; and Steve Schneider, Kris Swanson, Chris Caggiano, Kristen Sardis, Rod Siino, and Meghan Aftosmis.

My family and friends—my wife, Liz, in particular—were very supportive of me as I wrote this book. If being a teacher myself taught me anything, it is that we always do better under the tutelage, oversight, and care of people who not only believe we can do better but also sincerely wish to see us do so. I am fortunate to have been surrounded by such people all my life.

## A



## B



## C

# About the Author

After trying his hand at being a newspaper editor, reporter and critic; a production editor in book publishing; a managing editor for a bimonthly magazine; an English teacher; a freelance editor and writer; and a communications specialist in the corporate world, Tim Lemire still isn't sure exactly what he plans to do with his English major.

Royalties from this book are helping him pay off debt incurred earning his BA in English from Boston College and his MFA in creative writing from the University of Michigan. Lemire is also a graduate of the Radcliffe Publishing Course, now the Columbia Publishing Course in New York City.

Lemire's essays and humor have appeared in *The Writer* and *The Door*, as well as on PopPolitics.com and AlterNet.org. He is also a published cartoonist and illustrator.

Lemire lives in his native Rhode Island with his wife and children.